DON DELILLO,
JEAN BAUDRILLARD,
AND THE
CONSUMER CONUNDRUM

DON DELILLO, JEAN BAUDRILLARD, AND THE CONSUMER CONUNDRUM

Marc Schuster

CAMBRIA
PRESS

YOUNGSTOWN, NEW YORK

Requests for permission should be directed to permissions@cambriapress. com, or mailed to: Cambria Press, PO Box 350, Youngstown, New York 14174-0350.

Library of Congress Cataloging-in-Publication Data
Schuster, Marc, 1973-

   Don DeLillo, Jean Baudrillard, and the consumer conundrum / Marc Schuster.
       p. cm.
   Includes bibliographical references and index.
   ISBN 978-1-60497-504-8 (alk. paper)
   1. DeLillo, Don—Criticism and interpretation. 2. Baudrillard, Jean, 1929-2007. 3. Consumption (Economics) in literature. 4. Consumption (Economics)—Psychological aspects. I. Title.

   PS3554.E4425Z87 2008
   813'.54—dc22

   2007050143

for Kerri

TABLE OF CONTENTS

FOREWORD

Many critics have identified the affinities between French theorist
Jean Baudrillard and American author Don DeLillo; however, this is
the first detailed and sustained comparison between DeLillo's novels
and Baudrillard's works. Instinctive connections are easily, indeed
instantly, made between the two, but what this text does is explicitly
unpick and develop these connections. This thorough and thoughtful
reading of both writers not only acknowledges their affinities but
also exhaustively explores the ways in which their writings inform
and illuminate each other. By examining DeLillo's novels within
Baudrillard's theoretical framework, Marc Schuster has provided a
rich critical milieu in which an informed reading of both writers'
works may take place. A wealth of insights is offered to both the new
reader and the established fan. DeLillo is a major force in American
literature and, as a consequence, a collection like this, with allusions
ranging from T. S. Eliot to Slavoj Zizek, will prove invaluable to
scholars of all levels. Similarly, Baudrillard's place on reading lists,
especially for critical theory courses, is guaranteed, making this
book crucial reading for those with either an academic or general

interest. Connections to Saussure, Barthes, Marx, Derrida, et al. reinforce the strength of this book.

Comparisons of DeLillo and Baudrillard tend to focus on both writers' fascination with consumer ideology. Schuster's sophisticated reading develops this to point out the nuances in Baudrillard's canon and to investigate in particular his notion of "ambivalence," which is Baudrillard's term for the manner in which commodification may be resisted. Within consumer culture, subjects seek to advance their social standing by accumulating and displaying signs of affluence; ambivalence fractures this by allowing for loss. Schuster suggests that Baudrillard cites terrorism and art as potential forms of ambivalence, both favorite topics in DeLillo's work. He illustrates why Baudrillard sees acts of terror as the most likely way to implement social change and why DeLillo chooses art as the truly radical force which has the potential to remake, if not entirely overthrow, consumerism. Schuster locates DeLillo's difference in his belief that rather than sabotaging consumer culture, terror ultimately reinforces it.

Consumer ideology ensures that its subjects base their personal worth, their status, and their identity on the objects they own, buy, use, and consume, and the knowledge they possess. As Schuster points out, these facile, purchased identities ensure that humans, too, become commodities, replaceable subjects prone to decay and degeneration. This text displays the way in which DeLillo's work examines the effects of this phenomenon on interpersonal relationships together with the inevitable creation of a social hierarchy based upon prestigious possessions—Eric Packer's huge apartment in *Cosmopolis* is an obvious example. What might appear to otherwise be an insignificant, random object—to again reference *Cosmopolis*, a shark tank, or borzoi pen—is invested with value, hence encouraging consumers to amass quantities of material goods and surround themselves with objects they often do not need or even want, but instead think they ought to have. Schuster investigates the implications of overthrowing such a system and its artificial confines and wonders whether such a response would force contact with an elusive "reality."

The value attributed to objects is the fuel ultimately driving consumer ideology; this text develops this given to examine the values and beliefs that motivate terrorist activities and, furthermore, the clash of the values and beliefs of different cultures, often caused by a lack of communication. Schuster reminds us that words are the ultimate sign of value—hence such phrases as "invested with meaning" and "a wealth of meanings" are universally used and understood. In consumer society words become currency—invested with significance—and language is simultaneously both empowering and restrictive. Schuster's unpicking of Baudrillard's notion of ambivalence underpins the restricted economy of language. When language is invested with meaning, silence becomes a powerful weapon, stripping away, potentially, all significance. Similarly, Schuster posits, there is no way to analyze and assess value using language, as all language is already thoroughly entrenched with the concept of value.

The value of language also means that its use ranks and differentiates people, tying it ever more firmly to consumer ideology. Schuster uses DeLillo's and Baudrillard's works to demonstrate how art, terror, and language are all intrinsically locked into the manipulation of signs. Questioning meaning is cited as a potential tactic for rupturing the connection between language and value, as is the ambiguity of metaphor and the power of wordlessness—as with Mr. Tuttle of *The Body Artist*. Language is bent and distorted in graffiti—a concept examined by both writers. Consumer goods are used in an attempt to fill the unfillable gap which always remains outside of meaning or translation. As countries strive for global profitability, human capital becomes an increasingly debated concept—what exactly is a human worth?

Schuster unravels Baudrillard's writing on the complexities of war and terrorism both before and in the aftermath of 9/11, and illustrates the closer, more intimate picture given by DeLillo. This personal closeness can offer the reader a disturbing reminder of how much humans are influenced by consumer objects rather than by other humans, and the inevitable mutation of the species as a direct result of this. Schuster reminds the reader of DeLillo's quest to reclaim the small and the human, a philosophy not unlike that of Baudrillard's fellow countryman Jean Francois Lyotard. Baudrillard's idea that life and death are part of ambivalence should not be taken too literally, but demands decoding in much the same way as his proclamations about the Gulf War demanded decoding. He sees life and death as ambivalent states due to the way in which they balance each other and their incestuous closeness. Schuster reminds us that Baudrillard is not claiming that there is no difference between life and death, only that they are part of the same larger event.

This text demonstrates both art and terror as engaging with consumer ideology, and it places them at opposite ends of a continuum, with terror as a dehumanizing force whilst art emphasizes humanity. Schuster convincingly presents a case for developing the potential to destabilize both consumer beliefs and habits. He illustrates the way in which Baudrillard cites terrorists as having the ability to topple consumer ideology whilst DeLillo feels they instead reproduce and perpetuate it. DeLillo puts faith in artistic endeavors and feels that perhaps novelists can help to shield humanity from absorption into consumer society, in opposition to Baudrillard who believes it is too late for help. Ironically, it is not possible to influence consumer society without first joining it. Novels embrace consumerism with their need to be marketed, purchased, and consumed. Schuster ties this incestuous circularity to the potential to find all possible meaning within the text, tied up in the language used and the way in which that language and its values are interpreted.

Dr. Ruth Helyer
University of Teesside, UK

ACKNOWLEDGMENTS

Chapter 2 of this volume, "Escaping the Third Person Singular: *Americana* and the Semiotic Challenge," appeared in the autumn 2005 edition of *EnterText* (Volume 5, number 1) under the title "Escaping the Third Person Singular: Art and Semiotics in Don DeLillo's *Americana*."

I would like to thank Sheldon Brivic for guidance and support in bringing this book to fruition. I would also like to thank Ruth Helyer for providing the foreword for this volume.

DON DELILLO, JEAN BAUDRILLARD, AND THE CONSUMER CONUNDRUM

THE NUMBER JUSTIFIES ITSELF: DON DELILLO, JEAN BAUDRILLARD, AND CONSUMER CULTURE

Through much of Don DeLillo's *Cosmopolis*, protagonist Eric Packer rides a stretch limousine through the streets of Manhattan. His journey takes him past a presidential motorcade, a pop star's funeral procession, and a violent political demonstration. Along the way, Eric receives many visitors, including his proctologist, his currency analyst, his chief of finance, and his security advisor. He also makes time for a number of sexual encounters both within and beyond the confines of the limousine. Yet for all of Eric's wealth, he lacks any real connection to the world at large. His grasp of world events is based entirely on economic models, his sense of culture revolves around spectacle, and he rarely conceives of himself in more than the most superficial of terms—net worth and personal appearance, for example. In a phrase, Eric is completely self-absorbed. This trait, however, is exclusive neither to Eric nor to the exceedingly wealthy class he represents. Indeed, French social theorist Jean Baudrillard has argued throughout his career that the profit-driven framework of consumer culture has rendered everyone in the developed world incapable of meaningful exchange.

According to Baudrillard, we are so interested in accumulating and arranging signs of "good living" that we can no longer relate to each other in human terms. Consumer culture encourages us to believe that we can make ourselves appear more or less valuable to others by surrounding ourselves with more-or-less valuable commodities. By allowing us to measure self-worth in terms of value, however, consumer culture places us in the company of the commodities we value and renders us beholden to their laws; surrounded by commodities, we have come to view ourselves as commodities as well. This is precisely the position in which Eric finds himself throughout *Cosmopolis*, and the relationship between humanity and the commodities that constitute our cultural landscape is an issue with which DeLillo's characters struggle throughout the author's *oeuvre*. Given this overlap, my aim in this volume is to bring the works of DeLillo and Baudrillard into dialogue with each other in order to determine the potential for reversing the trends described by the French theorist. Specifically, this volume examines the ways in which DeLillo's novels interrogate the notion of ambivalence, a term Baudrillard uses throughout his career to denote the incessant potential for the destruction of the illusion of value that is at the heart of consumer ideology.

Ambivalence, as Baudrillard understands it, is a slippery term whose definition and significance have shifted throughout the theorist's career. One constant, however, is that ambivalence always calls into question the legitimacy of value. For Baudrillard, value is the principal illusion behind consumer ideology in that it imputes significance to otherwise insignificant objects and, in so doing, motivates us to amass vast quantities of the same. This concept is made particularly clear in *Cosmopolis* when Eric's "chief of theory," Vija

Kinski, questions the relationship between the design of his home and its price:

> What did you buy for your one hundred and four million dollars? Not dozens of rooms, incomparable views, private elevators. Not the rotating bedroom and computerized bed. Not the swimming pool or the shark. Was it air rights? The regulating sensors and software? Not the mirrors that tell you how to feel when you look at yourself in the morning. You paid the money for the number itself. One hundred and four million. This is what you bought. And it's worth it. The number justifies itself. (78)

In this passage, the sheer extravagance of the amenities that make up Eric's home underscores their uselessness. Nonetheless, Vija assures him that utility is beside the point. His home exists primarily as a sign of its own value, one hundred and four million dollars, and the main reason Eric must own it is to prove that he *can* own it.

From Baudrillard's perspective, the only way to alter social relations for the better is to reveal all forms of value as illusory. Such a revelation, he argues in his early works, will inevitably trigger the collapse of consumer ideology and, in so doing, allow individuals to regard themselves not as objects but as subjects. While this theory may not explain what ambivalence is or what forms it might take, it does demonstrate what ambivalence should do: serve as a catalyst for the destruction of consumer ideology. Nonetheless, Baudrillard's failure to provide a consistent definition of ambivalence or to offer compelling examples of ambivalence in action reveals one of the many limitations to his argument. As Douglas Kellner notes in *Jean Baudrillard: From Marxism to Postmodernism and Beyond*, Baudrillard presents neither a theory of the subject as an agent of social change nor a theory of class or group revolt (18). One reason Baudrillard cannot present such theories is that his argument denies agency altogether insofar as individuals, in his estimation, can only behave as objects within the confines of consumer culture. In other words, individuals are incapable of causing social change because they can only behave in a way that is amenable to the tenets of consumer ideology; as objects, they are neither agents of change nor capable of change themselves. Under such conditions, the denizens of the consumer society are in no position to enact any form of revolution, let alone one based on such esoteric theories as Baudrillard proffers.

Enter DeLillo. Sharing Baudrillard's interest in consumer culture, the American author has ruminated at length on the relationship between individuals and the (often brand-name) objects that constitute their environment. In *Americana*, DeLillo's first novel, protagonist David Bell strives to realize a sense of identity independent from that of his father, an advertising executive whose television commercials represent the most influential texts of David's childhood. In *White Noise*, which won the National Book Award in 1985, college professor Jack Gladney seeks to elude the specter of death by losing himself in the gleaming aisles of his local supermarket and by immersing himself in the study of Adolf Hitler's use of propaganda to become a larger-than-life (and, Gladney wants to believe, larger-than-death) historical icon. More recently, *Cosmopolis* follows the aforementioned young billionaire Eric Packer in his efforts, as the novel's dust jacket explains, "to pursue a cataclysmic bet against the yen and to get a haircut across town." Through these and all of DeLillo's novels, commodities and other signs of consumer culture do not serve as mere props; rather, as Frank Lentricchia notes in *Introducing Don DeLillo*, they are "of the essence" (6). That is, DeLillo's novels present consumer culture not just as a backdrop but as a matrix of contemporary values by, through, and against which his characters struggle to define and redefine themselves and, in so doing, reshape the culture that attempts to define them.

Unlike Baudrillard, DeLillo envisions a world in which subjectivity remains intact and the subject has the capacity to alter the ideological framework of society. According to Lentricchia, DeLillo writes in a mode that "marks writers who conceive their vocation as an act of cultural criticism; who invent in order to intervene; whose work is a kind of anatomy, an effort to represent their culture in its totality; and who desire to move readers to the view that the shape and fate of their culture dictates the shape and fate of the self" (2). Lentricchia made this assessment in 1991, and it was reaffirmed in 1999 when DeLillo was awarded the Jerusalem Prize for the Freedom of the Individual in Society. In "From Valparaiso to Jerusalem: DeLillo and the Moment of Canonization," John N. Duvall notes that DeLillo received this award because, in the words of the judges, his fiction partakes in "an unrelenting struggle against even the most sophisticated forms of repression of individual and public freedom" (563). Moreover, according to Duvall, DeLillo's novels "challenge the legitimacy of multinational capitalism and its manipulation of the image through media and advertising to construct first-world identity via the individual's acts of consumption" (563). DeLillo, then, offers solutions where Baudrillard only sees problems.

This is not to minimize Baudrillard's contribution to the field of social theory, particularly with regard to consumerism. To be sure, Baudrillard's unique intellectual pedigree makes him the perfect match for DeLillo. Trained as a sociologist, Baudrillard works within an intellectual framework that is Marxist in origin but also highly invested in the field of semiology, or the study of sign systems. Like many Marxist critics, Baudrillard is particularly concerned with ideology, or the means by which culture fosters the illusions that ensure the continued ascendancy of the dominating class. Yet for Baudrillard, the most instructive way to confront ideology is neither to critique the ways in which modes of production allow for the economic repression of the masses (as does traditional Marxism) nor, strictly speaking, to examine the ways in which the phenomena of everyday life reflect such repression (as does his first mentor, Henri Lefebvre). Rather, Baudrillard's critique of ideology focuses on the ways in which the structures of society mirror the structures of language. Following in the structuralist footsteps of Roland Barthes, whose own exploration of consumer and media culture draws heavily on the theories of linguist Ferdinand de Saussure, Baudrillard examines the ways in which all the elements of our cultural landscape interact to form a system that functions in much the same way as language.

Upheld by the tenets of consumer ideology, the system Baudrillard envisions has grown to such mammoth proportions as to enslave the heretofore dominating class as well. Like such post-Marxist critics as Walter Benjamin and T. H. Adorno, Baudrillard describes a world in which advances in communications technology have robbed the cultural landscape of a human presence. As a result of such technological advances, Baudrillard argues, we live in a state of hyperreality, or one in which models always precede reality. Such is the state of the developed world in DeLillo's novels as well, and this, Duvall notes, is where the projects of DeLillo and Baudrillard intersect:

> If DeLillo's work represents the theme of individual freedom, it is because he is willing to explore so thoroughly the way individual subjectivity is constrained and produced by the contemporary media, the electronic image, and by shopping, or as the French theorist Jean Baudrillard might put it, our social labor as consumers. DeLillo has captured in his fiction crystallizing examples of what Baudrillard identifies as the hyperreal and simulacrum. (563)

Where Baudrillard sees hyperreality as a state that can only stifle humanity, however, DeLillo recognizes the hyperreal landscape as a proving ground *for* humanity. As such, his novels explore the ways in which we might retain our humanity even in the dehumanizing face of hyperreality.

Building on such studies of DeLillo and Baudrillard as Duvall's, this volume examines the ways in which both figures critique the dehumanizing effects of consumer culture and, more specifically, the ways in which DeLillo's novels interrogate and refine Baudrillard's notion of ambivalence. To this end, my project is divided into three sections. The first section takes a broad view of DeLillo and Baudrillard and situates DeLillo's novels within Baudrillard's theoretical framework. This section begins with an examination of consumerism and the ways in which DeLillo's novels demonstrate that our fascination with commodities has caused us to regard ourselves as commodities as well. I then move into a discussion of ambivalence, offering a tentative definition of this slippery term and exploring the ways in which it is manifest throughout DeLillo's earlier works. Subsequently, the remainder of this volume examines the ways in which terror and art may or may not be effective responses to consumer culture.

Contrasting DeLillo's ruminations on terrorism with those of Baudrillard, I conclude that far from subverting consumer culture, acts of terror ultimately reinforce it. Conversely, I argue in the remaining chapters that DeLillo presents art and artists as agents of ambivalence. In contrast to Baudrillard, who sees artists as merely reproducing the social norms of consumer culture, DeLillo sees art—unlike terror—as a truly radical force with the potential to reshape, if not entirely subvert, that culture. This reading of DeLillo ultimately points to the author's own ambivalence toward consumer culture: while DeLillo recognizes consumer culture's potential for degrading and dehumanizing the masses, he also sees it as an arena in which the smallest acts of intimacy have the potential to take on the greatest significance. Thus where Baudrillard argues that the only hope for humanity lies in the total eradication of consumer culture, DeLillo's novels adopt a less vitriolic position and suggest that humanity will survive even in the shadow of consumerism. Thus, while Eric's limousine may insulate him from the world at large throughout much of *Cosmopolis*, he is by no means trapped within it.

CHAPTER 1

SHOPPING FOR ITS OWN SAKE: DON DELILLO'S SYSTEM OF OBJECTS

In *White Noise*, DeLillo presents the first-person narrative of Jack Gladney, a professor of Hitler studies whose fear of death is exacerbated when a cloud of toxic chemicals appears over his town. Brooding over the cloud and other phenomena that signal the imminence of death, Jack discovers that his wife, Babette, has been experimenting with Dylar, a drug that allegedly "speeds relief" to the "fear of death part of the brain" (200). When Dylar eventually proves ineffective, however, Jack and Babette retreat to the aisles of their local grocery store where the checkout line provides an opportunity to rehearse life's slow-moving march toward death. Thus, as the novel draws to a conclusion, the relationship between death and shopping (the two major themes of *White Noise*) comes clearly into focus: shopping is what we do to keep ourselves busy until we die or, to borrow an apt colloquialism, "check out." From this perspective, the novel as a whole amounts to an extended examination of consumer culture's efforts at organizing society in a way that proffers the ritual of shopping as a means of holding death at bay even as we move inexorably toward it.

To be sure, consumer culture can be regarded as largely benign; social theorists like Rob Shields and Michel de Certeau argue that consumption, the driving force behind consumer culture, allows for "an active, committed production of self and of society which, rather than assimilating individuals to styles, appropriates codes and fashions, which are made into one's own" (Shields 2). Accordingly, consumption provides a flexible social code within which the subject is free to produce a persona or multiple personae that are not mere embodiments of popular trends but reflect instead the attitudes and values of the subject. In *White Noise*, for example, Jack adopts the persona of "J.A.K. Gladney" whenever he appears on campus in his capacity as Chair of Hitler Studies. To bring this persona to life, Jack dons dark glasses and a black tunic (17). By arranging the commodities at his disposal in a particular way, then, Jack (the subject) creates "J.A.K." (the persona). This persona is more imposing and commands greater respect than the mild-mannered family man Jack embodies at home, and it also gives Jack the opportunity to allow certain of his quirkier personal traits to surface—his mild fetish for checking the time, for example, and his fascination with Adolf Hitler. This fascination with Hitler, however, draws attention to the ways in which Jack's adoption of the "J.A.K. Gladney" persona complicates the largely benign vision of consumption espoused by theorists like Shields and Certeau.

As Slavoj Zizek observes in *The Sublime Object of Ideology*, the purpose of culture is to limit and cultivate the death drive, which is exactly what consumer culture does in *White Noise*. Yet as Zizek further argues, fascism, which demands uniformity and forbids the reshaping of ideology, represents the concept of culture carried to an extreme insofar as "the source of the totalitarian temptation" is the aspiration to abolish (rather than to limit or cultivate) the death drive (5). In *White Noise*, this temptation is embodied in

Jack's fascination with Hitler, which itself stems from Jack's own aspirations of escaping death. When a mysterious old man appears in his backyard one morning, Jack mistakes him for "Death, or Death's errand runner" and tellingly hides behind a copy of *Mein Kampf* for protection (243–244). While the old man eventually proves harmless insofar as he is not Death but Jack's father-in-law, Jack's fear of dying persists, and he continues to seek asylum in his studies of Hitler and his continued outings to the grocery store, shopping mall, and other sites of consumption. What Jack ultimately wants from his culture is protection from death. As a result, his desire to yield to the temptation Zizek describes is particularly strong, and through much of the novel he demonstrates a willingness to forego subjectivity and the potential to reshape his cultural landscape in exchange for amnesty from death. Rather than empowering him, then, consumer ideology threatens to neutralize Jack and rob him of agency—a hazard Baudrillard views as a *fait accompli.*

Unlike Shields and Certeau, Baudrillard focuses primarily on the downside of consumer culture. In his first major work, *The System of Objects*, Baudrillard argues that the relationship between people and the objects that constitute their world stifles subjectivity. In other words, rather than allowing for what Shields describes as an "active, committed production of self and society," consumerism aims to assimilate everyone into what Baudrillard alternately terms the system of objects or simply "the system" (Shields 2). Within this system, according to Baudrillard, the apparent freedom to reshape ourselves and society through our purchases (i.e., "voting with our pocketbooks") is ultimately illusory; the only real "freedom" we have within the parameters of consumer culture is the freedom to accumulate and arrange commodities in a way that reflects our continuing advances in social status. Thus where Shields and Certeau might read Jack's adoption of the "J.A.K. Gladney" persona in *White Noise* as an instance of empowerment, Baudrillard might argue that Jack's dark glasses and robe serve primarily to insulate him from the world at large, that these accessories are arbitrary signs of differentiation which signal Jack's superiority in a particular social arena (that of academia and, more specifically, the field of Hitler studies), and that by investing these signs with such value, Jack and his associates neither strengthen nor weaken consumer ideology but simply confirm its authority.

Because the exhortation to accumulate and arrange signs of social status is at the root of consumer ideology, no combination of purchases or arrangement of goods can alter its basic dictum, which demands that we define ourselves in relation to the objects we possess. Hence Baudrillard's insistence upon the totalitarian nature of consumer ideology: the so-called "subject" has no power to alter consumer ideology and can only fall into line as an object within the system. Surrounded by objects, Baudrillard argues, we have come to behave as objects ourselves. That is, we no longer interact in a meaningful way with the world at large or the people who occupy that world. Instead, we situate ourselves within self-contained constellations of objects that insulate us from meaningful interaction of any kind. In short, we are too busy accumulating and arranging commodities in an effort to demonstrate that we live "the good life" (however it may be defined) to connect with each other or the world at large. Baudrillard illustrates the mechanics of this alienation by distinguishing between what he calls the utensil and the object:

> A *utensil* is never possessed, because a utensil refers one to the world; what is possessed is always an object *abstracted from its function and thus brought into relationship with the subject.* In this context, all owned objects partake of the same *abstractness*, and refer to one another only inasmuch as they refer solely to the subject. Such objects together make up the system through which the subject strives to construct a world, a private totality. (*System of Objects* 86)

As opposed to the utensil, then, the object takes on significance beyond its usefulness and becomes part of a complex system of objects that refer to each other and structure the subject's existence in a way that diminishes contact with the "real" world.

Even goods with apparent usefulness serve primarily as objects, Baudrillard argues, insofar as they seal the subject off from the world (111). Due to the overwhelming profusion of technology that isolates us from nature—including such innovations as the air conditioner, the refrigerator and television, as well as advances in agriculture, textiles, and manufacturing that provide us with an overabundance of commodities—humanity's relationship with need has become mystified; because we are immersed in a largely artificial environment, mere survival or protection from the elements is no longer a concern. Moreover, what presents itself as technological progress is not progress at all but stagnation. Minor improvements, refinements, and repackaging, or in Baudrillard's words, "anything to enhance the prestige of the object, but nothing by way of structural innovation," all pass for technological breakthroughs in present-day society (125). As a result, we live in a world of "pseudo-functionality" in which objects are meant not to be used but simply to be purchased (114, 162). Objects are "structured as a function neither of needs nor of a more rational organization of the world, but instead constitute a system determined entirely by an ideological regime of production and social integration" (174).

An example of the kind of regime Baudrillard describes appears in the opening paragraphs of *White Noise*. Here, a multitude of students descends upon the fictitious "College-on-the-Hill" in station wagons "loaded down with carefully secured suitcases full of light and heavy clothing; with boxes of blankets, boots and shoes, stationery and books, sheets pillows quilts; with rolled up rugs and sleeping bags; with bicycles, skis, rucksacks, English and Western saddles, inflated rafts" (3). Upon arrival, these students spring from their parents' cars to remove the objects inside:

> the stereo sets, radios, personal computers; small refrigerators and table ranges; the cartons of phonograph records and cassettes; the hairdryers and styling irons; the tennis rackets, soccer balls, hockey and lacrosse sticks, bows and arrows; the controlled substances, the birth control pills and devices;

the junk food still in shopping bags—onion-and-garlic chips, nacho thins, peanut creme patties, Waffelos and Kabooms, fruit chews and toffee popcorn; the Dum-Dum pops, the Mystic mints. (3)

That the students appear midway through this passage, buffered almost equally on both sides by descriptions of their possessions, suggests that the students, like their possessions, are links in a chain, comparable elements in what Baudrillard terms the system of objects. This impression is heightened in the subsequent paragraph when Jack describes the parents of these students as being nearly identical to each other, marked by well-made faces, wry looks, diet-trim bodies, and a sense of "massive insurance coverage" (3). What unites these parents more than anything else, however, is the long line of station wagons in which they have arrived, which "as much as anything they might do in the course of the year, more than formal liturgies or laws, tells the parents they are a collection of the like-minded and the spiritually akin, a people, a nation" (4). Here, the sense of collective identity the parents find in their cars mirrors the relationship between the students and their own possessions. Where the station wagons serve to set the parents apart from other groups (e.g., retirees, childless adults, those unable to afford college tuition), the stereo sets, radios, personal computers, and other paraphernalia belonging to the students speak a complex language that identifies those students as members of a relatively affluent youth culture and sets them apart from their parents and other groups, yet at the same time unites them with everyone who speaks their language, the language spoken by consumer culture, or in Baudrillard's terms, the language of the system.

In addition to illustrating ways in which parents and their children construct worlds through their possessions, the opening pages of *White Noise* also hint at the distinction Baudrillard draws between utensils and objects. The possessions in this passage place their possessors in a matrix of abstract values, many of which have less to do with the "real" world than with what Baudrillard describes as a "hyperreal" system of false needs; the English and Western saddles are not strapped to horses, the rafts are already inflated despite being far from any discernable bodies of water, the controlled substances foreshadow the appearance of Dylar (the fictional drug purported to insulate its users from anxiety over death), and the food is described as "junk"—suggesting that even provisions have ceased to function in any practical way insofar as they provide no real nourishment, only empty calories. As Richard Lane notes in *Jean Baudrillard*, this blurring of the line between reality and hyperreality is a major theme throughout *White Noise*, and the novel's characters are particularly concerned with the distinction between being in the world and being isolated from it: "There is a constant teasing-out of any hint of *inauthenticity*, a constant bantering between characters about the disjunction between information overload and the feeling that nothing about the world, about being in the world, is known" (Lane 122). For Baudrillard, however, this sense of isolation from the "real" world is not up for debate; it is a direct consequence of the proliferation of consumer goods throughout society.

Although he works within a Marxian framework through much of *The System of Objects* insofar as his rhetoric centers primarily on production, Baudrillard concludes with an attempt to define consumption. Consumption, he argues, has nothing to do with needs and is "surely *not* that passive process of absorption and appropriation which is contrasted to the supposedly active mode of production" (199). Rather, consumption is "an active form of relationship (not only to goods, but also to society and to the world), a mode of systematic activity and global response which founds our entire cultural system" (199). Where such "traditional symbolic objects" as tools and furniture "bore the clear imprint of the conscious or unconscious dynamic" of human activity, objects now function as signs, and their organization forms a signifying fabric constituting the "virtual totality of all objects and messages ready-constituted as a more or less coherent discourse" (200). This discourse encompasses everything and reduces all human relations to forms of consumption. We can neither live in the "real" world nor respond to each other as human beings because the objects we possess divorce us from both.

In *White Noise*, the alienation Baudrillard describes is best exemplified when Jack and his colleague, Murray Jay Siskind, pay a visit to "a tourist attraction known as the most photographed barn in America" (12). As they approach the site, they see a number of signs advertising the barn's imminence, and upon arrival they find droves of people either photographing or selling pictures of the attraction. Admiring the scene, Murray remarks that no one can actually see the barn itself; rather, they are all taking part in the prepackaged experience of the barn:

> Once you've seen the signs about the barn, it becomes impossible to see the barn…We're not here to capture an image, we're here to maintain one. Every photograph reinforces the aura…Being here is a kind of spiritual surrender. We see only what the others see. The thousands who were here in the past, those who will come in the future. We've agreed to be part of a collective perception. This literally colors our vision. A religious experience in a way, like tourism…They are taking pictures of taking pictures… What was the barn like before it was photographed?…What did it look like, how was it different from other barns? We can't answer these questions because we've seen the signs, seen the people snapping pictures. We can't get outside the aura. We're part of the aura. We're here, we're now. (12–13)

Serving no other purpose than to be photographed, the barn has ceased to function in its capacity as a barn and now functions only as the image or spectacle of a barn—a "barn," as it were, in quotation marks. For Baudrillard, this state of affairs typifies consumer culture: because nothing serves a real purpose, everything within this culture is nothing more than a spectacle. This dictum applies not only to objects, but to people as well, as exemplified by the connection Murray draws between the barn and its spectators. Self-consciously participating in a consumer phenomenon that might best be termed "the barn experience," these spectators cannot simply take pictures of the barn. Rather, they exist primarily to service the barn, to maintain, as Murray insists, its image. Just as the barn serves no other purpose than to be photographed, the tourists serve no other purpose than to photograph it. The tourists and the barn, then, are caught up in a tautological relationship in which each defines the other with no real reference to the outside world.

The relationship between the tourists and the barn in *White Noise* parallels the relationship Baudrillard sees between consumers and commodities within his system of objects in that no commodity within this system serves a purpose other than to signify the social status of its possessor while, in turn, the primary role of the commodity's possessor is to impute significance to the commodity. In *The Consumer Society*, Baudrillard expounds upon this theory by arguing that the proliferation of consumer goods in the developed world has caused us to "live at the pace of objects, live to the rhythm of their ceaseless succession" (25). This "ceaseless succession" stems from the fact that objects do not fulfill real needs but participate in what Baudrillard calls a "system of needs" in which objects produce neither enjoyment nor satisfaction but signify successful participation in society (75). Reinforced by the mass media, the system of needs presents a logic of social differentiation that induces individuals to "buy into an entire system of objects and needs through which one differentiates oneself socially, yet integrates oneself into the consumer society" (Kellner 15). Indeed, Baudrillard notes, the message broadcast by every outlet of the mass media is not necessarily to buy specific products but simply to participate in the system of needs (*Consumer Society* 122). Thus, borrowing Marshall McLuhan's famous phrase, Baudrillard argues that "the medium is the message," and that the function of the mass media is to "neutralize the lived, unique, eventual character of the world and substitute for it a multiple universe of media which, as such, are homogenous one with another, signifying each other referring back and forth to each other" (123). What results from this self-referential "multiple universe of media" is an abstract yet coherent system of logic that not only imposes an ideology of consumption upon the masses but also substitutes itself for the referential or "real" dimension of lived existence (124, 125). Within this context, the affluence to which the individual aspires does not really exist but "only has to make us believe it exists to be an effective myth" (193). Similarly, consumption itself is a myth or, more accurately, *the* myth of contemporary society insofar as it is an endlessly repeated idea that has gained the force of common sense and has become the "morality of modernity" (194).

When a colleague publicly belittles his off-campus fashion sense in *White Noise*, Jack suddenly finds himself "in the mood to shop" and embraces the morality of modernity that Baudrillard describes (83). Gathering his family together after the confrontation, Jack heads for the mall where he "shops with reckless abandon" to meet "immediate needs and distant contingencies" (84). The character of his purchases, however, suggests that Jack's sense of immediate "need" has less to do with practical necessity than with nursing his fragile ego:

> I shopped for its own sake, looking and touching, inspecting merchandise I had no intention of buying, then buying it. I sent clerks into their fabric books and pattern books to search for elusive designs. I began to grow in value and self-regard. I filled myself out, found new aspects of myself, located a person I'd forgotten existed. Brightness settled around me…I traded money for goods. The more money I spent, the less important it seemed. I was bigger than these sums. These sums poured off my skin like so much rain. These sums in fact came back to me in the form of existential credit. I felt expansive, inclined to be sweepingly generous, and told the kids to pick out their Christmas gifts here and now. I gestured in what I felt was an expansive manner. I could tell they were impressed. (84)

In addition to strengthening Jack's self-image, this shopping spree also strengthens his sense of belonging within his family. Thomas J. Ferraro notes in "Whole Families Shopping Together" that by shopping with his family, Jack "becomes 'one' with his family, which in turn achieves its 'oneness' through the activity of shopping" (22). Moreover, according to Ferraro, this passage demonstrates that the structure of Jack's family is itself grounded in consumption in that each of the Gladneys "knows his or her responsibilities, his or her privileges" within the context of the marketplace (23). Both as a unit and as individuals, Jack's family finds a sense of identity in the act of consumption.

Yet for all of Jack's magnanimity and the sense of family unity it appears to engender, the joy of shopping is markedly short-lived, and the members of Jack's family, as if to confirm Baudrillard's theory, gain no real satisfaction from their outing. Immediately after experiencing the "buzz" of their shopping trip, the Gladneys drive home in silence, then retreat to their respective rooms, "wishing to be alone" (*White Noise* 84). Not much later, Jack finds his daughter sitting in front of the television, moving her lips and "attempting to match the words as they [are] spoken" (84). This image is echoed throughout the novel whenever the children of Jack's marriage mutter the names of products and corporate slogans in their sleep, and confirms a theory Murray espouses early in the novel when he argues that children are the primary targets of "advertisers and mass-producers of culture" (50). Children, Murray says, understand something that adults seem to have forgotten—that the purpose of television is to indoctrinate them into society; in addition to offering "incredible amounts of psychic data," television also, according to Murray, "welcomes us into the grid" by presenting us with "the bright packaging, the jingles, the slice-of-life commercials, the products hurtling out of the darkness, the coded messages and endless repetitions, like chants, like mantras" of consumer culture (51).

Unlike Baudrillard, Murray sees television's power to indoctrinate as a positive phenomenon insofar as it offers society a shared sense of history and purpose. From Jack's perspective, however, this shared sense of history and purpose is illusory as demonstrated by the isolation ultimately engendered by consumption and television. The ideology of consumption that the medium enforces strips Jack's family of what Baudrillard calls the "real" dimension of lived existence and replaces interpersonal relationships with relationships among individuals and the objects they possess. As Jack's family is loath to discover, the latter type of relationship cannot deliver the degree of fulfillment it promises. In *The Consumer Society,* Baudrillard argues that the discrepancy between what consumer culture tells us the object will do for us and what the object actually does robs us of our ambivalence toward objects. Moreover, this lack of ambivalence leads us into an unhealthy relationship with the objects that surround us:

> Forced to adapt to the **principle of need**, to the **principle of utility** (the principle of economic reality) or, in other words, to the ever full and *positive* correlation between a product of some kind (object, good or service) and a satisfaction through the one being indexed to the other; forced into this concerted, unilateral and ever positive finality, *the whole of the negativity of desire*, the other side of **ambivalence**, and hence all the things which do not fit into this positive vision, *are rejected, censored by satisfaction itself* (which is not enjoyment [*jouissance*]: enjoyment, for its part, is ambivalent), and, no longer finding any possible outlet, crystallize into a gigantic fund of anxiety. (177)

While Baudrillard's definition of ambivalence gains greater nuance in his later works, he uses the term broadly in this passage; ambivalence is a sense of both fulfillment and nonfulfillment, or gain and loss, in relation to the object of desire. Because consumer ideology does not allow for ambivalence and, instead, forces the consumer to view the business of consumption only in terms of gain, the consumer cannot help but feel inadequate in relation to the objects he or she possesses.

The trouble with consumer ideology, Baudrillard argues, is that it tells us (via advertising, media images, and the like) that the commodities we purchase will bring us absolute fulfillment, that for every need we may experience, an object exists within the system that will bring us unconditional satisfaction. This reasoning, Baudrillard notes, ignores the fact that needs can never be satisfied in full, and that "a completed process, where there is only positivity, is something which is never found" (203). Hence the consumer's "giant fund" of anxiety: our natural ambivalence toward objects is repressed insofar as consumer ideology tells us that our enjoyment of objects should be unconditional. As with the Gladneys, our dissatisfaction with the objects that surround us will inevitably surface. Yet because consumer ideology tells us that these objects can truly bring absolute fulfillment, we have no alternative but to locate the problem within ourselves, and the only option consumer ideology provides to fix this problem or to fill the void left when we fail to be satisfied by the objects we acquire is for us to acquire more objects.

Despite our constant disappointment with objects, we continue to believe the promise of consumer ideology—that consumption will improve our lives and increase our sense of self-worth. This notion is underscored in *White Noise* when Jack reflects that his purchases allow him to "grow in value and self-regard" (84). Indeed, that the massive sums he spends return to him "in the form of existential credit" suggests that even the act of spending does not entail loss, and that, in line with Baudrillard's argument, consumer culture only allows for gain. Which begs an important question: what exactly does Jack think he is gaining? For Baudrillard, the answer to this question is the key to understanding the distinction between the "real" world and the "hyperreal" realm of consumer culture: Jack thinks he is gaining "value," a concept that causes him to view his activities in the "real" dimension of lived existence as tangential to the business of accumulating good credit—existential or otherwise. This sense of value is explained earlier in the novel when Jack checks his bank balance. Upon discovering that the number on the ATM screen roughly corresponds with the number in his head, Jack experiences a rush of "relief and gratitude" that stems from his belief "that something of deep personal value, but not money, not that at all, had been authenticated and confirmed" (46). When Jack speaks of value, then, he is not referring to a dollar amount, but something much greater: a sense of having been, in his words, "blessed" by "the system" (46). Such blessings, according to Baudrillard, amount to a dangerous illusion that allows people to view themselves as they do the commodities that constitute their environment: as markers of greater or lesser value within the system of objects. In other words, consumer ideology reduces our status to that of objects insofar as it renders us, like objects, signs of value.

Building on the above observation, Baudrillard argues in *For a Critique of the Political Economy of the Sign* that all "repressive and reductive strategies of power systems are already present in the internal logic of the sign" and that, as a result, Marxism must be reevaluated in relation to structuralism and semiotics in order for the analysis of consumer ideology to be effective (163). While Marx correctly perceived the radical discontinuity between feudalism and early capitalism, he failed to recognize the cleft between early and late capitalism, the latter being fundamentally different from the former due to what Kellner calls a new logic of sign value and fetishism. Under the rule of sign value, Kellner explains, "consumption and display become a central locus of value, and are as important as production is in determining the logic, nature and direction of social processes" (21). While this argument appears in various forms throughout *The System of Objects* and *The Consumer Society*, Baudrillard's project in *For a Critique* is to dissect the logic of consumption at its most basic level, the level of the sign, because, the theorist argues, it is the internal logic of the sign that provides an "alibi" for the illusion of value that regulates consumer ideology.

Ironically, Baudrillard traces consumer ideology's alibi to Marx, who defines the commodity as an object with both exchange value and use value. In plain terms, this distinction means that while the commodity may be sold at a certain price, its actual utility may be deemed more or less valuable than that price. For Marx, this binary model reveals the inequality between the forces of capital and labor since capital remunerates labor with less than the exchange value of labor's product. As Marx argues in "Estranged Labour," this arrangement results in the commodification of the worker:

> The worker becomes all the poorer the more wealth he produces, the more his production increases in power and range. The worker becomes an ever cheaper commodity the more commodities he creates. With the *increasing value* of the world of things proceeds in direct proportion the devaluation

of the world of men. Labour produces not only commodities; it produces itself and work as a *commodity*—and does so in the proportion in which it produces commodities generally. (Tucker 71)

Here, Marx associates the commodification of the individual with commodity fetishism, the process by which capital mystifies or conceals the relationship between labor and its product. The laborer will only cease to be a commodity, Marx argues, when the mystifying nature of commodity fetishism is revealed and use value, which satisfies real human needs, emerges as the "true" form of value.

Where Marx locates the commodification of the individual in the mystified relationship between labor and its product, Baudrillard locates such commodification in the ideology of consumption, which finds a false alibi or justification in the hypothetical priority Marx places on use value. As noted throughout Baudrillard's *oeuvre*, the consumption of goods is not a function of need but of social differentiation. In this sense, Baudrillard argues, "it is absurd to speak of a consumer society as if consumption were a system of universal values appropriate to all men because of being founded upon the satisfaction of individual needs, when really it is an institution and a morality, and in this way an element of the strategy of power in any society, past or future" (*For a Critique* 62). Use value, then, is an illusion that makes exchange value seem somehow rational by providing it with what Baudrillard calls "the guarantee of the real" (137). Yet because this guarantee is based not on real needs but on the artificial system of needs described in *The System of Objects*, the notion of value can only direct the individual's attention away from the real dimension of lived existence and toward the abstract realm to which Jack looks for validation when he checks his bank account in *White Noise*. Such faith in the abstract realm of value, Baudrillard further argues, stems from the parallel he sees between the structure of the commodity and the structure of the sign.

Because the commodity is binary in nature, it bears the structure of what Ferdinand de Saussure calls the linguistic sign. In "Nature of the Linguistic Sign," Saussure notes that the linguistic unit, or sign, is "a double entity formed by the associating of two terms" (65). These two terms are *the concept* and *the sound-image* or, as Saussure later dubs them, *the signified* and *the signifier*. From Baudrillard's perspective, however, the relationship between the signifier and the signified is not balanced; as with use value in relation to exchange value, the signified provides the signifier with "the guarantee of the real" (*For a Critique* 137). Yet this so-called guarantee is illusory in that it conceals what Baudrillard considers the true relationship between the signifier and the signified: that the signified is an effect of the signifier, that without the signifier, the signified would not exist. Nonetheless, Baudrillard argues, consumer ideology assures us that the signified (or concept) is the guarantor of the signifier's real and, more importantly, that this signified is best understood in terms of value, the validity of which is itself guaranteed by the Marxian notion of use value.

The logic of consumer ideology, then, hinges upon the notion of value. As in *White Noise*, this notion is connected to money insofar as it can be measured in terms of Jack's bank balance but is also, as Jack insists, "not money, not that at all" (46). Rather, as Jean-Joseph Goux asserts in *Symbolic Economies*, value is the object's ideal form or that aspect of the object which "can be compared measured and equated despite differences" among it and other objects (98). This form, according to Goux, is what allows for the existence of social castes or classes; because all people are essentially the same, the upper or ruling classes must look elsewhere to justify their standing in society. This is why idealism, "which affirms the primacy of idea, consciousness, mind (and, we might add, value, meaning, essence, form) and the subordination of matter" is "the philosophical ideology of the dominant classes" (98). In this regard, consumerism might best be thought of as a democratized form of idealism: rather than pointing to such ineffable phenomena as the divine right of kings, we can now look to the individual's skill as a consumer, the measure of which can be gleaned with some (but by no means absolute) accuracy by assessing his or her net worth, to establish the value of the individual. Despite this apparent democratization, however, consumer ideology continues (according to Baudrillard) to be a repressive force insofar as its privileging of the ideal (or signified) over the physical (or signifier) renders us beholden to the logic of the sign, which in turn renders us beholden to the logic of the system of objects.

Ultimately, Baudrillard argues, it is the logic of the sign itself that restricts the subject's ambivalence in relation to objects. The sign, as Baudrillard and Saussure agree, is marked by an arbitrary nature (Baudrillard, *For a Critique* 148). Baudrillard's definition of arbitrary, however, goes beyond that of Saussure. Where Saussure notes that the sign is arbitrary because there is no causal link between the signifier and signified, Baudrillard argues that arbitrariness is rooted in the fact that consumer ideology would have us believe that the signifier both equals and is discreet from the signified (149). So while the signifier is not the signified, it nonetheless "equals," "means," or even "is" *in the realm of circulation and exchange* that which can neither be spoken nor represented except through the signifier: the signified and the signified only. For the sake of economy, the sign reduces, represses, and annihilates "all that which overflows the schema of equivalence and signification" and eliminates ambivalence in the name of "a fixed and equational structure" that ultimately denotes value and nothing more (149). As a result, the subject loses ambivalence toward objects and relates to them only in terms of positive sign value (i.e., what the object says to the world at large about the subject's status in relation to all other objects).

Here, ambivalence continues to mean for Baudrillard roughly what it meant in *The Consumer Society*: the coexistence of fulfillment and nonfulfillment of desire. At the same time, however, his argument takes a major step forward. By linking the principle of utility (the positive correlation of some product with the satisfaction it supposedly engenders) with the signified, Baudrillard locates the repression of ambivalence within the structure of the commodity, which follows the logic of the sign. According to this logic, if the object is the commodity's signifier, then its signified is its positive sign value:

$$\frac{\text{Signifier}}{\text{Signified}} = \frac{\text{Object}}{\text{Positive Sign Value}}$$

Because it is a sign itself, positive sign value has as its components both a signifier and a signified or, according to Baudrillard's model, exchange value and use value. Thus the commodity has a compound structure:

$$\frac{\text{Object}}{\text{Positive Sign Value}} = \frac{\text{Object}}{\text{EV/UV}}$$

In other words, the object signifies positive sign value, which can be described as exchange value legitimized by use value. Thus if the root of the commodity's "meaning" is its use value, then the commodity's promise is that of fulfillment or satisfaction of needs. As noted, however, the validity of this promise is inconsequential in that we continue to believe it regardless of how many times commodities let us down. Insofar as we continue to place our unflinching trust in the promise of consumer ideology—that is, the promise that commodities will bring us satisfaction—we confirm our faith in the imaginary realm of value and, in so doing, lose our ambivalence in relation to objects. This is what Baudrillard means when he says that the entire process of signification results in "nothing but a gigantic *simulation model of meaning*" (*For a Critique* 160). Our absolute faith in the notion of value causes us to perceive the world as an array of signs that we can only read in terms of value. Moreover, because we perceive the world in this fashion, we ourselves become signs of value and come to regard ourselves in much the same way that we regard all other elements within the system of objects: as commodities.

Like the denizens of consumer culture Baudrillard describes, Jack views himself in binary terms throughout *White Noise*. Early on, he describes himself in relation to his on-campus persona as "the false character that follows the name around" (17). In other words, Jack sees himself as inferior to the image he projects or, more accurately, to the name or signifier "J.A.K. Gladney." Later, Jack measures his self-worth in terms of his bank account and, after he is exposed to the chemical agent Nyodene D, a medical technician informs Jack that he is the "sum total" of all his data (141). This second revelation helps to explain what Jack intuits when he gleans "something of deep personal value, but not money" upon checking his bank account: a quantifiable figure consisting of a seemingly infinite number of variables, for which his bank account serves as a powerful (yet by no means singular) index. When Jack is told that he is the sum total of all his data, his suspicion that his self-worth (or, more accurately, that he himself) can be reduced to a single number is confirmed. Moreover, that the name on Jack's medical file is not "Jack" but "J.A.K." suggests that Jack's identity is bound up in two components: the signifier "J.A.K. Gladney" and the sum total it signifies (141). Yet while this binary structure parallels that of the commodity, it fails to account for one thing: the neurotic voice that agonizes over the meaning of life, death, and all phenomena in between throughout the narrative.

Jack's suspicion that he is "the false character that follows the name around" suggests that he partakes in what Baudrillard refers to in *The Consumer Society* as the "giant fund of anxiety" generated by consumer ideology's restriction of ambivalence. Nonetheless, Jack is not entirely paralyzed by this anxiety; when he is not obsessing over his failure to live up to the "J.A.K. Gladney" image and all that it signifies, Jack's interactions with his family and friends are marked by what Babette describes in a conversation regarding their sexual preferences as "balance, a sort of give and take" (29). This sense of balance, Jack explains, is rooted in the fact that he and Babette "tell each other everything," a practice that has become for the couple "a form of self-renewal and a gesture of custodial trust" (29). Such trust, according to Jack,

> helps us develop an identity secure enough to allow itself to be placed in another's care and protection. Babette and I have

> turned our lives for each other's thoughtful regard, turned
> them in the moonlight in our pale hands, spoken deep into
> the night about fathers and mothers, childhood, friendships,
> awakenings, old loves, old fears (except for fear of death). No
> detail must be left out, not even a dog with ticks or a neigh-
> bor's boy who ate an insect on a dare. The smell of pantries,
> the sense of empty afternoons, the feel of things as they rained
> across our skin, things as facts and passions, the feel of pain,
> loss, disappointment, breathless delight. In these night recita-
> tions we create a space between things as we felt them at the
> time and as we speak them now. This is the space reserved for
> irony, sympathy and fond amusement, the means by which we
> rescue ourselves from the past. (30)

Revolving around such unquantifiable perceptions as pain, loss,
and disappointment, the kind of communication Jack describes in
this passage is certainly not beholden to the logic of value, nor can
the kinds of experiences he and Babette relate to each other be subsumed in the sum total of their data. Rather than arranging the signs
at their disposal to demonstrate their value as individuals, then, Jack
and Babette surrender the notion of value in favor of vulnerability
and intimacy. In so doing, they provisionally escape the gravitational
pull of Baudrillard's system of objects.

Despite the intimacy they share, however, Jack and Babette never
discuss their mutual fear of death. It is no coincidence, then, that
this fear motivates the couple to embrace the drug Dylar. Much to
their chagrin, however, Jack and Babette learn that Dylar does not
deliver on its promise. Instead of quelling the fear of death, the drug
causes its *habitués* to enter the gigantic simulation model of meaning Baudrillard describes. Ingesting Dylar tablets by the handful, the
drug's inventor, Willie Mink, lives in a world in which signs are,
for all practical purposes, indistinguishable from the things they
represent. Thus when Jack utters the phrase "plunging aircraft,"
Willie folds into a crash position, "head well forward, hands clasped
behind his knees" (309). While the somewhat absurd nature of the
passage in which this exchange occurs casts doubt on Baudrillard's
assertion that we currently live in a world consisting only of signs,

Jack's desire for Dylar coupled with Willie's prediction that a more effective version of the drug will eventually come on the market underscores DeLillo's concern that while the world Baudrillard envisions has not yet come to pass, such a world may very well be waiting in the wings.

Baudrillard contends that all forms of exchange within consumer society are governed by the value-laden logic of signification. The members of the society he envisions are so beholden to the notion of value that they cannot conceive of any frame of reference beyond that of value. As a result, the members of this society read all things—including commodities, language, other people, and even themselves—as signs of value and nothing else. Intent upon amassing vast quantities of the "existential credit" to which Jack refers in *White Noise*, consumers lack ambivalence, or the capacity to recognize anything that overflows the binary schema of the commodity. Moreover, because value is an illusory and completely arbitrary notion rooted not in the real world but in the abstract realm of the ideal, adherence to the tenets of consumer ideology can only result in complete alienation from reality. Yet as *White Noise* suggests, this alienation is not as complete as Baudrillard would have us believe. While Jack frequently attempts to make up for the disjunction between his outward signs of social ascendancy and his inner sense of value by increasing his rate of consumption, he also recognizes that some phenomena, like the confidences he shares with Babette, cannot be quantified. Thus where Baudrillard argues that ambivalence is so foreign to the system of objects as to render it inimical to that system, DeLillo sees ambivalence as a phenomenon that may be threatened, but not entirely extinguished, by consumer culture.

CHAPTER 2

ESCAPING THE THIRD PERSON SINGULAR: *AMERICANA* AND THE SEMIOTIC CHALLENGE

In a 1991 interview titled "I Don't Belong to the Club, to the Seraglio," Jean Baudrillard described the period in which he studied under Roland Barthes as the point in his intellectual development at which "everything changed" (Gane, *Live* 20). Drawing heavily on Ferdinand de Saussure's study of the linguistic sign, Barthes' exploration of consumer and media culture gave Baudrillard the impetus to study such "life signs within society" as myths, ideologies, fashion, and the media as functions of language (Kellner 4). As Mike Gane notes in *Baudrillard: Critical and Fatal Theory*, Barthes' reading of Saussure not only provided the general methodological guidelines Baudrillard would use throughout his career, but also provided Baudrillard with the semiological background needed to examine the ways in which all objects interact to form a system that functions much like language (34). This so-called "system of objects,"

Baudrillard argues, is regulated by the same logic of value that regulates signification. This logic, moreover, is dehumanizing insofar as it renders objects of all elements within the system—including what might otherwise be considered the human subject.

By grounding all meaning in the abstract realm of value, consumer ideology creates a framework that forces us all to regard ourselves as commodities. Nonetheless, Baudrillard argues, the very knowledge "that the Object is nothing and that behind it stands the tangled void of human relations" offers hope that "violent irruptions and sudden disintegrations" will inevitably and unexpectedly arise to destroy consumer ideology (Baudrillard, *Consumer Society* 196). Such "violent irruptions and sudden disintegrations," moreover, will consist not only of subversive acts against the bourgeois power structures that victimize labor but also, and more importantly, of a complete rethinking of communication and exchange that will allow for the reemergence of ambivalence, a term Baudrillard uses to denote the incessant potential for the "destruction of the illusion of value" (Baudrillard, *For a Critique* 209). Yet as the inevitable and unexpected nature of these "irruptions" might suggest, one of the major drawbacks of Baudrillard's argument is, as Douglas Kellner notes in *Jean Baudrillard: From Marxism to Postmodernism and Beyond*, that Baudrillard presents neither a theory of the subject as an agent of social change nor a theory of class or group revolt (18). That is, although these irruptions will inevitably occur, we have no power to bring them about.

Given the lack of a place for the human subject in Baudrillard's revolutionary vision, his call for ambivalence has little bite beyond the realm of theory. Moreover, the contrast he draws between the "real" world and the abstract realm of value raises the issue of whether moving beyond value is a viable proposition. Baudrillard's dichotomy suggests that the "real" world exists outside of language or, at the very least, can be reached via a mode of language that is not grounded in value. Whether such a mode of language can exist is certainly debatable, as are the practicality and practicability of abandoning value. Yet if Baudrillard's assessment of consumerism (i.e., that it renders us objects) is even marginally correct, these issues must be examined—a task rendered less daunting and perhaps more rewarding in the light of Barthes' work in the field of semiology and Don DeLillo's first novel, *Americana*.

Describing the role of semiology some years after the publication of Baudrillard's landmark *For a Critique of the Political Economy of the Sign*, Barthes argues in *The Semiotic Challenge* that the study of signs should yield answers to the issues Baudrillard raises. Regarding the "ideological commitment" of semiology, Barthes explains that attacking "the petit-bourgeois good conscience" is not enough (8). Semiology must also interrogate "the symbolic and semantic system of our entire culture; it is not enough to change contents, we must above all aim at *fissuring* the meaning-system itself" (8).

As with Baudrillard, the meaning-system Barthes envisions is predicated on value, which he defines as "the redeeming concept which permits saving language's permanence and surmounting what we must call *fiduciary anxiety*" (155). In other words, value amounts to an unspoken agreement or social contract much like that which regulates currency: in order for language (like currency) to work, we must agree to regard the artificial and arbitrary connection between signs and concepts as if it were natural and purely logical.

To illustrate his point, Barthes examines a pair of lavatory doors at the University of Geneva respectively marked *Messieurs* and *Professeurs*:

> On the level of pure signification, the inscription has no mean-
> ing: are not "professors" "gentlemen"? It is on the level of value
> that the opposition, as bizarre as it is ethical, is explained: two
> paradigms enter into collision, of which we read no more than
> the ruins: *messieurs*/dames//*professeurs*/étudiants: in the play
> of language, it is indeed value (and not signification) which
> possesses the apparent, symbolic, and social charge: here that
> of segregation, pedagogical and sexual. (155)

For Baudrillard, such segregation results in commodification: because all elements of the system are segregated by their apparent value, they become nothing more than signs of value (i.e., commodities). Hence Baudrillard's interest in ambivalence—by destroying the illusion of value, ambivalence effects the very fissuring of the meaning system for which Barthes calls in *The Semiotic Challenge*.

Here, however, we return to the frustrating impasse that naturally lies at the heart of Baudrillard's position. Because consumer culture allows us to view ourselves only in terms of value, we lack the capacity to behave as anything other than objects. Or to put it another way, our lack of ambivalence renders us completely beholden to the laws of consumer ideology. From this perspective, action on the part of the individual is impossible. As a result, the destruction of the system can only come, so to speak, at the hands of the system itself.

Of course, Baudrillard's position hinges on the contention that consumer ideology has suppressed ambivalence completely and has therefore eradicated the potential for human subjectivity. Taking a comparatively humanist approach, however, DeLillo depicts a world in which civilization is certainly entranced but by no means ensnared by the lure of consumerism. Curtailed but not entirely repressed under the conditions DeLillo envisions, ambivalence remains a bulwark against the crushing onslaught of consumer ideology and so prevents the total assimilation of the consumer into what Baudrillard terms the system of objects. For DeLillo, then, the cultivation of ambivalence serves as a preventive measure: either we strive to view the world at large in terms beyond value or we run the risk of becoming commodities, or signs of value, ourselves. Setting the tone for many of DeLillo's later works, *Americana* explores the viability of life outside the grip of consumer culture and, by extension, beyond the logic of value that regulates the language of that culture.

In order to escape the complex and conflicting feelings he holds with regard to his mother, *Americana*'s protagonist, David Bell, learns at an early age to retreat into the idealized world depicted in the television commercials his father has crafted in his capacity as a Madison Avenue adman. In so doing, David begins to place his faith in television and all that it offers, as reflected in the words he puts into his father's mouth when he eventually films a mildly fictionalized autobiography: "The TV set is a package, and it's full of products. Inside are detergents, automobiles, cameras, breakfast cereals, other television sets. Programs are not interrupted by commercials; exactly the reverse is true. A television is an electronic form of packaging. Without the products there's nothing" (270). Just as packaging serves not only to protect goods in transit but also (and perhaps more importantly) to present those goods as desirable, television's message is simple: happiness can be achieved through the acquisition of commodities. Or, as David's fictionalized father further observes, "In this country there is a universal third person, the man we all want to be. Advertising has discovered this man. It uses him to express the possibilities open to the consumer. To consume in America is not to buy; it is to dream. Advertising is the suggestion that the dream of entering the third person singular might possibly be fulfilled" (270).

David's description of himself as "an extremely handsome young man" who takes the "simple step" of lathering up and shaving whenever he begins to wonder who he is, combined with his self-described resemblance to movie stars Kirk Douglas and Burt Lancaster, suggests early on that he has attained the American dream of entering what his father calls "the third-person singular" (11, 12). Insofar as his sense of identity depends primarily upon the image he sees in the mirror and its resemblance to celebrities, David appears to have reduced his life to the two-dimensional world of appearances that he associates with his father and, in so doing, to have distanced himself from the disturbing conflicts embodied by his mother. In this way, David's behavior sheds light on the relationship between Sigmund Freud's notion of ambivalence and that of Baudrillard. In *Inhibition, Symptoms and Anxiety*, Freud notes that a patient's fear of horses represents an attempt to resolve an Oedipal attitude toward his father: "a well-grounded love and a no less justifiable hatred directed towards one and the same person" (16). While such conflicts are common, Freud notes, they generally do not result in phobia. Rather, the child's affection tends to intensify at the expense of his hatred; this phenomenon, which Freud terms a reaction formation, stems from a need to repress the disagreeable instinct to desire the mother at the expense of the father's life (16, 17).

Where the reaction of Freud's patient to his disagreeable Oedipal instincts is a fear of the horses he associates with his father, David's is a more typical reaction; he simply represses the ambivalence he feels toward both parents. One thing that allows him to do so is the model provided by the advertisements his father has created. In Baudrillard's terms, because these advertisements proffer the illusion of a world in which commodities can meet all human needs, they eliminate David's ambivalence toward objects. In so doing, these advertisements also create an environment that eases to the point of suppression the ambivalence he feels toward the members of his family even as it reduces him to a two-dimensional commodity, the third-person singular image of himself. As a result, David comes to define himself solely in terms of value. In this context, what Tom LeClair refers to as "the new consumerism of communications, with its entropic tendency toward the most probable and reductive state" takes on heightened significance: the most probable and reductive state proffered by television advertisements is value, and David's entrance into the third person singular, his "buying into" the ethos of advertising, is at the same time his crossing over into what Baudrillard terms the system of objects (LeClair 49).

If David's passage into the system of objects tends to isolate him, it also proves an attractive alternative to living in the often painful "real" world precisely because it offers order in the face of apparent chaos; the conflicts and contradictions embodied in David's mother are denied by what DeLillo refers to in his 1983 *Rolling Stone* article, "American Blood," as "the artificial and dulling language" of the consumerist dream (27). From Barthes' perspective, such language can only result in the suppression of meaningful communication because the message of advertising always boils down to a single notion: the unparalleled excellence of all commodities (Barthes, *Challenge* 174). The problem, of course, with this mode of language is that it eliminates difference and, in so doing, "entirely exhausts the intention of communication" (175). If every brand of mouthwash, for example, is touted as "the best," then only the most superficial (if any) difference exists between the messages of each brand's advertisement.

In *Americana*, David's father demonstrates the validity of Barthes' argument when he describes his own efforts at devising an ad campaign for Dentex mouthwash:

> Okay, so we zero in on one of the essential ingredients, quasi-cinnamaldehyde-plus. QCP. We take the hard-sell route. Dentex with QCP kills mouth poisons and odor-causing impurities thirty-two percent faster. Be specific. Be factual. Make a promise. Okay, so some little creep says to me in a meeting: thirty-two percent faster than what? Obvious, I tell him: thirty-two percent faster that if Dentex didn't have QCP. The fact that all mouthwashes have this cinnamaldehyde stuff is beside the point; we were the only ones talking about it. This is known as pre-empting the truth. (273)

Citing QCP as the ingredient that makes Dentex "the best" mouthwash even as he admits that all mouthwashes contain this ingredient, David's father reveals that there is, in fact, no "best" and, by extension, that the hierarchy established by the concept of "the best" is entirely artificial. Nonetheless, the concept of the "the best," which is the benchmark for the concept of value, continues to serve as the governing myth of David's culture, as evidenced by his friend Pike's obsession with establishing a universal pecking order for such mismatched animals as polar bears and tigers, as well as David's obsession with his own place on the corporate ladder.

Like his fellow employees, David sees the workplace as a battleground rife with signs that he is either gaining or losing ground in his efforts at being recognized as "the best" in his field. Indeed, so convinced is David that everything in the workplace is a sign that he begins to agonize over the décor of his fellow workers' offices. After providing an exhaustive list of his coworkers and the colors of their sofas and office doors, David explains, "I had all this down on paper. On slow afternoons I used to study it, trying to find a pattern. I thought there might be a subtle color scheme designed by management and based on a man's salary, ability, and prospects for advancement and decline" (88). Rooted in paranoia though David's theory may be, his coworkers all subscribe to a system of measuring success in which "points" are scored for ruthlessness, personal appearance, cleverness, and (ironically) humility (13).

Measuring his performance in all personal encounters against those of the idealized figures of Kirk Douglas and Burt Lancaster (i.e., "the best" men he can imagine), David can only relate to other people in competitive terms. In the social world as in the business world, his quest to set himself off as "the best" renders him an advertisement for himself, but as an advertisement, he is limited to repeating the same message that all of his friends and coworkers must also repeat: that he is "the best," and as with Barthes' critique of the language of advertising, the seemingly universal desire to prove oneself "the best" renders meaningful communication impossible in David's world. Describing meetings with his coworkers as "drone-fests," David explains that the language of these meetings is such that words are always "at odds" with their meanings and that they do not "say what [is] being said, nor its reverse" (63, 36). Rather, the message David receives at these drone-fests is that he is, indeed, a drone and that his job as such is to avoid independent thinking (36). Thus while David initially claims to have mastered "the special elements" of the "new language" he discovers in the workplace, he eventually confesses that the tongue has mastered him: "Words blow in and out. I can hear them perfectly, with astounding clarity, but I can't believe they're coming from my mouth" (36, 97). In short, after relentlessly reproducing the unvarying message of corporate America for so long, David comes to realize that he has no voice of his own.

In an effort to reclaim his voice, David embarks upon a cross-country quest to discover what he calls the "yin and yang in Kansas" (10). While this metaphor appears early in the novel, David does not understand its implications until much later. Rather than seeking the kind of balance that the "yin and yang in Kansas" implies, David's initial instinct is to sabotage the "yin" of the corporate world with the "yang" of his preferred artistic medium, film. Yet as David's adaptation of the medium to corporate ends in the dog-eat-dog world of television programming demonstrates, his use of film only serves to reproduce the underlying logic of consumerism that he is trying to resist. From Baudrillard's perspective, this is because the work of art, like any commodity, ultimately serves as a sign of value or "part of the package, the constellation of accessories by which the 'socio-cultural' standing of the average citizen is determined" (Baudrillard, *Consumer Society* 107). Far from interrogating the logic of value, then, art, in Baudrillard's opinion, has been co-opted by consumer culture and, as a result, has become a sign of acculturation.

Arguing that the essence of consumer acculturation is distilled in the phrase "Beethoven is fabulous," Baudrillard notes that the accul-turated consumer is less concerned with the aesthetics of Beethoven's music than the social cachet attached to recognizing the "quality" of the composer's works (108). In *Americana*, this example takes an appropriately cinematic twist as David moves from group to group at a party "so boring that boredom itself soon becomes the topic of con-versation," and he "hears the same sentence a dozen times. 'It's like an Antonioni movie'" (DeLillo, *Americana* 4). Like the women who come and go "Talking of Michelangelo" in T. S. Eliot's "The Love Song of J. Alfred Prufrock," the partygoers in this passage appear less interested in art itself than in using their knowledge of it to dem-onstrate social ascendancy. While repeated references to Antonioni fail to advance the party's conversational discourse, these references underline the desire among David's friends and coworkers to prove their acculturation or, in plain language, to show that they are among "the best" at engaging in witty banter at cocktail parties.

That David retreats to the bathroom to check for dandruff shortly after hearing several identical versions of the Antonioni conversa-tion suggests that such public displays of what passes for wit among his friends and coworkers are akin to personal appearance in the social realm. In both cases, the goal is to impress; good grooming and wit go hand-in-hand. To be ignorant of Antonioni is to have dandruff, but appreciating art—or better yet, possessing it—is a sign of social ascendancy that operates in much the same way as personal appearance. Under such conditions, however, there can be little potential for art to undermine the consumer mindset.

Upon entering his host's bathroom, David notices six framed graffiti hanging on the wall: "The words were set in large bold type, about 60-point, on glossy paper; they were set in a scripted typeface to look real. Three of the graffiti were blasphemous and three were obscene. The frames looked expensive. I noticed some dandruff on my shoulders" (4). Though blasphemous and obscene, these graffiti fail to evoke the defiance David wishes to voice. That they are "set in a scripted typeface to look real" recalls Baudrillard's notion of the hyperreal, or a world consisting of models based on models, insofar as these pieces are not reproductions of "real" graffiti but merely models loosely based on some artist's notion of what graffiti might be like. Moreover, the expensive frames in which they appear underline the fact that these ersatz graffiti pose no threat to the order of consumption. Indeed, as Baudrillard points out in *The Consumer Society*, blasphemy and obscenity do not exist in consumer culture: "If all the denunciations, all the disquisitions on 'alienation,' and all the derisive force of pop and anti-art play so easily into establishment hands, that is because they are themselves part of the myth" (196). The only "true" blasphemy within the system of objects is to fail to partake in what Baudrillard refers to as the "formal liturgy" of consumption, but the affluence of the Western world precludes this option. Far from encouraging him to resist consumer ideology, the painting reminds David of his dandruff, perhaps the most subtle of all social diseases invented by Madison Avenue to move merchandise from store shelves to consumers' bathrooms.

According to Baudrillard, what suffers when art serves only to indicate the socio-cultural standing of the individual who either possesses or appreciates it is a sense of confrontation. Rather than interrogating consumer ideology, the work of art serves only to reinforce that ideology. To appreciate the work of art is to accept and reaffirm its value and, in turn, to legitimate the practice of using commodities to signal social standing. In other words, to demonstrate an appreciation of art is to demonstrate that one is "in on the joke." In

Americana, however the "joke" of consumer ideology is revealed to be obscene when David emerges from the bathroom to find his host entertaining partygoers with a spate of racist anecdotes:

> Quincy was in rare form, telling a series of jokes about Polish janitors, Negro ministers, Jews in concentration camps and Italian women with hairy legs. He battered his audience with shock and insult, challenging people to object. Of course we were choking with laughter, trying to outdo each other in showing how enlightened we were. It was meant to be a liberating ethnic experience. If you were offended by such jokes in general, or sensitive to particular ones which slurred your own race or ancestry, you were not ready to be accepted into the mainstream. B.G. Haines who was a professional model and one of the most beautiful women I have ever known, seemed to be enjoying Quincy's routine. She was one of four black people in the room—and the only American among them—and she apparently felt it was her diplomatic duty to laugh louder than anyone at Quincy's most vicious color jokes. She almost crumpled to the floor laughing and I was sure I detected a convulsive broken sob at the crest of every laugh. (6)

Like the acculturated individual who agrees that Beethoven is fabulous, Haines has no choice but to laugh lest she signal her divergence from the mainstream. Belying her repressed sadness and rage, however, her sobs reveal that, like the graffiti David finds in his host's bathroom, Quincy's race jokes serve only to uphold the status quo even as they purport to undermine it.

The same, according to Baudrillard, can be said for art. In *The Consumer Society*, Baudrillard argues that in what he terms our generalized neo culture "there is no longer any difference between a delicatessen and an art gallery" (28). This is because the art object, like all objects of consumption, "loses its symbolic meaning and tends to peter out into a discourse of connotations which are...simply relative to one another within a framework of a totalitarian cultural system (that is to say, a system which is able to integrate all significations whatever their provenance)" (115). Within this system, objects and images operate as signs of value, which serves as the controlling myth of consumer culture. Beholden to this myth, consumer culture cannot regard itself from a critical distance; because all language speaks of value, there is no critiquing value through language. As a result, Baudrillard argues, "there can be no contemporary art which is not, in its very existence and practice, compromised and complicit with that opaquely self-evident state of affairs" (116). This is to say that art, like language, is bound up in the manipulation of signs for the sole purpose of indicating social status.

Although Baudrillard posits pop art as the first medium to explore its own status as a "signed" and "consumed" object, he also argues that pop artists "forget that for a painting to be a super-sign (a unique object, a signature, the object of a noble, magical commerce), it is not sufficient to change the content of the picture or the artist's intentions: it is the structures of the production of culture which decide the matter" (119). Like the graffiti David finds in his host's bathroom, pop art does not challenge consumer culture. Instead, the medium operates on the same level as Quincy's race jokes. Baudrillard notes that many works of pop art

> provoke a moral and obscene laugh (or hint of a laugh)—the canvases being indeed obscene to the classical gaze—followed by a derisive smile, which might be a judgment on either the objects painted or the painting itself. It is a smile which willingly enters into the game: 'This isn't very serious, but we aren't going to be scandalized by it. And, deep down, perhaps... [Baudrillard's ellipses]' But these reactions are rather strained, amid some shameful dejection at not knowing quite what to make of it all. Even so, pop is both full of humour and humourless. Quite logically, it has nothing to do with subversive, aggressive humor, with the telescoping of surrealist objects. It is no longer a question of short-circuiting objects in their function, but one of juxtaposing them to analyse the relations between them. This approach is not terroristic. (120–121)

The laughter evoked by Quincy's jokes and many works of pop art is that of cynical distance, a term Slavoj Zizek uses in *The Sublime Object of Ideology* to describe seemingly subversive acts and attitudes that are, in the end, "part of ideology's game" (Zizek 28). Thus while offering what might be considered humorous, even "revolutionary," content, even pop art—the mode of expression most aware of the logic behind consumer ideology—is powerless to change that ideology or the means by which culture is produced. According to Baudrillard, then, art is bound by the logic of consumption, and the best the artist can hope for is to be named in statements like "Beethoven is fabulous" or "It's like an Antonioni movie."

Given Antonioni's position in the constellation of signs of acculturation that constitute David's social world, the art of cinema, like pop art and the "art" of the dirty joke, poses little threat to the dominant culture. In fact, throughout the early days of his marriage, attending movies provides David with little more than an opportunity to demonstrate his fashion sense:

> We saw all the new movies and went to a lot of parties. We seemed to believe that everything we did was the most wonderful thing that had ever been done. We wore certain clothes to certain movies. Grays for black and white. Boots, leather, chino, flag shirts and the like (our pre-acid gear) for Technicolor. Dressing, we matched each unmatching item with great care and spent several minutes assuring each other that we were ready for the waiting line at Cinema I. Each movie we saw was the greatest. Merry would talk about it constantly for two days and then forget it forever. There was no time for remembering things because something else was always coming along— another great movie, a great new pub or restaurant, a great new men's shop, boutique, ski area, beach house or rock group...
>
> Soon I was no longer content merely to make love to my wife. I had to seduce her first. These seductions often took their inspiration from cinema. I liked to get rough with her. I liked to be silent for long periods. The movies were giving difficult meanings to some of the private moments of my life. (34–35)

In this passage, seeing the movie and being seen by other moviegoers are of equal importance to David, and the movies he and his wife take in are not only disposable insofar as they are forgotten after two days but also because they are interchangeable with all the other opportunities for consumption their world offers. Perhaps more importantly, film in this instance also serves as a prescriptive medium for David, both inspiring and giving meaning to the particulars of his sex life.

Just as the work of art functions only as a sign of acculturation in consumer society, so too does lovemaking. In the context David describes, to make love well is to demonstrate one's prowess as a consumer. Yet even as he seduces his wife, David reveals a degree of social impotence. He cannot change consumer culture, cannot argue with its logic. He can only take cues from his environment and learn how to behave by watching the objects around him. Or, to reverse the formula, far from causing David to question consumer ideology, the objects in David's life—including those which might be described as "art"—provide models for acceptable behavior even in so private a realm as the bedroom. While it may be overstating the case to argue that consumer culture, rather than David himself, makes love to his wife in the above passage, David's attitude toward his own sexual activity clearly confirms the power of the marketplace to dictate cultural norms.

Yet David continues to hold out for a mode of art that is as transgressive as the motorcycle gang that rumbles through his boyhood town and causes his neighbors to look out their windows with "a strange mixture of longing and terror" (DeLillo, *Americana* 183). Although they are "gone in seconds," the gang of twenty marauders leaves a young David with the impression that "a hurricane or plague had struck the town," and as the gang disappears in the distance, he realizes that he and his neighbors are "not quite the same people" they had been just seconds earlier (182–183). To effect a similar change in himself as an adult, David begins to shoot a "long messy autobiographical-type film" when he arrives with his entourage in a small town in what he simply calls "Middle America" (205, 207).

Describing the film as "the strangest, darkest, most horrifying idea" of his life, David initially models his work after his friend Bobby Brand's novel-in-progress, *Coitus Interruptus* (125, 205).

Touted as "the novel that would detonate in the gut of America" and cause everyone in the country to "puke blood when they read it," *Coitus Interruptus* is, to all appearances, the literary equivalent of the motorcycle gang that briefly terrorized David's neighborhood in his youth (112, 205). Moreover, Brand's project is similar to that of Baudrillard and Barthes in that it seeks to reform society at the level of language. "I plan to take out the slang and replace it with new forms, new modes," Brand explains; "Maybe I'll eliminate language itself. It may be possible to find a completely new mode" (288). Yet while Brand fantasizes that *Coitus Interruptus* will put him in good stead with "famous old French intellectuals," the project ultimately proves unfruitful when he reveals that his manuscript consists of eleven pages, seven of which "don't have any words on them" (291, 307).

The author's apparent lack of productivity notwithstanding, *Coitus Interruptus* can only fail to provide the new mode of language Brand seeks because the seemingly revolutionary concept behind the novel only reinforces the logic of value. Although the novel exists largely in Brand's imagination, he explains that it is about a former president of the United States who has been succeeded by the first African-American president and subsequently begins to turn into a woman (205). While this configuration reverses the order of the hierarchy Barthes sees as implicit in the lavatory doors at the University of Geneva (i.e., *messieurs*/dames//*professeurs*/étudiants and, to add race to the mix, *white*/black), it leaves the notion of hierarchy—and, by extension, value—intact. In other words, while Brand's novel replaces *messieurs*/dames and, in this case, *white*/black with their opposites, sexual and racial segregation continue to exist as functions of language and value. As his name suggests, Brand is merely substituting one mode of hierarchy for another, positing his own "brand" as the best. In so doing, he continues in the tradition of David's father, whose affinity with Brand is further revealed when the would-be author claims that the theme of his novel is immaterial "because appearance is all that matters" (205). While *Coitus Interruptus* might (as Brand claims) cause the whole country to "puke blood," it would do little to undermine the logic of value that undergirds consumer ideology.

In contrast to the hierarchical dichotomies *Coitus Interruptus* continues to uphold, a fellow traveler and artist named Sullivan presents David with "a strange painted wood-and-wire doll" that represents a "menacing bitchy hermaphroditic divinity" (289). Neither man nor woman, the doll dissolves the bar between the terms of the sexual binary Barthes describes and thereby nullifies the hierarchy that his binary implies. Rather than substituting *dames*/messieurs for *messieurs*/dames (as Brand's novel would), the hermaphrodite divinity short-circuits the distinction between sexes and, as a result, imparts meaning that is not predicated on value. In other words, the doll's hermaphroditic nature allows for ambivalence. And while the doll certainly suggests to David that a mode of communication may, in fact, exist beyond that of signification, his memory of a class in Zen philosophy gives him the theoretical framework in which to discover that mode.

Referencing John Keats' "Ode On a Grecian Urn," David draws attention to similarity of the poet's notion of "negative capability" to the distrust of words that marks Zen philosophy. "Beauty was too difficult and truth in the West had died with Crazy Horse," David explains before describing Professor Hiroshi Oh's lectures on Zen (175).

> Oh spoke of Emptiness. The mind is an empty box within an empty box. With his index finger he made a sign in the air, one motion, name-shape, the circle's single fulfilling line...Oh hummed and chanted. Note the paradox. Empty box within empty box. He went into more paradox, more gentle conflict, more questions of interpretation in which ancient masters nodded their disagreement. It was Oh's practice to reveal some deep Zen principle, carefully planting evidence of its undeniable truth, and then confront us with a totally different theory of equally undeniable truth. He seemed to enjoy trying to break our minds, crush us with centuries of confusion as if to say: If the great teachers and enlightened ones of history cannot find a common interpretation, how will you ever know what to believe, you poor white gullible bastards? (176)

In Oh's lessons, the empty boxes of Zen philosophy are similar to the urn depicted in the Keats poem in that both contain their share of paradoxes. The tension between the temporal and everlasting in Keats, for example, and the logical impasse of a box that is both empty and not empty are reminiscent of the poet's praise of negative capability, a state in which "man is capable of being in uncertainties, Mysteries, doubts, without any irritable reaching after fact and reason" (Keats 60). This aversion to fact and reason reflects a dissatisfaction with signification that is common to Baudrillard and practitioners of Zen philosophy alike.

D. T. Suzuki, whom David references as the author of the text used in Oh's class, explains in *Zen and Japanese Culture* that the philosophy of Zen is invested in engendering a quality very similar to negative capability. Appealing to an intuitive mode of understanding known in Japanese as *satori*, Zen aims to abandon concepts "in order to reach the truth of things" (Suzuki 218). Concepts, Suzuki notes, "are useful in defining the truth of things but not in making us personally acquainted with it. Conceptual knowledge may make us wise in a way, but this is only superficial. It is not the living truth itself, and therefore there is no creativeness in it, being a mere accumulation of dead matter" (218). To this end, Zen practitioners subvert the rationality of words through paradox. Zen is not necessarily against words, Suzuki notes, "but it is well aware of the fact that they are always liable to detach themselves from realities and turn into conceptions" (5). What concerns Zen is not words or language but "something" hovering wordlessly in the mind, "an unnamable 'X.' It is no abstraction; it is concrete enough, and direct, as the eye sees that the sun is, but it is not to be subsumed in the categories of linguistics. As soon as we try to do this, it disappears" (7).

Suzuki's distinction between conceptual knowledge and intuitive knowledge of "the living truth itself" mirrors the distinction Baudrillard draws between the object and the utensil: where the utensil grounds the individual in the world and allows for what Suzuki calls a personal acquaintance with the truth of things, the object can only be "read" in terms of value (Baudrillard, *System of Objects* 86).

In this context, Zen's wariness toward words is well founded: by denoting value, as Baudrillard contends, words do indeed, to borrow Suzuki's phrase, "detach themselves from realities and turn into conceptions" (5). As the nature of the koan, a paradoxical statement or riddle peculiar to Zen philosophy, demonstrates, however, words do not necessarily have to follow the logic of the sign. For example, the empty box within an empty box to which Oh alludes in *Americana* has no signified; just as there is no way to imagine a square circle, the notion of an empty box containing anything represents an impossible proposition. Divorced from any sensible signified, the phrase "empty box within an empty box" cannot be considered a signifier. Rather, the phrase is a conglomeration of words that must be considered independent of their "meaning," words *qua* words. Because these words do not signify, they take on gravity and alert us to their own tangibility. Like the primitive tools and furniture to which Baudrillard alludes in *The System of Objects*, the words of the Zen koan function as "traditional symbolic objects" that bear the imprint of human activity insofar as their organization does not form a signifying fabric constituting the "virtual totality of all objects and messages ready-constituted as a more or less coherent discourse" (200). No longer simply a means of exchanging abstract concepts, the words of the Zen koan do not share the sign's conceit that the signifier can name the otherwise-unspeakable signified. In other words, the language of the Zen koan "speaks" yet refrains from signifying value.

Like the Lacanian Real, the "unnamable 'X'" to which Suzuki refers in his discussion of the Zen koan cannot be reached through language. Rather, language bars us from that X through the construction of what Zen philosophy dubs conceptual knowledge and Marxist philosophy calls ideology. In the context of consumer culture, Baudrillard argues, the concept to which ideology reduces everything through the process of signification is value. Taken together, then, it is not surprising that David's interests in Zen philosophy and consumer culture combine to form an amalgam that is remarkably similar to Baudrillard's critique of the sign. Informed by Zen's inherent distrust of language in general and words in particular, David's later artistic endeavors aim at subverting the reductive logic of value and substituting for it a mode of communication that allows for ambivalence to operate. Attempting to bypass what Baudrillard describes in *For a Critique of the Political Economy of the Sign* as the "fixed and equational structure" of the sign, David's goal as he becomes more involved with his project is to create a film that, like the language of the Zen koan, allows ambivalence to surface by rupturing the connection between language and value (149).

Unlike Brand, David explains that his project is not to reduce the value of language, but to reinforce it (DeLillo, *Americana* 288). This explanation puts David's project at odds with that of Baudrillard insofar as Baudrillard calls for the destruction of value while David's project is merely one of displacement: his aim is to increase the value of language by rescuing meaning from the contingency of value. In other words, David wants to strengthen language by divorcing its capacity to be meaningful from what Barthes sees as its unerring tendency to root all meaning in hierarchy. In order to bring this mode of language into being, David shoots his film in a fashion that reduces "the kind of movement that tells a story or creates harmony" (288). Doing so, he argues, will allow "language to evolve from static forms" as opposed to adhering to a preordained sense of order (288). Echoing the language of the Zen koan, David describes one of his characters as "standing still but moving" and "silent with answers" (309). As with the Zen koan, these apparent contradictions divorce David's words from abstract concepts and, by extension, from value. Moreover, David confronts the ambivalence of his Oedipal guilt when he films a scene in which Sullivan, portraying David's mother, appears to merge with a teenage boy portraying David: "I could see it in the foreflash, underexposed, their bodies incomplete…and I wondered why this mute soliloquy of woman and boy should mean anything more, even to me, than what it so clearly was, face of one and head of the other" (317). Like the "menacing bitchy hermaphroditic divinity" Sullivan presents to David earlier in the novel, the single figure created by Sullivan and the boy is neither male nor female but partakes in the essence of both genders and, in so doing, eliminates the sense of hierarchy implied by the male/female binary.

Yet even as David frames what might be termed his primal scene, he returns to the language of value by referring to his project as a "commercial" and wonders if it will "sell the product" (317). While David's regression to the very idiom he seeks to interrogate suggests the failure of his project, it must be remembered that David does not aim to subvert consumer ideology entirely but to demystify it: where consumer ideology generally forces us to interpret all manner of phenomena in terms of value, David's purpose is to allow us to recognize the illusory nature of value via the reemergence of ambivalence. By nature, this project is distinctly non-utopian: far from positing an ideal world, it forces us to recognize the "bad" of the world along with the "good" or, more accurately, to recognize that the world cannot be broken down along such binary lines as good or bad, or even, as Madison Avenue might have us believe, into discreet shades of better or worse judged in relation to "the best." Thus David cannot view his project along the lines of a purely *anti-commercial*/commercial dichotomy but as a commingling of both elements—hence David's eventual assertion that his film "functions best as a sort of ultimate schizogram, an exercise in diametrics to unmake meaning" (347).

As an artist, David's purpose is to "deal in the complexities of truth," an endeavor in which he considers himself "most successful" (347). This success is due in large part to his ability to recognize that while his culture may be schizoid in nature, the pieces of that culture form a coherent if conflicted whole. While such truths are beyond the ken of Madison Avenue, they are well within the purview of DeLillo's artistic vision, and his first novel fittingly offers a glimpse of two Americas: one steeped solely in the logic of value, and one fraught with ambivalence. In the first America, the notion of "the best" segregates all elements of society along arbitrary lines. From Baudrillard's perspective, this first America is the only America consumer ideology will allow; even art allegedly aimed at subverting consumer ideology will ultimately be assimilated by it.

From DeLillo's perspective, on the other hand, art has the potential to dissolve such dichotomies as *good*/bad in order to reveal the second America. This America is certainly no utopia, but because its language is not based entirely on value, its internal conflicts can be confronted more honestly than those repressed by the artificial strictures of consumer ideology. In this sense, the America that David discovers is not the monolithic America that is a product of its own national mythology but is rather a complex and flawed state that encompasses both fulfillment and discontent. While this complex vision of America may generally be repressed by the value-laden logic of Madison Avenue, DeLillo demonstrates throughout *Americana* that art does indeed have the potential to allow this America to emerge—if only provisionally.

CHAPTER 3

ANOTHER MEDIA EVENT?
PLAYERS AND THE SPECTER
OF TERRORISM

As protagonist Lyle Wynant becomes increasingly involved with a loosely organized terror cell in *Players*, a terrorist known only as J. Kinnear explains the motivation behind a plan to bomb the New York Stock Exchange. The explosion will accomplish nothing, he says: "It's another media event. Innocent people dead and mutilated. Toward what end? Publicize the movement, that's all. Media again. They want coverage. Public interest. They want to dramatize" (180). Later, however, a terrorist named Marina proves more optimistic when she explains that the explosion will not only "cause serious damage at the Exchange" but also, given the setting of the attack, amount to a "a fantastic moment" (183). Building upon Marina's rationale, Lyle suggests that her goal is to attack "the idea of their money" and agrees that doing so is the best way to topple the status quo: "The system. The secret currents. Make it appear a little less inviolable. It's their greatest strength...and to incapacitate it, even briefly, would be to set loose every kind of demon" (183). As the divergence between Kinnear's expectations and those shared by Marina and Lyle suggests, the ultimate effect of acts of terror is debatable.

From Kinnear's perspective, acts of terror amount to nothing more than grotesque publicity stunts. From Marina's perspective, such acts have the potential to cause serious damage to what Lyle refers to as "the system." Examining this controversy throughout *Players* and returning to the issue in the wake of the terror attacks of September 2001 in an essay titled "In the Ruins of the Future: Reflections on Terror and Loss in the Shadow of September," DeLillo intimates that what both perspectives fail to acknowledge is the human toll that acts of terror exact. For DeLillo, acts of terror occur largely because terrorists view the world not on an individual, human level but in terms of competing ideologies or systems of belief. Coincidentally, critics have made the same claim against Baudrillard; because his work focuses almost entirely on systems, he fails to address the needs of individuals caught within those systems. Yet for Baudrillard, there can be no other way. The system, from his perspective, is a unified whole, and all parts working within the system—including those we might otherwise consider individual subjects—are bound by its logic. To speak of freeing the individual, then, is to speak of shattering the system; each event is contingent upon the other.

According to Baudrillard, the alternatives posed by Kinnear and Marina are not mutually exclusive. Discussing the terror attacks of September 11, 2001, in *The Spirit of Terrorism*, Baudrillard argues that because Western culture is one in which images take precedence over the real, "the white magic of cinema and the black magic of terrorism" combine to give "unprecedented impact" to the act of terror (29, 27). "Reality and fiction are inextricable, and the fascination with the attack is primarily a fascination with the image," Baudrillard argues (29). Moreover, the media are "part of the event, they are part of the terror, and they work in both directions" (31). By taking advantage of all forms of what Baudrillard terms the "perverse circulation" available to Western culture, then, the terrorist does indeed set loose every kind of demon, as Lyle asserts in *Players*, and it is precisely because the act of terror is a public spectacle that it does so much damage: within the system, all is spectacle.

Or, more accurately, everything within the system is a sign—a theory Baudrillard has developed throughout his career. In *Symbolic Exchange and Death*, he argues that we are no longer governed by the laws of reality. Rather, we have moved from reality into a state Baudrillard describes as hyperreal, "the meticulous reduplication of the real, preferably through another reproductive medium such as advertising or photography" (71). What we generally consider "reality" is not real at all but a closed system of signs that protects itself "from the referential and the anxiety of the referential, as well as from all metalanguage" by "operating its own metalanguage, that is, by duplicating itself as its own critique" (74). In other words, hyperreality has no external point of reference against which to gauge its laws. Rather, hyperreality generates its own origin; it is a model based upon a model with no equivalent in reality. This realm, Baudrillard argues, "is no longer a space of production, but a reading strip, a coding and decoding strip, magnetised by signs" (75). Because the hyperreal lacks any basis in reality, signs are all it can accommodate.

The controlling metaphor in this system of signs is that of value, and the most basic sign of value is money. However, Baudrillard argues, the notion of value is ultimately meaningless insofar as it, like everything else in hyperreality, has no external point of reference: wages are severed from labor, and currency is severed from the gold standard. As a result, "value" becomes nothing more than an abstract means of gauging political economy (i.e., the production and distribution of wealth), and money becomes speculative, a "floating signifier" with no real signified to serve "as a brake to its proliferation and unlimited play" (22). This notion is played out in *Players* when Lyle speculates that he and his fellow stock traders have "effectively negated" the outside world with their economic models and forecasts (23). Studying yellow teleprinter strips, he sees an "artful reduction of the external world to printed output, the machine's coded model of exactitude," and a glance at a series of numbers and stock symbols gives him "an impression of reality disconnected from his own senses" (70). From Baudrillard's perspective, this seemingly "disconnected" reality is actually the basis for what Lyle considers the external world insofar as the commodities that abound throughout this so-called external world serve no real purpose other than to reflect the status of their owners on a scale of political economy. That is, they can only signify value. Thus their meaning derives solely from the abstract realm of numbers, which itself is a "coded model" of the world of objects it defines. The solipsistic essence of hyperreality, Lyle's world is modeled after a model of itself.

Within the parameters of market-driven hyperreality, Baudrillard argues, even people become commodities. Stripped of any real referents,

> labour and non-labour, labour and capital, become commutable, all logic has dissolved; and we discover this in the flotation of all categories of consciousness where the *mental equivalent of the gold standard*, the subject, has been lost...There are no more authorities to which to refer, under whose aegis a subject could exchange objects dialectically, or exchange their determinations around a stable identity in accordance with definite rules: the end of the conscious subject...The logical consequence of this is, if the conscious subject is the mental equivalent of the gold standard, then the *unconscious is the mental equivalent of speculative currency and hot money* [a term Baudrillard uses to characterize the senseless circulation of the monetary sign]. Today, individuals, disinvested as subjects and robbed of their fixed relations, are drifting, in relation to one another, into an incessant mode of transferential fluctuations: flows, connections, disconnections, transference/countertransference. (*Symbolic Exchange* 23)

We are caught up, then, in the ebb and flow of market conditions, and the best we can hope for (if, indeed, we are capable of hope under the conditions Baudrillard describes) is to become "valuable" commodities ourselves, so we go about accumulating objects that will serve as outward signs of our own worth. Evaluating such objects subconsciously, we are always defining ourselves in terms of our possessions.

Although Lyle abhors the aspect of modern living that Baudrillard describes, his wife Pammy is so thoroughly immersed in consumer culture that she imputes moral value to even the smallest of financial transactions, as when she deems a purchase of fresh fruit an "act of moral excellence" (32). Despite the sense of moral excellence she gains from this purchase, however, Pammy never gets around to eating more than a "little bit" of the fruit, and the rest goes "in the fruit bin to shrivel like fetuses" (33). In short, the fruit serves no purpose but to make Pammy feel like a good consumer—that is, a "valued" member of consumer society. Along similar lines, Pammy jokes that she washes a set of drinking glasses by hand because she "wants them to know what it feels like to be washed by human hands" and doesn't "want them to grow up thinking everything's done the easy way, by machine, with impersonal detergent" (85). That her real motivation is that the dishwasher is broken does not detract from the import of this passage: the line between the human and the inanimate has become blurred.

Further blurring of the line between the human and the inanimate occurs when a Mister Softee ice cream truck passes by Lyle and Pammy's bedroom window. The truck announces itself with a "cranked out mechanical whine," and Lyle explains that there "really is a Mister Softee" (36). According to Lyle, "He sits in the back of the truck. That's him making the noise. It's not music on a record or tape. That's his mouth. It's coming out of his mouth. That's his language. They speak that way in the back of ice cream trucks all over the city" (36). Moreover, Lyle notes, Mister Softee is "very fat and pastelike. He can't get up. He doesn't have the right consistency" (36). Though clearly a joke, Lyle's description of Mister Softee applies just as easily to himself. When Pammy requests that they have a serious conversation, Lyle makes "gulping sounds," which "interest him more than most noises" he makes (36). In this and other passages throughout the novel, Lyle demonstrates that like Mister Softee, he is incapable of meaningful exchange; he cracks jokes, speaks in odd dialects, makes clever remarks, and frequently changes the subject of conversation, but Lyle rarely if ever says anything meaningful to Pammy or any of the other people in his life. As Mark Osteen notes in *American Magic and Dread*, Lyle and Pammy "play" at intimate exchange, but "each has retired to a private box" from which real communication is impossible (145). Just as Mister Softee sits alone and immobile in the back of an ice cream truck, Lyle and Pammy are both isolated and immobilized by their inability to communicate. Pammy's observation that Mister Softee has no genitals, then, can apply to Lyle as well; both lack the "balls" to effect any kind of change—social or otherwise.

Underlining the parallel between Mister Softee's apparent lack of genitals and Lyle's social impotence is his initial motivation for joining the terror cell: he is attracted to a woman named Rosemary Moore, who is affiliated with the terrorists. Beginning a clandestine sexual affair with Rosemary, Lyle gains the opportunity to reveal that his own genitals, like Mister Softee's, are "in there somewhere." From the beginning of his involvement with the cell, however, Lyle feels powerless. Realizing that his position within the organization is much like that of an actor in a play, Lyle immediately grows bored. Addressing Lyle's concerns, Kinnear explains that even as the cell attempts to topple the system, it must continue to play by the system's rules—hence Lyle's perception that all of his actions are scripted in advance. While the cell purports to operate on "basic, really visceral levels" in its efforts at ridding society of its repressive elements, the terror cell is ultimately bound by what Kinnear refers to as "the nature of the game" (103). That Kinnear is eventually revealed to be a double-agent only blurs the line between the allegedly opposing sides of the dialectic in which Lyle is attempting to engage; playing by the same rules, the terrorists and their oppressors are no more than evenly interchangeable commodities within a system that is larger than both parties. Under such circumstances, no true dialectic can take place, and the only hope for liberation from the system appears to stem from the potential for the system's own self-destruction.

In *Symbolic Exchange and Death*, Baudrillard argues that the system will never fall to a "direct, dialectical revolution of the economic or political infrastructure" because everything produced within the system "will only feed back into the mechanism and give it impetus, following a circular distortion similar to a Moebius strip" (36). In other words, all "traditional" forms of revolution adhere to the basic tenets of consumer ideology that regulate the system. As in *Players*, revolutionaries must stockpile weapons in order to overthrow their oppressors. However secretive or off the books they may be, the transactions involved in such stockpiling only strengthen the system; money is money regardless of the circumstances of its exchange. More to the point, so-called "subversive" acts of violence amount only to signs that one side of a given conflict has gained the upper hand. The only appropriate response within the system is for the powers that be to respond with further acts of violence in order to score more "points" and regain any ground that they may have lost as a result of the instigating act of violence. Consequently, Baudrillard argues that "the worst error of all revolutionary strategies is to believe that we will put an end to the system on the plane of the real: this is their imaginary, imposed on them by the system itself, living or surviving only by always leading those who attack the system to fight amongst each other on the terrain of reality, *which is always the reality of the system*" (36, Baudrillard's emphasis). The logic of violence and counter-violence—which is to say the logic of escalating violence—that marks the cat-and-mouse game between terrorists and their oppressors only strengthens the system by increasing the number of signs in circulation.

In order to topple the system, Baudrillard argues, the terrorist must abandon traditional forms of violence for those he describes as symbolic. Rather than engaging in a "violence 'of signs,' from which the system draws strength," the terrorist must challenge the logic of consumer ideology through his or her own suicide (36). The only means of turning the system's power against itself, according to Baudrillard, is to *"defy the system with a gift to which it cannot respond save by its own collapse and death"* (37, Baudrillard's emphasis). Because the system cannot "lose face," it must *"commit suicide in response to the multiplied challenge of death and suicide"* (37, Baudrillard's emphasis). Moreover, because death has no equivalent in the realm of hyperreality,

> it opens up an inexpiable overbidding…Nothing *corresponds* to death. Which is precisely what happens in this case: *the system itself is driven to suicide in return*, which suicide is manifest in its disarray and defeat. However infinitesimal in terms of relations of force it might be, the colossal apparatus of power is eliminated in this situation where (the very excess of its) derision is turned back against itself…The system can only die in exchange, defeat itself to lift the challenge. Its death at this instant is a symbolic response, but a death which wears it out. (38, Baudrillard's emphasis)

Modifying this position to account for the failure of such suicide missions as those that continue to plague the Middle East to bring about any real change, Baudrillard notes in *The Spirit of Terrorism* that if terrorists merely use their own deaths to combat the system, they will "disappear…in a useless sacrifice" (21). However, as soon as terrorists learn to combine "all the modern resources available to them" with the "highly symbolic weapon" of their own deaths, the destructive potential of their actions "is multiplied to infinity" (21).

A similar result is arguably what Marina has in mind in *Players* when she couches her plan for bombing the New York Stock Exchange in a discussion of her brother's willingness to die for the cause. "Rafael was willing to die," she explains; "This is the single most important thing about him" (182). Combined with Kinnear's warning that Lyle's life will be sacrificed if he continues his association with the terror cell, Marina's praise of her brother amounts to a challenge: in order to demonstrate his commitment to "the cause," Lyle must die in the planned explosion. Moreover, her choice of target ensures that Lyle's death will be a matter of public spectacle in that any attack on the New York Stock Exchange will surely attract the attention of the media. Yet when Lyle's only sexual encounter with

Marina leads him to realize "the critical nature of his involvement," the reality of the situation becomes too much for Lyle to bear (188). As a result, he flees to Canada where he trades the "great shoaling transit" of sex with Marina for the relatively artificial experience of sex with Rosemary, who has "a plastic phallus harnessed to her body" (190, 197).

Abandoning the plot to bomb the New York Stock Exchange, Lyle effectively relinquishes his only weapon against the system, the power to enact symbolic exchange through his own death. That such "power" seems self-defeating and ultimately ineffective, however, cannot be denied. Indeed, when Pammy's friend Jack Laws commits suicide, the system barely flinches. Although the tragedy initially strips Pammy's world of signifiers by rendering "everything nameless" for her, the "surreal torment" and the "sense of aberration" she associates with Jack's death lifts when Lyle summarizes what happened "in short, declarative sentences" (199, 200). Here, Lyle's efforts to calm Pammy echo the mission statement of her employer, the Grief Management Council, which, for a fee, serves "the community in its efforts to understand and assimilate grief" (18). For Pammy, this amounts to offering those who have experienced loss a "means to codify their emotions" (19). Or, in Baudrillard's terms, a means to commodify their emotions.

In *Symbolic Exchange and Death*, Baudrillard argues that "The consummate enjoyment…of the signs of guilt, despair, violence and death are replacing guilt, anxiety, even death in the total euphoria of simulation" (74). In other words, within the system Baudrillard describes, real emotions take a backseat to the enjoyment of the signs of emotions; people speak of enjoying a "good cry" or a "good laugh," but neither experience carries any cathartic effect. One example of this phenomenon occurs shortly after Pammy stifles her own grief over Jack's death; watching an "inept and boring, fifties vintage" tragedy on television, she cannot help but feel awash in ersatz grief despite "the artificiality of the movie, its plain awfulness" and the "blaring commercials" that are broadcast alongside it (204, 205). Despite the seeming intensity of this grief, however, Pammy realizes that such films are formulated to "to make people react to a mass market stimulus," and after succumbing to what she considers "a few bogus sentiments" she leaves her apartment to satisfy a craving for a roast beef sandwich and a cold beer (206). Far from aiding in the destruction of the system, the mass market medium of television, as depicted in *Players*, serves only to siphon off the real emotions Pammy experiences with regard to her friend's suicide and to return her to the "real" world as a healthy consumer.

To play the media game, then, is to play by the rules of the system. Regardless of content, the mass media's coverage of events can only reinforce the governing logic of the system (i.e., that everything is ultimately a sign of value) and cannot allow for symbolic exchange. Baudrillard himself makes this clear in *For a Critique of the Political Economy of the Sign* when he argues that "by trying to preserve (even as one 'dialectically transcends' them) any separated instances of the structural communication grid, one obviates the possibility of fundamental change, and condemns oneself to fragile manipulatory practices that would be dangerous to adopt as 'revolutionary strategy'" (184). True dialectic, Baudrillard argues, will only occur when the code itself is eliminated, and the only way to eliminate the code is to allow for response, which the code prohibits.

Because use of the media amounts to no more than "an objectified support for answerless messages, a transmission system at a distance," Baudrillard argues that revolutionaries should engage in modes of exchange that are marked by "an *immediate* inscription, given and returned, spoken and answered, mobile in the same place and time, reciprocal and antagonistic" (176). According to Baudrillard, such modes of exchange include the use of silkscreen banners and hand-painted notices. Though seemingly quaint, a similar non-technological alternative to the mass-mediated bloodshed espoused by terrorists appears early in *Players* when an anonymous protester raises a sign that is "hand-lettered on both sides, political in nature" (13). Although passers by are too distracted to notice the protester, he reappears throughout the novel, "professing clearly his opposition" to "the banks, the tanks, the corporations" (28, 27).

When Lyle finally approaches him, he learns that the protester has been holding the sign for eighteen years to no apparent avail. His reason for holding the sign, the protester explains, is that people "want to be dazzled" (151). By giving them the opposite of what they want—that is, by giving them something unremarkable—he avoids playing by the rules of the system and thus refuses to validate the system's hegemony. Holding his sign in silent protest, he offers not another media event, but an event that cannot be mediated at all.

Because the man with the placard must be confronted directly, he does not participate in the play of signs that is the lifeblood of the system and thus does not help to strengthen the system. Simply "not strengthening" the system, however, is not Baudrillard's goal, and the fact that the protester and his placard go largely unnoticed throughout *Players* underscores the relative ineffectiveness of such low-tech means of confronting consumer ideology as Baudrillard espouses—hence the eventual shift in Baudrillard's thinking regarding the use of the mass-media for the purpose of effecting social change through terrorism. In "Baudrillard, September 11, and the Haunting Abyss of Reversal," Leonard Wilcox explains that the theorist's "middle period" is marked by a realization that while image and spectacle "function to absorb the alterity of terrorism, terrorism has adapted adroitly to the logic of sign exchange and sign value" (21). Moreover, contemporary terrorism, as Baudrillard assesses it in this middle period, "usurps the mechanisms of simulation in order to inhabit the system from the inside; like a viral organism, it multiplies from within, pushing the very logic of the system to a point of extremity" (21). Along these lines, Baudrillard argues in *The Spirit of Terrorism*, pushing the logic of the system to such a point of extremity was the very goal of the terrorists who brought about the collapse of the World Trade Center towers on September 11, 2001.

Baudrillard's contribution to a February 2002 debate on the previous year's terror attacks (titled "Requiem for the Twin Towers") and his subsequent analysis of those attacks in *The Spirit of Terrorism* suggest that, in some instances, the terrorist act can restore the potential for meaningful exchange in a world where the technocratic machinery of global capitalism allows for no form of thinking except that governed by the dictates of consumerism. Within consumer culture, Baudrillard argues, language lacks ambivalence because the purpose of every utterance (as with all aspects of that culture) is to signify value—both moral and economic insofar as consumer culture associates piety with wealth. Lacking a capacity for ambivalence, we are unable to communicate beyond the code of value; we cannot engage in what Baudrillard calls symbolic exchange, or exchange predicated on loss. Indeed, Baudrillard describes the attacks of September 2001 as symbolic insofar as the terrorists' willingness to die "restores an irreducible singularity to the heart of a system of generalized exchange" (9). Where consumer culture revolves around the generalized exchange of infinitely replaceable, repeatable, and reproducible signs (e.g., currency), the terrorist act introduces a new element to the economy: that which is irreplaceable, unrepeatable, and irreproducible. That is, terrorism counters the unending, soul-numbing exchange of signs that is at the heart of consumer culture with the self-sacrifice of the individual and, in so doing, targets and wounds consumer culture via what Baudrillard describes as a "genu-inely adversarial" relationship (26).

While DeLillo does not use Baudrillard's terminology, much of his writing is suggestive of the theorist's call for ambivalence as a means of restoring symbolic exchange in the face of an otherwise-intractable consumer ideology. Yet where Baudrillard sees symbolic exchange and consumer culture as mutually exclusive concepts, DeLillo does not reject their potential to coexist. In an essay titled "In the Ruins of the Future: Reflections on Terror and Loss in the Shadow of September," DeLillo argues that the "daily sweeping taken-for-granted greatness of New York" is that the city will continue to accommodate "every language, ritual, belief, and opinion" of its denizens even as the terrorist impulse strives to eliminate difference, upon which meaningful exchange is based (40). Moreover, DeLillo argues that by focusing solely on ideology, terrorists lose the capac-ity to confront their rivals as individuals or, to borrow Baudrillard's terminology, in a "genuinely adversarial" fashion. This critique might just as well apply to Baudrillard himself: where DeLillo's often-critical depictions of contemporary life are both tempered and strengthened by his interest in individuals who strive to make genuine connections within the limits of consumer ideology, Baudrillard's overwhelming interest in systems (or "the system," as he frequently refers to consumer culture) usually comes at the expense of his attention to the particular. Painting in broad strokes, Baudrillard fails to recognize that symbolic exchange and genuinely adversarial relations can and do exist within consumer culture while DeLillo's interest in individuals offers a more-balanced critique of that culture as well as a critique of the terrorist impulse to confront it with violence.

DeLillo and Baudrillard agree on two central points: that the terrorist attacks of September 2001 represent a reaction against globalization and that the suicidal nature of those attacks gave the terrorists an advantage over their enemies. Referencing such contemporary phenomena as the surge of capital markets, the speed of the internet, and "the utopian glow of cyber-capital," the opening paragraph of DeLillo's essay all but invokes Baudrillard, who is widely regarded as a prophet of postmodern technological and economic theory, by name (33). Fueled by these phenomena and the "high gloss of modernity," the power of American culture to penetrate "every wall, home, life, and mind" presented the September terrorists with their primary target, DeLillo argues (33). Similarly, Baudrillard argues that the central antagonism operating in the world today pits globalization against itself. This conflict "goes far beyond hatred for the dominant world power among the disinherited and the exploited," Baudrillard explains in *The Spirit of Terrorism*, because "even those who share in the advantages of that order" desire to destroy it (6). As American culture continues to saturate the globe, reactions against that culture become increasingly inevitable because "[a]llergy to any definitive order, to any definitive power, is—happily—universal" (6).

The extreme violence of the attacks in question underscores the intensity and virulence of the allergy Baudrillard describes—particularly among the terrorists, whose collective suicide demonstrates how deeply their animosity toward American culture must have run. Moreover, their seemingly eager acceptance of death proved their most effective weapon. "We are rich, privileged and strong, but they are willing to die," writes DeLillo; "This is the edge they have, the fire of aggrieved belief" ("Ruins" 34). Placing American culture on equal footing with that of the terrorists in terms of wealth and privilege, Baudrillard takes DeLillo's argument a step further:

> Suicidal terrorism was a terrorism of the poor. [The attacks of September 2001 are] a terrorism of the rich. This is what particularly frightens us: the fact that they have become rich (they have all the necessary resources) without ceasing to wish to destroy us. Admittedly, in terms of our system of values, they are cheating. It is not playing fair to throw one's death into the game. But this does not trouble them, and the new rules are not ours to determine. (*Spirit of Terrorism* 23)

"Playing" by rules that are inimical to the American value system, terrorists have gained the upper hand in their struggle against globalization. While DeLillo and Baudrillard agree that this is the case, each sees a different "strength" in the terrorists' suicide. Where Baudrillard argues that suicidal terrorism has the potential to broaden the scope of interpersonal exchange, DeLillo argues that such behavior is predicated upon and aims only to promulgate a mode of exchange that is decidedly limited.

Baudrillard has long argued that the overarching logic of Western culture is one of accumulation: we define ourselves in terms of the vastly complex constellations of commodities we own. Because the value of these commodities exists only in the abstract, it cannot be destroyed; even as we discard or exchange certain commodities, we do so to signal that we have consumed well, and, in so consuming, have lived well. Insofar as the purpose of every exchange within consumer culture is to signal a rise, however incremental or illusory, in social status, "the system" does not allow for loss. By way of contrast, however, the voluntary death of the terrorist demands that the system recognize loss. In turn, this recognition can only prove fatal to the system, "which cannot operate on the terrain of symbolic exchange and death—a thing of which it no longer has any idea, since it has erased it from its own culture" (15). The distinction here (again) is between symbolic and sign exchange. Where sign exchange is predicated on the ability to substitute a sign (such as a dollar amount) for any commodity, the symbolic object has no substitute or equivalent. As a result, the logic of symbolic exchange demands that one party must lose what the other gains. Because consumer culture is so heavily invested in the exchange of signs, however, symbolic exchange and death are both inimical to the system. Thus, Baudrillard argues, terrorists "have succeeded in turning their own deaths into an absolute weapon against a system that operates on the basis of the exclusion of death, a system where the ideal is an ideal of zero deaths" (16). By introducing loss to a system that precludes loss, the terrorist's suicide begins to unravel the fabric of consumer culture.

In addition to introducing loss to the system, symbolic exchange also alters the relationships among those engaged in exchange. Baudrillard's assertion that everything within consumer culture ultimately signifies value applies to people as well as commodities. Indeed, because people can be so reduced, they are, in fact, commodities themselves. This applies not only, as in Marx, to laborers whose value is determined by the profits they generate for their employers, but to consumers who, as in *Players*, define themselves in terms of the commodities they own: within consumer culture, we are only as good or as valuable as our possessions tell people we are. As commodities, Baudrillard argues in *Symbolic Exchange and Death*, people are incapable of meaningful exchange: "The arbitrariness of the sign begins when, instead of bonding two persons in an inescapable reciprocity, the signifier starts to refer to a disenchanted universe of the signified, the common denominator of the real world, towards which no-one any longer has the least obligation" (51).

Endlessly repeated signs of value themselves, consumers can only engage in an eternal and meaningless swapping of signs. We do not address each other as individuals but as commodities; we are signs trading signs within a system of signs. In contrast, the symbolic nature of the September attacks allowed the terrorists to engage the system on a personal level:

> Now, it is a mistake to see terrorist action as obeying a purely destructive logic. It seems to me that the action of the terrorists, from which death is inseparable (this is precisely what makes it a symbolic act), does not seek the impersonal elimination of the other. Everything lies in the challenge and the duel—that is to say, everything still lies in the dual, personal relation with the opposing power...Apart from the pact that binds terrorists together, there is also something of a dual pact with the adversary. This is, then, precisely the opposite of the cowardice of which they stand accused, and it is precisely the opposite of what the Americans did in the Gulf War (and which they are currently beginning again in Afghanistan), where the target is invisible and liquidated operationally. (25–26)

Because the terrorist is sacrificing his life rather than trading signs, he confronts the opposing power directly; the exchange is meaningful because it involves loss. This strikes a blow to consumer culture in that the terrorist's self-sacrifice removes the act of exchange from the province of value and, in so doing, robs all signs of meaning insofar as all meaning within consumer culture stems from value. Or, more accurately, the self-sacrificing nature of the terrorist act reveals all meaning within consumer culture to be illusory. In other words, the terrorists responsible for the attacks of September 2001 restored ambivalence to interpersonal exchange by short-circuiting the code of value. For Baudrillard, this represents a step forward: by restoring the potential for loss, the ambivalence of the terrorist act restores meaning to every mode of exchange, including communication. From DeLillo's point of view, however, nothing could be further from the truth.

Although DeLillo agrees that a willingness to die gives the terrorist an "edge," his interpretation of this willingness is different from Baudrillard's. Where Baudrillard argues that the terrorist's death allows for the kind of face-to-face confrontation that consumer culture precludes, DeLillo sees the terrorist's zeal as blinding. "Does the sight of a woman pushing a stroller soften the man to her humanity and vulnerability, and her child's as well, and all the people he is here to kill?" DeLillo asks rhetorically ("Ruins" 34). His answer is that this sight has no effect on the terrorist:

> This is his edge, that he does not see her. Years here, waiting, taking flying lessons, making the routine gestures of community and home, the credit card, the bank account, the post-office box. All tactical, linked, layered. He knows who we are and what we mean in the world—an idea, a righteous fever in the brain. But there is no defenseless human at the end of his gaze. (34)

From this point of view, the terrorist's behavior is much like that of Baudrillard's depiction of the consumer. Where the consumer is forever engaged in a tactical, linked, and layered effort to manipulate signs of wealth in order to "keep up with the Joneses" (as it were), the terrorist, too, manipulates such signs in order to blend in with the Joneses, if not to keep up with them. Yet like Baudrillard, the terrorist does not see beyond what DeLillo describes as "the routine gestures of community and home" and is therefore blinded to anything but ideology. If the terrorist were to acknowledge the defenseless human at the end of his gaze, he would run the risk of replacing his hatred for the idea of "Americans" with his compassion for *an* American, and thus lose his edge. While the terrorist's death may allow him to confront consumerism or "the system" directly, it does not allow him to confront individual consumers at all. Likewise, Baudrillard's position allows for a largely valid critique of consumer ideology in general but ignores the potential for individuals to exchange anything but signs of wealth. For DeLillo, this extreme focus on ideology is exactly what allows acts of terror to occur.

Looking beyond ideology, DeLillo emphasizes the need to consider individual stories by examining the power of such stories himself. Stories abound regarding people's whereabouts on September 11, DeLillo notes: stories of life-saving coincidence, of bravery and heroism, and of "encounters with dread" (34). The power of these stories, according to DeLillo, is that they "take us beyond the hard numbers of dead and missing and give us a glimpse of elevated being. For a hundred who are arbitrarily dead, we need to find one person saved by a flash of forewarning" (34). In so doing, DeLillo explains, we create counter-narratives from the single grand narrative of the attacks, and these counter-narratives are helpful insofar as they give us something "to set against the massive spectacle that continues to seem unmanageable, too powerful a thing to set into our frame of practiced response" (35). Although this so-called "frame of practiced response" is reminiscent of the meaningless exchange of signs that Baudrillard associates with consumer culture, the fact that we can, when necessary, exchange the kinds of counter-narratives DeLillo describes suggests that Baudrillard's pessimism regarding our potential to engage in anything more than the exchange of meaningless signs is overblown if not misplaced.

One of the stories DeLillo tells with regard to the attacks of September 2001 is that of his nephew, Marc, and Marc's wife, Karen. Living in an apartment complex a short distance from the World Trade Center, Marc and Karen are largely ignorant of the events that are unfolding; they know for sure that at least one plane has struck one tower, but beyond that they can only speculate. When the first tower falls, Karen initially mistakes the rumble for a bomb blast. Certainly no one in their building is concerned with the political motives or ideological underpinnings behind the attack; they are simply frightened. As ash blacks out the windows and smoke pours into the stairwell where the residents of the apartment complex have taken shelter, Marc realizes that death might be imminent. Calling her father in Oregon, Karen says goodbye to him. "Not hello-goodbye," DeLillo explains, but "goodbye-I-think-we-are-going-to-die" (37). Meanwhile, the residents of the apartment complex discuss practical matters and sing songs with the children who are present. After an improvised rescue, everyone arrives safely at a shelter where a line eventually forms along a food counter. "I don't want cheese on that," one survivor says (37). "I like it better not so cooked," says another. These culinary critiques are not so incongruous with the events that have just occurred, DeLillo explains. The survivors are simply "alive and hungry, beginning to be themselves again" (37).

One of the most striking things about this story is the contrast between the two kinds of conversations DeLillo describes. When death is imminent, Karen's "goodbye" takes on heightened significance. Indeed, Karen's conversation with her father might be described in Baudrillard's terms as symbolic in that one of its underlying assumptions is that Karen will soon die. Under these conditions, Karen's words are certainly in short supply. Thus they are not infinitely reproducible signs but special words that must be used sparingly. "Goodbye" is not simply the appropriate rejoinder to "hello" in this instance. Rather, it operates as a gift. Because this goodbye is Karen's last word to her father, it is clearly marked by a certain ambivalence. It speaks of love and imminent loss, but more importantly it cannot be traded in the general economy of casual conversation. Because there can only be *one* last goodbye, because that goodbye has no substitute and no equivalent rejoinder, Karen must give it to her father without expecting anything in return. This, in a phrase, is the nature of symbolic exchange.

As Karen's seemingly final conversation with her father demonstrates, the nearness of death allows symbolic exchange to occur within consumer culture. Moreover, there is nothing particularly unique about their conversation insofar as countless similar conversations must occur on a daily basis throughout any culture. Although consumer ideology may attempt to shield us from death, death continues to touch all of our lives. It occurs every day, and as those who are able say goodbye (not "hello-goodbye" but "goodbye-I-think-I-am-going-to-die"), the dying engage in symbolic exchange. Their abundance does not make these final words any less important, but does demonstrate that symbolic exchange can occur outside the context of a suicidal terrorist mission. Thus while the voluntary death of the terrorist may indeed be a symbolic act, it is nothing "the system" cannot handle and is certainly no more symbolic than anyone's last words. Moreover, as Marco Abel suggests in "Don DeLillo's 'In the Ruins of the Future': Literature, Images, and the Rhetoric of Seeing

9/11," DeLillo's writing is itself marked by the kind of ambivalence that arguably allows symbolic exchange to occur.

For Abel, the power of DeLillo's essay on the terror attacks of September 2001 is that it "invents a view of reality that invites readers to shape and reshape reality into different impressions of equal value" (1240). As a result, DeLillo's writing does not present a "correct" interpretation of the terror attacks as do George W. Bush's exhortations to bring the "evil ones" to justice or, for that matter, Baudrillard's assertion that the attacks amounted to a deadly blow to "the system." Instead, DeLillo's essay "tries rhetorically to induce in the reader a certain kind of response-ability" by alternating between "impressionistic close-ups of the event and distanced, intellectual analyses of what happened—but without ever arriving at a resolution" (1241). This distinction is important, Abel argues, because reducing the event's complexity "to a (moralizing) explanation" produces "a culture of judgment instead of prompting an investigation of how values function" (1246). This argument suggests that DeLillo's writing puts into practice the kind of language Baudrillard can only describe in theory: ambivalent language, or language that operates beyond the code of value. By eschewing the notion of a more or less morally, politically or historically "correct" interpretation of events, DeLillo avoids what Abel describes as a "dialectical us-versus-them rhetoric," and transcends the issue of rightness-versus-wrongness or good-versus-bad that provides the underlying logic behind the concept of value.

Needless to say, DeLillo's ability to suspend judgment in a way that allows for what Baudrillard describes in *For a Critique of the Political Economy of the Sign* as the incessant potential for the destruction of the illusion of value is not limited to "In The Ruins of the Future," nor is DeLillo unique among artists for demonstrating this ability. Indeed, by suspending judgment via constant oscillation between, to borrow Abel's terminology, "impressionistic close-ups" of his characters and "distant, intellectual analyses" of the ideological concepts that frame their lives, DeLillo demonstrates throughout his *oeuvre* that underscoring the ambivalence of human existence is the province of both the artist in general and the novelist in particular. That is, where consumer ideology and all of its machinations (as described by Baudrillard throughout his career) arguably exist to streamline society so that all of its components become markers of value or signs of affluence, the artist reminds us that life exists beyond value, beyond ideology. By way of contrast, the act of terror, as DeLillo suggests in both *Players* and "In the Ruins of the Future," can only reinforce the illusion of value; it is an act that asserts the superiority of one culture, one perspective, one way of life over another, and the superiority of ideology over individuals. Where the act of terror is as dehumanizing as the system it is allegedly intended to overthrow, the work of art strives to underscore our humanity by rescuing ambivalence from the artificial positivity of consumer ideology.

CHAPTER 4

CALCULATING TERROR: SIGNIFICATION AND SYMBOLIC EXCHANGE IN *THE NAMES*

Jacques Derrida famously argues in *Of Grammatology* that "[t]here is nothing outside of the text" (158). To this argument, Jean Baudrillard adds that the text of consumer society is entirely regulated by value. In other words, all of consumer society can be read as a single text, and every element of that text ultimately serves as a sign of social ascendancy or value. Value, however, is an ideological construct that mystifies social relations and precludes meaningful exchange, as evidenced by what Douglas Keesey refers to as the "abstract business English" spoken by James Axton and his fellow expatriates in Don DeLillo's *The Names* (121). Such language, Keesey argues, causes Westerners to lose touch with "the basic joys of human life on earth: true involvement, meaningful conversation, the satisfaction of common desires" (121). In order to restore the Western world's potential for what Keesey describes as meaningful conversation and true involvement in the world, Baudrillard calls for a mode of exchange that operates beyond the code of value: symbolic exchange, or exchange predicated on loss. Yet where Baudrillard argues that acts of terror have the potential to effect symbolic exchange, DeLillo's exploration of the relationship between language and terrorism in *The Names* suggests that terror only reproduces the code of value that Baudrillard seeks to dismantle.

In *For a Critique of the Political Economy of the Sign*, Baudrillard argues that consumer culture is a system that maintains unequal power relations among those beholden to its laws by regulating the exchange of signs (85). One way to understand this argument is in terms of money: if money is a sign of wealth, and wealth is a sign of power, then consumer ideology (i.e., the governing logic behind consumer culture) regulates power by ensuring, to borrow a phrase, that the rich get richer and the poor get poorer. For the most part, this argument is in line with a basic premise of Marxism—that the capitalist takes advantage of the laborer by setting the value of commodities higher than the value of the labor that produces them (Tucker 316). Yet for Baudrillard, consumer ideology is far more insidious than capitalism. Where Marx sees a distinction between use value (the degree to which a commodity meets a need) and exchange value (the degree to which the capitalist profits from the sale of a commodity), Baudrillard argues that need "can no longer be defined adequately in terms of the naturalist-idealist thesis—as innate, instinctive power, spontaneous craving, anthropological potentiality" (*For a Critique* 82). Rather, need must be seen as "a function induced (in the individual) by the internal logic of the system" (82). Alienated from any real sense of need, Baudrillard argues, we have lost touch with what we might consider the "real" world. In its place, we have entered a world of imagined needs, and because these needs are merely imagined, the commodities that allegedly satisfy them serve no real purpose. Rather, these commodities are simply signs of our successful participation in the dominant culture (33). Money, then, is not the only sign of ascendancy within consumer culture; *everything* is. Our "success" as individuals is gauged in terms of how well we consume, or, more accurately, how well we display the signs of having consumed.

Divorced from the "real," living world throughout much of *The Names*, James and his fellow expatriates live in a world of signs that is strikingly similar to the one Baudrillard describes. Where Americans once traveled to places like Athens "to write and paint and study, to find deeper textures," James explains in his capacity as the novel's narrator, their current purpose for such travel is simply to "do business" (6). "Recyclers of petrodollars" and "handlers of huge sums of delicate money," the Americans in the novel regard the world with a strong sense of detachment (98). As James further explains,

> We were a subculture, business people in transit, growing old in planes and airports. We were versed in percentages, safety records, in the humor of flaming death...Open seating never caught us by surprise and we were quick to identify our luggage on the runway where that was the practice and we didn't exchange wild looks when the oxygen masks dropped during touchdown...We knew where martial law was in force, where body searches were made, where they engaged in systematic torture, or fired assault weapons into the air at weddings, or abducted and ransomed executives. This was the humor of personal humiliation. (6–7)

For all their experience, the travelers James describes perceive themselves as insulated from the dangers that haunt the locales to which they travel. Living like tourists, they not only escape accountability (as James observes), but also avoid experiencing anything that resembles need: because they take their meals in restaurants and sleep in hotels, the needs of these travelers are always already met long before they have the opportunity to arise. Thus travelers like Ann Maitland can discuss traumatic personal experiences involving house arrest, deportation, heavy mortar shelling, and outbreaks of infectious hepatitis "in a tone of remote sadness, as if they were things she'd heard about or read in a newspaper" while others, like Dot Borden, are perpetually "ready to lead expeditions to American brand names" (40, 53).

Alienated from any real sense of need, the travelers in *The Names* can only trade signs of their expertise as consumers of what might best be termed "the foreign experience"—not travel itself, but the prestige of having traveled to so-called foreign lands. They understand the world in terms of "foreign exchange factors, inflation rates, election possibilities, imports and exports" and distill the places they visit into "one-sentence stories" that can be traded like currency (50, 94). At the same time, James is only capable of using language in a way that further alienates him from the world at large. On one hand, he recognizes that the speakers of foreign tongues who surround him, and for whom "Conversation is life," engage in a mode of discussion that amounts to "a shared narrative, a thing that surges forward" (52). On the other hand, conversations with Tap and Kathryn, James' son and estranged wife, only serve to remind him that he is "the outsider in their group," as do the simple furniture and spare decorations that adorn their home (8). Discussions with Kathryn are known to deteriorate into recitations of what James refers to as his "27 Depravities," among which is his tendency to "advertise" himself "as refreshingly sane and healthy in a world of driven neurotics," and Tap's frequent lapses into Ob, "a coded jargon he'd learned from Kathryn," only support James in his suspicion that he is, indeed, an outsider (17, 10). Not a speaker of Ob himself, James cannot proffer signs that he is part of Tap and Kathryn's group and therefore cannot gain social ascendancy within it as he can in mainstream society by advertising himself as sane. In short, the conversations James has with Tap and Kathryn help to exemplify the distinction Baudrillard draws between symbolic exchange and signification: where symbolic exchange draws parties together, the ultimate purpose of signification is to designate social rank, and thus to differentiate.

The sign is never given, Baudrillard argues: "it is appropriated withheld and manipulated by individual subjects…as coded difference" (*For a Critique* 65). From this perspective, the code that regulates signification bears no relation to the "real" dimension of lived existence. Rather, the code's authority is rooted in the abstract and artificial concept of value, which Baudrillard sees as denigrating to meaningful exchange. Because the sign garners meaning from value rather than the act of exchange itself, it cannot "speak" of the relationship between or among those engaged in the exchange:

> It is from the (theoretically isolatable) moment when the exchange is no longer purely transitive, when the object (the material of exchange) is immediately presented as such, that it is reified into a sign. Instead of abolishing itself in the relation that it establishes, the object becomes autonomous, intransitive, opaque, and so begins to signify the abolition of the relationship. Having become a sign object, it is no longer the mobile signifier of a lack between two beings, it is "of" and "from" the reified relation. (65)

In contrast to signification, symbolic exchange does not depend entirely on an external, artificial code for meaning. Rather, symbolic exchange is predicated on loss; what marks the object as symbolic is "that one separates himself from it in order to give it" (65). To clarify: one cannot lose signs because the code renders all signs interchangeable; what matters is not which particular signs one possesses, but the total effect of those signs on the public perception of one's social rank (i.e., the total value imputed to those signs by the code). Because symbolic exchange does not rely solely upon the abstract notion of value for meaning, "the symbolic object...is not only the concrete manifestation of a total relationship (ambivalent, and total because of its ambivalence) of desire, but also, through the singularity of an object, the transparency of social relations in a dual or integrated group relationship" (65). Thus where sign exchange is ultimately meaningless beyond its capacity to designate social status, symbolic exchange, in Baudrillard's words, constitutes "an act which is significant in itself as the basis, simultaneously, of both the mutual presence of the terms of the relationship and their mutual absence (their distance)" (65).

Always a combination of "love and aggression" (65), symbolic exchange substitutes an interpersonal relationship based upon mutual need for the cold, calculating jockeying for social ascendancy Baudrillard associates with sign exchange. In *The Names*, this distinction is best illustrated by Charles Maitland's assertion that the best way to travel in foreign countries is to "learn the language...but not to let them know" (41). In so doing, Charles effectively accumulates linguistic signs without ever returning them. That is, there is no give and take between Charles and the native speakers of foreign tongues; their exchanges are not based upon mutual need and do not draw the parties together in a common bond. Rather, by refusing to speak, by accumulating signs without returning them, Charles isolates himself from those with whom he would communicate. In contrast to Charles, James, and the other Americans who speak the "secret language" of "loans, arms credits, goods, technology," Kathryn and Tap operate according to a logic that has less to do with accumulation than with meeting human needs (114).

Preferring "basic" satisfactions, Kathryn lives with Tap on a Greek island "with no wandering shoppers or places to shop" (15). She works in a trench at the site of an archaeological dig "with trowels, root clippers, dental picks, tweezers" and speaks Greek with the owner of a restaurant where octopus carcasses hang over a clothesline near the tables (15, 18). Stemming from a lifestyle that demands greater involvement with the world at large, this communication strategy certainly differs from that of Charles. Moreover (and her estranged husband's paranoia notwithstanding), Kathryn's conversations with James are marked by the combination of love and aggression that Baudrillard sees as the hallmark of ambivalence; when James states that his job allows him to feel "involved" in the world, Kathryn challenges him with the assertion that "there ought to be something higher than the corporation" (12). Although James blithely replies that the only thing higher than the corporation is the orgasm, his own orgasms are few and far between, and he secretly yearns for the kind of real-world involvement Kathryn experiences: visceral engagement with one's immediate environment and communication based on mutual need.

Motivated by a similar desire, the archaeologist Owen Brademas is intent on discovering the remains of entire cultures for whom survival once depended upon the mutual satisfaction of needs. What draws

Owen to archaeology is a sense of mystery at the forces that formerly drew communities together and rendered them dependent upon the land and their own ingenuity for survival. Arguing that the site of his excavation is "one of those Greek places that pits the sensuous against the elemental," Owen describes the lives of those who once inhabited the region as being marked by a "physical...fertile slow-working delight" (26). "People must devise means to collect rain-water, buttress their houses against earthquakes, cultivate on steep, rocky terrain," Owen explains, adding that the goal of the people who once inhabited the area was not the accumulation of wealth but mere subsistence (26).

Such implements of self preservation as Owen describes speak directly to the distinction Baudrillard draws between utensils and objects in *The System of Objects*: "A *utensil* is never possessed, because a utensil refers one to the world; what is possessed is always an object *abstracted from its function and thus brought into relationship with the subject*" (86). As opposed to the object, then, the utensil derives its meaning not from an arbitrary code of value but from its capacity to connect its user to the world. Where the "primitive" people with whom Owen is fascinated once used utensils to ensure their own survival, the overwhelming majority of professional people in Western culture are, as Baudrillard agues, alienated from a real sense of need and thus have no true use for utensils. As a result, the commodities these people possess are no more than objects that "together make up the system through which the subject strives to construct a world, a private totality" (86). Thus in order for James to satisfy his desire for a sense of involvement with the real world, he must abandon his own "private totality" and enter the slow-working realm of rainwater, earthquakes, and rocky terrain that Owen describes.

Although he does not use the theorist's terminology, James is clearly interested in substituting the kind of mutually inclusive bond Baudrillard sees operating in symbolic exchange for the cold, calculating, and divisive code of value that marks signification. Moreover, James, like Baudrillard, sees language as the key to reestablishing his own connection with the "real" world and its inhabitants. In short, James wants to learn to use language as a utensil rather than as an object. As with his desire to return to a state of existence that pits the sensuous against the elemental, this focus on language is largely influenced by Owen, whose "first and current love" is epigraphy, or the study of inscriptions (DeLillo, *The Names* 29). Although Owen admits that the ancient inscriptions with which he is infatuated reflect the "routine stuff" of "land sale contracts, grain payments, records of commodities," he also recognizes "the mysterious importance in the letters as such, the blocks of characters" (35). Such characters are much more than the ephemeral signifiers Baudrillard sees operating in consumer culture; Owen's "unreasoning passion" for letters (as such) stems from their physicality and the information they reveal about the people who used them.

Reflecting upon the importance of a clay tablet he once had the opportunity to examine, Owen explains,

> The tablet at Ras Shamrah said nothing. It was inscribed with the alphabet itself. I find this is all I want to know about the people who lived there. The shapes of their letters and the material they used. Fire-hardened clay, dense black basalt, marble with a ferrous content. These things I lay my hands against, feel where the words have been cut. And the eye takes in those beautiful shapes. So strange and reawakening. It goes deeper than conversation, riddles. (35–36)

Here, Owen's description of the ancient alphabet echoes a piece of information offered earlier in the novel—that the word "character" comes from a Greek verb meaning "to brand or sharpen" and from its noun form, which refers to a "pointed stake" or an "engraving instrument or branding instrument" (10). This explication underscores the multifaceted nature of letters in the ancient world: the character is not only the mark left on the clay tablet, but the act of forging the mark, and the tool with which the mark is forged as well. The ancient character, then, served as a utensil that allowed for a connection between its user and the tactile world of "routine stuff," and Owen's recognition of this connection lends him the sense of "deep and complicated passion" for life that James envies (20). Moreover, that James experiences a childlike "surge of pride" each time he discovers for himself the etymology of a new or foreign word suggests that he, too, has the potential to find such passion in the raw stuff of language (81).

In all fairness, the suggestion that his use of language always leaves James with a sense of isolation is somewhat misleading. While the majority of his conversations operate according to the logic of signification (i.e., as a means of differentiation for the sake of signaling social value), James does, on occasion, experience the sense of mutual connection Baudrillard sees operating in symbolic exchange. For example, James reflects that discussing such topics as "nephews and nieces, other family matters, a cousin taking trumpet lessons, a death in Winnipeg" with Kathryn renders their conversations "almost tactile," and that conversations like these allow him to experience "a close-up contact warmth in the names and images" (31). Talk of familiar things, James explains, yields a sense of "the nameless way in which we sometimes feel our connections to the physical world. *Being here*. Everything is where it should be. Our senses are collecting at the primal edge" (32). This sense of connection, however, is always short-lived, and it is never long before talk of familiar things gives way to the petty bickering that characterizes their relationship; when one conversation turns immediately to a contest, James laments that he and Kathryn must too soon revert to their old, combative selves (74). Yet because he is so deeply habituated to the logic of signification, James cannot see that the kind of conversation for which he longs cannot be reduced to a system or code. As a result, he places a quasi-religious faith in the power of systems to return him to a state of communion not only with Kathryn but also with the world at large.

Reflecting at some length on the topic of religion, James notes that he and Kathryn are both "Skeptics of the slightly superior type" and that their "only sources of speculation and wonder" are the "quasi stellar object" and the "quantum event" (92). "Our bones were made of the material that came swimming across the galaxy from exploded stars," James explains; "This knowledge was our shared prayer, our chant" (92). Yet for all of his skepticism, James returns to the "grim" and "inexplicable" concept of a looming "god-mass" to account for the orderly nature of the universe—hence his praise for the "mind-scorched, empty-eyed" men James imagines moving their lips "to the endless name of God" in India (92). On one hand, their prayer may be interpreted in purely secular terms as a paean to the orderly nature of the universe. However, that James juxtaposes his reference to "the endless name of God" with a two-word paragraph that simply reads "The alphabet" suggests that this name is less a meditation on the wonders of the universe than an artificial construct, a code that renders the chaos from which humanity emerged intelligible, an attempt to project order onto that chaos. Thus even as he professes his doubt in the existence of God, James expresses a deep and abiding faith in systems that are no less arbitrary in nature than those over which he holds a "slightly superior" attitude. As a result, his faith in the alphabet is markedly different from Owen's fascination with the same. Where Owen focuses his attention on the shapes and material composition of "letters as such," James hopes to find in the letters a pattern that will, in the words of Kathryn, "subdue and codify" the mysteries of the universe and allow him to reconnect with the world (80). Yet by placing his faith in such a code, James reveals the limits of his skepticism and ultimately precludes his potential for attaining the state he so strongly desires.

James, moreover, is not alone in his fascination with the alphabet as a system. Shortly before a brutal murder takes place on the island of Kouros, Owen tells James of a chance meeting with a small band of travelers in the rugged hills of that island. These travelers, Owen explains, have a lifestyle that closely resembles that of the ancient cultures he studies: huddling around a stone fireplace for warmth, they sleep in a cave, and their hair is stringy with that "particular clinging dirt of people who no longer notice" (29). This lifestyle so intimately roots the travelers in the visceral experience of their immediate surroundings that Owen describes dirt as "their medium" and reads into their interactions "a curious force in the air, as though each of them sat in a charged field and these fields had begun to overlap" (29, 30). In other words, these travelers appear to be connected to each other and their world in much the same way James wishes to maintain lasting connections with his own world and the people who inhabit it. Additionally, that the travelers express more than a passing interest in the alphabet suggests that the faith James places in systems is not entirely misplaced. When Owen describes the tablet at Ras Shamrah to them, the travelers attempt to conceal their excitement. The reason for their interest in the tablet, however, proves different from Owen's own. Where Owen is interested in "history, gods, tumbled walls, the scale poles and pumps of the excavators," the travelers want only to know about the alphabet itself, "letters, written symbols, fixed in sequence" (30). Indeed, so strong is their interest in the topic that James is moved to ask whether these travelers might be a religious cult, and when the seemingly senseless murder of a feeble-minded old man coincides with the disappearance of the travelers, James describes them as "zealots of the alphabet" and begins to suspect that they might somehow be involved in the killing.

Reinforcing James' suspicion of the travelers, Owen asserts that the murder was not a senseless act but an example of "how far men will go to satisfy a pattern" or, in Kathryn's words, how far they will go to "subdue and codify" the world (80). Yet the pattern in this case is strikingly arbitrary: according to a cult member named Andahl, the travelers killed the feeble old man because "the letters matched" (209). That is, the victim's initials matched the initials of the town in which the travelers murdered him. Explaining the rationale behind this murder and others like it, Andahl can do little more than assert that something in the cult's method finds a "home" in James' unconscious mind, a "curious recognition" that James "seem[s] to understand and find familiar, something [he] cannot analyze" (208). This recognition, Andahl explains, allows members of the cult—known only as *Ta Onómata* or The Names—to share a "permanent bond" (208). "How could it be otherwise?" he asks; "We have in common that first experience, among others, that experience of recognition, of knowing this program reaches something in us, of knowing we all

wanted at once to be a part of it" (208). When James presses him on
the ethical implications of the cult's "program," Andahl replies that
the murder of the old man was justified: "I knew at once it was right.
I cannot describe how fully and deeply it reached me...Shatter his
skull, kill him, smash his brains" (209). In a fairly lengthy and graphic
description of one such murder, Andahl further argues that the physical, "hands-on" nature of the cult's violence allows its members to
realize the gravity of their actions and proves the "rightness" of their
program (209, 211). While James is initially sickened by the gruesome
nature of this program, he continues to be fascinated by the cult insofar as its members' faith in codes and systems appears to allow them
the kind of involvement with the world for which he himself yearns.

Because of its intensely physical and, one might argue, intimate nature, the cult's method of killing stands in contrast to the
"wrong kind of killing" James sees occurring in America (115).
Such killing, James argues, is "a form of consumerism...the logical
extension of consumer fantasy. People shooting from overpasses,
barricaded houses. Pure image" (115). In other words, the American
style of murder is like all forms of exchange within consumer culture: cold, impersonal, and disconnected from any sense of reality
insofar as the victim is not an individual but an image or a sign.
Along similar lines, Baudrillard argues throughout *The Gulf War
Did Not Take Place* that while Operation Desert Storm did, in fact,
occur, media coverage rendered its victims nonexistent to world
audiences; though we saw buildings reduced to rubble, we never
saw human casualties. Returning to this theme in *The Spirit of Terrorism*, Baudrillard argues that America's campaign in Afghanistan
after the terror attacks of September 11, 2001, called not for soldier-
to-soldier confrontation but the operational liquidation of invisible
targets (26). Conversely, the perpetrators of the September attacks
did not seek "the impersonal elimination of the other," but through
the suicidal nature of their actions engaged in a "dual, personal relation with the opposing power" (25, 26). This face-to-face, interpersonal mode of engagement, Baudrillard argues, forced Americans
to deal with the terrorists in a way with which they were completely

unaccustomed: on the terrain of symbolic exchange and death. That is, where consumer ideology had theretofore allowed Americans a "zero-death" view of war and murder that was in line with their unspoken conviction that all things were mere signs of social ascendancy, the terror attacks proved so devastating not because of the magnitude of destruction but because the terrorists engaged in something more than sign exchange, something more than the safe, anonymous, victimless mode of killing that James and Baudrillard both describe. The terrorists, like the cult members in *The Names*, replaced the arbitrary, disengaged, and calculating logic of sign exchange with the mutually binding sense of loss that characterizes symbolic exchange.

Or so the argument goes.

According to Baudrillard, terrorism is an effective means of revolution because the terrorist does not confront consumer ideology on "the terrain of reality" (i.e., according to the laws of reality as dictated by the system) but in terms to which the system cannot respond except through its own self-destruction (*Symbolic Exchange and Death* 36). In response to the willing death of the terrorist, Baudrillard explains, the system "turns on itself, as a scorpion does when encircled by the challenge of death. For it is summoned to answer, if it is not to lose face, to what can only be death. The system must *itself commit suicide in response to the multiplied challenge of death and suicide*" (37, Baudrillard's emphasis). In other words, because the logic of consumer ideology is one of constant increase, the only way to win against this system is to lose; its logic demands that the only appropriate response to the suicide of the terrorist is a bigger, better, new-and-improved suicide. This logic applies not only to the death of the terrorist, but to the death of the terrorist's victims as well:

> On the symbolic or sacrificial plane, from which every moral consideration of the innocence of the victims is ruled out, the hostage is the substitute, the alter-ego of the "terrorist"—the hostage's death for the terrorist's. The hostage and terrorist may thereafter become confused in the same sacrificial act. The stakes are death without any possibility of negation, and therefore return to an inevitable overbidding. (37)

By bringing the reality of death to the bargaining table (as it were), terrorists force the collapse of consumer ideology insofar as death shuts down the potential for negotiation: death (like its counterpart, life) has no equivalent, and therefore no combination of signs can properly respond to it. The reality of death, then, renders signs valueless. Or, more accurately, the imminence of death reveals the illusory nature of all signs: they are not meaningful (as consumer ideology would have us believe), nor have they ever been meaningful beyond the code of value that regulates the system.

By subverting the code of value that regulates consumer culture, the act of terror (theoretically) allows symbolic exchange to take place. As Baudrillard notes in *For a Critique of the Political Economy of the Sign*, ambivalence and symbolic exchange do not confront the discourse of value with an opposing code but with the rejection of codes altogether (209). Because the "pact and sacrificial obligation" that unites them is not predicated on an external code but upon their mutual recognition of the imminent reality of death, terrorists share a bond that, like the bond Andahl imputes to the members of his cult in *The Names*, is "immune to any defection or corruption" (Baudrillard, *Spirit of Terrorism* 23). In fact, Baudrillard and Andahl both appear to be making the same argument: intimacy with death restores the subject's involvement with the world by subverting the nonpersonal mode of exchange that marks consumer ideology. In other words, death allows symbolic exchange to operate in place of signification. In "The Baudrillardian Symbolic, 9/11, and the War on Good and Evil," however, Bradley Butterfield notes that while the terror attacks of September 2001 presented an "irreducible, singular and irrevocable challenge to each and every imagination," this challenge did little to alter the logic of consumer ideology: "What the system did in response to 9/11, or instead of responding to it, was to reabsorb its symbolic violence back into the never ending flow of anesthetized simulation" (18, 25). In *The Names*, James' position as a risk analyst for an insurance company underscores Butterfield's argument and gives the lie to Baudrillard's assertion that consumer culture cannot respond to acts of terror except through its own demise; by charging increasingly higher insurance premiums to protect the financial interests of potential terror targets, the company for which James purportedly works demonstrates the uncanny fashion in which consumer culture can assimilate even the most dangerous phenomena.

During his final meeting with Owen, James confesses that although his own life "eludes" him, he feels a sense of connection with the cult (DeLillo, *The Names* 300). Nonetheless, when Owen offers a tortured first-hand account of a cult murder, James realizes that his fascination is misplaced. The cult does not, as James wants to believe, provide a means of reconnecting with the world at large. Rather, as Owen explains, the cult offers nothing more than another means of reducing the world to an orderly nature: "These killings mock us. They mock our need to structure and classify, to build a system against the terror in our souls. They make the system equal to the terror. The means to contend with death has become death" (308). This mockery is not intended, Owen adds; a system itself, the cult mocks all other systems by virtue of its extreme nature. Thus rather than allowing James the kind of direct route to a natural sense of truth DeLillo imputes to Tap's mode of language in a 1988 interview with Anthony DeCurtis, the cult can only preclude James' true involvement with the world at large in much the same way as his use of abstract business English protects him from meaningful interaction with the people in his life (DeCurtis 64). Indeed, Owen's argument echoes a suspicion James initially entertains shortly before his meeting with Andahl—that the cult is engaged in a "painstaking denial" of death (DeLillo, *The Names* 175). While James sees humanity's knowledge of death as "our saving grace" as well as "our special sadness...and therefore a richness, a sanctification," the cult's ritualistic murders deny "our base reality" by producing a "needless death," a "death by system, by machine intellect" (175). Just as consumer culture promises that accumulating and arranging signs of value will result in the abolition of our "special sadness," and just as religious fervor promises paradise beyond death (as in the case of suicide bombers), the cult in *The Names* opposes death by systematically preempting it. Because the result of this preemption is not, as Baudrillard and Andahl assert, a stronger bond with the world and others but a form of totalitarianism, James must look elsewhere for the sense of connection he desires.

Shortly after leaving Owen, James overhears a violent argument that rekindles his desire to connect with Kathryn and Tap, who have left Greece for British Columbia. Ruminating over the distance between himself and his family, James realizes that he has "no idea what kind of house they live in, what the street look[s] like, how they go about their daily routine" (311). Rather than approaching these details as signs of social differentiation that can only underline his status as an outsider in their group, James comes to recognize their "haunting importance" (311). Recalling his father's interest in the seemingly minor details of his own life, James arrives at the conclusion that such details as "the petty facts of time and weather" do, in fact, have the potential to "connect people across a distance" and allow them to recognize each other "as real" (311). Such an approach to language, however, does not come naturally to James. While he admires a novel Tap is writing for its "spirited misspellings," it takes two readings for James to realize that his son's "mangled words" make language "new again" and allow him to see how words work, what they really are: "ancient things, secret, reshapable" (313). This epiphany echoes Owen's assertion earlier in the novel that "[t]he word in India has enormous power. Not what people mean but what they say. Intended meaning is beside the point. The word itself is all the matters" (294). Divorced from "what people mean," each word takes on a gravity of its own; its meaning is not in its definition but in the fact of its existence. Under such conditions, each word serves as a gift, and the sharing of words places speakers and writers, listeners and readers in binding relationships predicated not on the differential logic of political economy but on a mutual understanding that all gains must produce corresponding losses.

In an age where the reproduction of signs is instantaneous and largely effortless, such a view of language is certainly foreign; the notion that one can somehow "lose" a word—printed, spoken, or otherwise—when so many exact duplicates are available at the touch of a button appears, on the surface, to be patently ridiculous. Yet as Owen points out, even in modern times, the Hindu woman "tries to avoid speaking her husband's name" because each utterance of that name "brings him closer to death" (294). Additionally, the major-ity of ancient Indian literature "has been eaten by white ants. The bark and leaf manuscripts nibbled, gnawed and consumed" (295). In both instances, the potential for loss is integral to the significance of the words in question. Because each utterance of her husband's name points up the relative brevity of life, the Hindu woman must take great care in deciding when and how often to speak that name. Similarly, the complete disappearance of an entire body of literature underlines the fact that words can, in fact, be lost forever if steps are not taken to preserve them. Likewise, James' initial impulse to cor-rect Tap's errors spells the demise of the very quality that makes the child's writing unique. Yet by preserving these errors, by cultivating an appreciation for the words as words, James comes to the realiza-tion that they speak not only their intended meanings but also, and more importantly, of his relationship with Tap.

While escaping textuality may be, as Derrida argues, impossible, the distinction Baudrillard draws between signification (i.e., the lan-guage of value) and symbolic exchange (i.e., language not predicated on value) suggests that different modes of language can allow for more-or-less meaningful readings of the phenomena that constitute our world. In *For a Critique of the Political Economy of the Sign*, Baudrillard notes that where the object of symbolic exchange is "inseparable from the concrete relation in which it is exchanged, the transferential pact in which it seals two persons," the sign "only refers to the absence of relation itself, and to isolated individual subjects" (64, 65). Symbolic exchange, then, not only represents "the concrete manifestation of the total relationship" but also allows for "the total transparency of social relations in a dual or integrated social relation-ship" (65). In other words, symbolic exchange allows us to recognize our duties and obligations to each other, to understand without pre-varication the ties that bind. In contrast, sign exchange "no longer gathers its meaning in the concrete relationship between two people" but does demonstrate "the *total constraint of the code* that governs social value: it is the specific weight of *signs* that regulates the social logic of exchange" (66, Baudrillard's emphasis). Hence Baudrillard's call for a return to symbolic exchange: by abandoning the codes that regulate sign exchange, we will substitute real interpersonal relations for those whose "meaning" only exists in relation to arbitrary systems of value.

In *The Names*, James is motivated by an interest similar to that of Baudrillard. Because the complex systems of modern communication to which the likes of Charles Maitland are beholden "don't shrink the world" but only "make it bigger"—that is, they only widen the gaps among those who would communicate with each other—James must find a new means of communicating (323). Although the cult to which he is initially attracted appears to have found the solution to James' quandary, their guiding logic, like that of the terrorists whose actions Baudrillard praises, is arguably no different from the value-laden logic that regulates signification: an arbitrary system that only serves to hinder human relations. Turning away from the cult, James looks to words themselves as a means of reconnecting with his family and the world at large; by developing an appreciation for his son's "spirited misspellings" James allows himself to recognize that what binds him to his family is not always *what* they are saying but *that* they are saying. It is this approach to language that James envies early in the novel when he remarks that the simplest greetings not only convey information but also "bridge the lonely distances" (53). Likewise it is this same approach to language that, in Tap's words, connects us with "the nightmare of real things, the fallen wonder of the world" (339).

CHAPTER 5

SEDUCTION OF THE AMBIVALENT: FATAL STRATEGY IN *LIBRA*

Early in *Libra*, a young Lee Oswald (as he is called in the novel) offers a critique of capitalism that resonates closely with that of Jean Baudrillard. In addition to exploiting workers, Lee argues, capitalism exploits consumers as well: "Everything is based on forcing people to buy. If you can't buy what they're selling, you're a zero in the system" (40). Despite his apparent antipathy toward American consumer culture, however, Lee cannot help defining himself in terms dictated by "the system." What motivates Lee throughout the novel is a desire to be more than a zero, to be a historical force. Ironically, however, this desire only strengthens the system Lee so fervently despises. His involvement in the assassination of President Kennedy not only fails to trigger the kind of revolution he desires, but also renders Lee a commodity: upon his capture, Lee ceases to be Lee Oswald, a zero in the system, and becomes instead "Lee Harvey Oswald," a looming presence in the system of signs Baudrillard sees as detrimental to meaningful exchange. At the same time, however, Lee's transformation to Lee Harvey Oswald is suggestive of fatal strategy, a notion espoused in Baudrillard's later writings as humanity's only viable means of adapting to the harsh and lifeless conditions of consumer culture. *Libra*, then, underscores the fatalistic nature of Baudrillard's fatal strategy. As Lee's transformation to Lee Harvey Oswald demonstrates, far from being subversive, Baudrillard's fatal strategy largely reinforces consumer ideology.

In *The Consumer Society*, Baudrillard describes consumption as the organizing force behind everyday life in the developed world (29). Because technological innovation has largely alienated humanity from a real sense of need, Baudrillard argues, the value of the commodities we consume lies not in what Marx considers their use value but in their capacity to serve as markers of status. Simply put, we consume not to satisfy needs but to signal our prowess as consumers. One result of this phenomenon is that our dealings no longer involve personal interaction, "but rather—on a rising statistical curve—with the reception and manipulation of goods" (25). We combine and arrange such goods according to a complex "calculus of objects," which demands that we continue to accumulate without any goal (other than the continued accumulation of goods) in sight (27). Measuring personal worth only in terms of affluence, this calculus of objects—that is, consumer ideology—places us squarely within a matrix of signs that mean nothing except in relation to each other. Sheltered within this matrix of signs—this system of objects, to use Baudrillard's term—we live in denial of the real (34). Moreover, we have lost the ability to relate to each other in human terms; surrounded by objects, which themselves serve as no more than signs of affluence, we have come to regard ourselves and others as objects as well. That is, within the system of objects, we measure self-worth using the same calculus of objects we use to determine the worth of commodities. As a result, everything within the system Baudrillard describes, including the individual, is reduced to a sign, the value of which is determined by its position in relation to all other signs within the system.

Baudrillard's strategy for subverting the system he describes has evolved over the course of his career. Early on, Baudrillard argued that the cultivation of ambivalence, or the recognition of both positivity and negativity in the fulfillment of desire, would lead to the knowledge "that the Object is nothing and that behind it stands the tangled void of human relations" (196). Such knowledge, Baudrillard further argued, would inevitably result in "violent irruptions and sudden disintegrations" that would tear the system asunder (196). More recently, Baudrillard has adopted what he terms a fatal strategy, which, Douglas Kellner notes in *Jean Baudrillard: From Marxism to Postmodernism and Beyond*, focuses on "the triumph of objects over subjects within the obscene proliferation of an object world so completely out of control that it surpasses all attempts to understand, conceptualize and control it" (155). From this perspective, the individual must concede to the overwhelming power of the system and adopt the position of the object in order to survive. Or, as Kellner explains, "in fatal strategies, the subject recognizes the supremacy of the object, and therefore takes the side of the object and attempts to reproduce its strategies, ruses and rules" (160). Baudrillard's adoption of fatal strategy, then, represents a concession of defeat: if one cannot subvert consumer ideology, one might as well learn to partake in it with a vengeance. To a large extent, this is also the perspective Lee adopts as events unfold in *Libra*.

Like Baudrillard, DeLillo also envisions a world in which individuals surround themselves with objects that serve primarily as signs of affluence. This environment, DeLillo notes in an interview with Anthony DeCurtis, is in some ways responsible for contemporary violence:

> I see contemporary violence as a kind of sardonic response to the promise of consumer fulfillment in America. Again, we come back to these men in small rooms who can't get out and have to organize their desperation and loneliness, who have to give it a destiny and who often end up doing this through violent means. I see this desperation against the backdrop of brightly colored packages and products and every promise that American life makes day by day and minute by minute everywhere we go. (DeCurtis 58)

The desperation DeLillo describes here is much like the desperation Lee experiences throughout *Libra*; his initial critique of capitalism and its twentieth century counterpart, consumerism, is based upon his own struggle to resist being identified as a zero in the system. While his classmates discuss the virtues of fast cars and breath mints in a vernacular limned from television commercials, his mother, Marguerite, cites her own efforts to provide a home "with bright touches and not a thing out of place" as proof that Lee's tendency to "dress below the level" is not a sign of the family's indigence (7–9, 11). Despite Marguerite's faith in the inherent value of a well-appointed home, Lee looks upon his mother with a mixture of "pity and contempt" for her failure to recognize that they are both "locked in a process, a system of money and property that diminishe[s] their human worth every day, as if by scientific law" (35, 41). Nonetheless, Lee cannot help but play by the rules of the very system he despises. Rather than aiming to dismantle the power structure that renders him a zero, Lee's goal is to raise his own social status by any means necessary. Hence his enlisting in the Marine Corps and subsequent attempts at espionage: military service offers Lee a clear-cut system through which he might gain ascendancy, and, as Mark Osteen observes in *American Magic and Dread: Don DeLillo's Dialogue with Culture*, his involvement with Soviet agents allows Lee to enter a linguistic realm of social exchange from which he might otherwise be barred (155). In other words, his access to American military secrets renders Lee a valuable commodity to the Soviets.

And here lies the rub: the system that renders Lee a zero operates in both US and Soviet territories, regardless of apparent differences in ideology. Manipulating and arranging certain signs (i.e., military secrets), Lee seeks to gain social ascendancy within Soviet circles. Yet even as he defects to the Soviet Union, Lee comes to the startling realization that he is still a "zero in the system" when the officials with whom he meets regard him with a terrifying blankness and cannot "distinguish him from anyone else" (DeLillo, *Libra* 151). Unlike those "who defect for practical reasons," Lee has heretofore idealized communism as "the system that doesn't exploit" and thus can only be disappointed when the system does, in fact, exploit him (165, 40). After denouncing his US citizenship and revealing nearly everything he knows about American military operations to the KGB, Lee is sent to Minsk, where his "dull and regimented" life as a factory worker leaves him yearning to "get ahead" (198). Moreover, and much to Lee's dismay, the citizens of Minsk are as enchanted with commodities as are the Americans he despises; despite (or perhaps because of) the high price of chocolate, the people of Minsk have a "vicious sweet tooth," and Lee laments that their "small" lives revolve around confection, record players, and meals at the automat (199). Meanwhile, even the most hard-line Communists attend political sermons for the sole purpose of "looking for any bonus-making catch of inattentiveness on the part of any worker" (206). Although Lee's earlier assertion that the "main thing in communism is that workers don't produce profits for the system" may be true, the system itself continues to follow the dictates of consumer ideology, and those who live within its parameters can hope for no more than to arrange the signs at their disposal in a way that might enhance their own standing within that system. Whether those signs are tangible commodities like chocolate and record players, or intangibles like secrets and information, their purpose remains the same: to signify value in the generalized economy of an artificial code.

As noted in Mark Poster's introduction to *The Mirror of Production*, Baudrillard argues that one reason Marxism fails to dismantle (and even partakes in) capitalism is that "Marx's theory of historical realism...is too conservative, too rooted in the assumptions of political economy, too dependent on the system of ideas it seeks to overthrow to provide a framework for radical action" (1–2). Where Marx locates the "determinant instance" of capitalism "in the structure of the means of production and the relations of production," Baudrillard's critique focuses on the political economy of the sign and argues that "the investment of things with value...the placing of a sign on a thing and the logic of this process of signification is the true essence of capital" (5). According to Baudrillard, Marx's

> presupposition of use value—the hypothesis of a concrete
> value beyond the abstraction of exchange value, a human
> purpose of the commodity in the moment of its direct rela-
> tion of utility for a subject—is only the effect of the system of
> exchange value, a concept produced and developed by it. Far
> from designating a realm beyond political economy, use value
> is only the horizon of exchange value. (22–23)

In other words, the notion of use value is itself a myth that ultimately provides an alibi for the notion of exchange value, which
Marx seeks to reveal as mystifying. Moreover, by exalting labor,
or the work of production, "as value, as end in itself, as categori-
cal imperative," Marx can only conceive of social progress in terms
of material gain and thus ignores the potentially beneficial effects
of "discharge, waste, sacrifice, prodigality, play and symbolism"
that stem from the destruction of value (35, 42). Where Baudrillard
argues that primitive man "does not chop one tree or trace one fur-
row without 'appeasing the spirits' with a counter-gift or sacrifice,"
Marx ignores the potential for loss in human activity and substitutes
linear accumulation for the primitive cycle of gifts and counter-
gifts Baudrillard describes (83). Accordingly, the first principle of
political economy is "not in the exploitation of labor as a productive
force...but in the imposition of a form, of a general code of rational
abstraction, in which capitalist rationalization of material production is only a particular case" (129).

Because the counter-system to capitalism envisioned by Marx "is
structurally incapable of liberating human potentials except as productive forces, that is, according to an operational finality that leaves
no room for the reversion of the loss," it is also particularly vulnerable to the overarching logic of consumer ideology, which itself
measures all signs in terms of value (144). In other words, Marxism
values people only in terms of productivity, which, in line with the
demands of consumer ideology, does not allow for loss. One result of
this is that Marxism, like consumer ideology, forces people to measure self-worth in terms of value: the laborer is only valuable insofar as he or she is productive. Yet, Baudrillard argues, the notion of

"man's own power to give rise to value by his labor" is a fiction that gives rise to alienation:

> Everywhere man has learned to reflect on himself, to assume himself, to posit himself according to this scheme of production which is assigned to him as the ultimate dimension of value and meaning. At the level of all political economy there is something of what Lacan describes in the mirror stage: through this scheme of production, this mirror of production, the human species comes to consciousness...in the imaginary. Production, labor, value, everything through which an objective world emerges and through which man recognizes himself objectively—this is imaginary. Here man is embarked on a continual deciphering of himself through his works, finalized by his shadow...reflected by this operational mirror, this sort of ideal of a productivist ego. This process occurs not only in the materialized form of an economic obsession with efficiency determined by the system of exchange value, but more profoundly in this overdetermination by the code, by the mirror of political economy: in the identity that man dons with his own eyes when he can think of himself only as something to produce, to transform, to bring about as value. (19–20)

This "something to produce, to transform, to bring about as value" is a sign, and under the conditions Baudrillard outlines, the laborer ultimately, if not consciously, conceives of him or herself as a sign of value, as does the consumer.

In "Lee Harvey Oswald and the Postmodern Subject," Thomas Carmichael uses reasoning similar to Baudrillard's to explain Lee's sense of identity in *Libra*: emerging "only as an effect of the codes out which he is articulated," Lee "is haunted by doubling and the sense of his own subjectivity as an entity realized only in the field of the Other" (207, 210). Moreover, Carmichael argues, Lee's angst-ridden obsession with his own place in history demands that we read the Other against which he defines himself as an "already represented history which is in turn governed by the logic of exchange and indifference" (210). That the language Carmichael uses to describe the governing logic of this history bears some resemblance to that which Baudrillard uses to describe consumer culture is no coincidence; Carmichael goes on to note that while Lee can be read "as paradigmatic of the situation of postmodern subjectivity," his "seeming confirmation of the Lacanian subject takes place within a culture which itself is governed, as Baudrillard terms it, by 'the radical negation of the sign as value' through the arrival of the simulacrum as the 'death sentence of every reference'" (211). That is, Lee must be read as a sign within the artificial system Baudrillard describes. Yet where Carmichael reads Lee as a postmodern subject attempting to locate himself within "an intertextual network of endlessly dispersed and displaced writing," Lee's status as a sign problematizes the notion of subjectivity (211). If Lee is indeed a sign, how is he different from the other signs that surround him? In other words, how can Lee be a subject, even of the postmodern variety Carmichael describes? The answer, Baudrillard might argue in his later career, is that he cannot.

In "Fatal Strategies," Baudrillard argues that "the position of the subject has become simply untenable" (qtd. in Kellner 158). This argument, Douglas Kellner notes in *Jean Baudrillard: From Marxism to Postmodernism and Beyond*, reflects Baudrillard's career-spanning interest in the "growing power of the world of objects over the subject" but differs from his earlier theories in that it precludes the potential for the subversion of consumer ideology (159). Describing what he calls "the sovereign power of the object," Baudrillard claims that while philosophers have always celebrated the supremacy of the subject over the object, the object now reigns supreme (156). Where such philosophers as Descartes and Sartre "endowed the subject with all the splendid features of freedom, creativity, imagination, certitude, objectivity and knowledge" and conceptualized the object as "an inert thing in a causal order," Baudrillard calls the inert nature of the object into question (157). Rather than manipulating objects, Baudrillard argues, so-called subjects have been manipulated and seduced *by* objects throughout history (157). Discounting religious and philosophical perspectives that posit seduction as an "evil and worldly" phenomenon that causes "misguided souls" to miss out on "the reality behind the seductive veil of perceptual illusion,"

Baudrillard here interprets seduction "not primarily in the sense of enticing someone to have sexual relations, but as a ritual, a game with its own rules, charms, snares and lures" (143–144). Fundamentally artificial, seduction is the means by which objects charm and fascinate us. Thus, Baudrillard argues, "if we can understand seduction properly, then we can grasp the ubiquity and supremacy of objects in our lives" (157). Such an understanding, moreover, will allow the subject to recognize the untenable nature of its own position and take up that of the object instead, "learning its ruses, strategies and modes of seduction" in order to thrive within the system of objects (160). Fatal strategy, then, represents a departure from Baudrillard's attempts to formulate a viable means of subverting consumer ideology and posits instead a kind of cynical resignation: rather than trying to control objects as subjects might, our best course of action is to accept our place as objects and operate accordingly.

Even as Lee clings to the notion that he might have a hand in shaping history throughout *Libra*—that is, that he is a subject—he, perhaps unwittingly, begins his apprenticeship as an object early in the novel. While a young teen in the Bronx, Lee learns a basic lesson in the seductive language of objects when a television commercial tells him that the name of a particular product is "Natures spelled backwards": in order to entice consumers, products need memorable names and clever slogans (5). This lesson, Lee later realizes, applies not only to products but to historical figures as well: "Trotsky was not his real name. Lenin's name was not really Lenin. Stalin's name was Dzhugashvili" (34). Applying a strategy similar to that which allowed Stalin to adopt a *nom de guerre* meaning "man of steel," Lee begins to play games with his own name (40). Among the aliases he adopts while imagining himself in the role of a double agent during his stint as a Marine in Atsugi, Japan, is Hidell, which, Lee tells himself, "means don't tell" (89). This name, moreover, is accompanied by a somewhat-absurd slogan that attempts to mimic the mnemonic nature of the advertising Lee recalls from his childhood; in place of "Natures spelled backwards," Lee posits, "Take the double-*e* from Lee./ Hide the double-*l* in Hidell./ Hidell means hide the *L*./ Don't tell" (90). Still ruminating on the seductive power of names after defecting to the Soviet Union, Lee learns of the capture of US pilot Francis Gary Powers, whose own name, Lee realizes, is already being incorporated into the fabric of history:

> It occurred to Oswald that everyone called the prisoner by his full name. The Soviet press, local TV, the BBC, the Voice of America, the interrogators, etc. Once you did something notorious, they tagged you with an extra name, a middle name that was ordinarily never used. You were officially marked, a chapter in the imagination of the state. Francis Gary Powers. In just these few days the name had taken on a resonance, a sense of fateful event. It already sounded historic. (198)

Blinded by his own desire to become a historical figure himself, Lee fails to recognize that Powers is no more than a pawn of forces beyond his control and that becoming Lee Harvey Oswald will render Lee an object within the matrix of history rather than a subject with the power to shape that history.

Lee's assessment of Powers as a "hardworking, sincere, honest fellow [who] has found himself in a position where he is being crushed by the pressure exerted from opposite directions" might also be read as a self-evaluation (198). As noted, Lee's own disappointment in the Soviet lifestyle is matched only by his distaste for American consumer culture. According to DeLillo, Lee's life is largely "the antithesis of the life America promises its citizens: the life of consumer fulfillment" (DeCurtis 52). At the same time, however, DeLillo notes that Oswald's return to the United States from the Soviet Union with a wife who "was completely amazed by this world of American consumer promise" must have been a source of "enormous tension in his life" (52). Moreover, Marina's "desire to become more fully a part of this paradise she'd been hearing about all her life" could only exacerbate Lee's "ambivalent feelings about being a husband who provides for his family and at the same time being a leftist who finds an element of distaste in consumer fulfillment" (52). Although this ambivalence prevents Lee from exclusively embracing one (allegedly distinct) ideology over another, it also represents, according to Baudrillard's early writings, Lee's only means of escaping the system of objects. Crushed by the pressure "exerted from opposite directions" himself, Lee remains a zero in both Soviet and American circles. As a zero, however, he lacks value, and this lack of value is exactly what prevents Lee from being both a sign and an object. That is, as a zero, Lee lacks the social cachet needed to gain entry to the system of objects. Nonetheless, the system proves so enticing that Lee cannot resist its allure. His determination to become a driving force in history allows Lee to accept the illusion of value and to believe that he might begin to accumulate value himself (and, in turn, raise his own social standing) through the labor of political assassination.

While his increasing involvement in the plot to take Kennedy's life appears to rob Lee of what Baudrillard terms ambivalence in his earlier writings, it is also suggestive of the fatal strategy the theorist espouses in his later work. In his translation of "Fatal Strategies," Poster notes that Baudrillard's use of the word "fatal" not only implies doom or destruction but also (and more importantly) a sense of fate and predestination (206). Humanity's fate is not to conquer objects, Baudrillard argues, but to follow their lead and engage in the "obscenity which…has become their immanent purpose and insane justification" (184). Given the "infinite proliferation" of objects in our world, humanity's best course of action is not to "distinguish the true from the false" but to "seek what is more false than false: illusion and appearance" (184). "[C]ompletely absorbed by models," humanity has moved to a state of ecstasy, "that quality specific to each body that spirals in on itself until it has lost all meaning, and thus radiates as pure and empty form" (187).

Citing television as an example of empty form, Baudrillard notes that simulation amounts to "the ecstasy of the real":

> To prove this, all you need to do is watch television, where real events follow one another in a perfectly ecstatic relation, that is to say through vertiginous and stereotyped traits, unreal and recurrent, which allow for continuous and uninterrupted

juxtapositions. Ecstatic: such is the object of advertising, and
such is the consumer in the eyes of advertising. (187)

Watching television shortly before the assassination, Lee himself
enters a state much like the one Baudrillard describes. While viewing a pair of movies that focus on political assassination, Lee senses
that he is "connected to the events on the screen" and begins to feel as
if he is "in the middle of his own movie" (DeLillo, *Libra* 370). Completely absorbed by these movies, Lee also succumbs to the promise
of consumer fulfillment as "loud late-night commercials coming one
after another" convince him to "start saving right away for a wash-
ing machine and car" (370, 371). That Lee views such commodities
as "the standard ways to stop being lonely" suggests that he has
bought into the ecstatic message of television hook, line, and sinker
(371). A character in his own movie, Lee can believe in the promises
of advertising because neither he nor the products advertised exist in
reality. That is, television has stripped both Lee and those products
of reality. As a result, Lee's only recourse is to become the "star" of
his own movie by assassinating Kennedy.

In his volume on DeLillo, Douglas Keesey notes that the Kennedy
assassination can be read as the ultimate act of consumption, a notion
underlined by the fact that Lee sees himself moving toward the event
like a "shopping cart rolling slowly out of an alley" (165). Moreover,
Keesey argues, *Libra* continually "reminds us that Oswald killed
Kennedy for the publicity and was in turn killed by another publicity-
seeker...and suggests that the endless media simulations and inves-
tigatory reconstructions of the assassination...serve mainly to repeat
the assassin's act, making him famous and implicating everyone
in violence and death" (175). Yet for Lee, the stakes involved in
assassinating Kennedy are much higher than gaining mere publicity.
As DeLillo explained in a 1993 interview with Adam Begley, Lee's
story is "the story of a disaffected young man who suspects there are
sacred emanations flowing from the media heavens and who feels
the only way to enter this heavenly vortex is through some act of
violent theater" (Begley 303).

While Lee does indeed want to be remembered as a historical figure (as evidenced by his keeping of a "historic diary"), Lee also aims to prove his own existence. That is, if the world in which he lives truly is, as Baudrillard argues, an ecstatic simulation, then he must produce himself as a sign (that amounts to more than a zero in the system) in order to become "real." Since his financial situation bars Lee from gaining social ascendancy through the "traditional" channels of consumption, he must find alternate means of doing so. What matters, he realizes after being arrested for disturbing the peace, are not necessarily his actions but "documenting the experiences" (327). Hence his incessant interest in creating a paper trail; by leaving such textual footprints as the historic diary, a criminal record, and the now infamous photograph of "Lee Harvey Oswald" brandishing a rifle, Lee attempts to leave evidence of having passed through the system. Despite his best efforts at documenting his own existence, however, Lee fails to materialize in any substantial way insofar as even the degree of his involvement in the assassination remains questionable at best.

DeLillo's portrayal of the assassination places Lee at the scene of the crime and has him firing two non-lethal shots at Kennedy. The third and fatal shot, however, is fired by one of his coconspirators an instant before Lee fires his last shot. Or is it? Although we are told that Lee allegedly "knew he missed with the third shot," Lee only comes to this conclusion as he begins to formulate an alibi: "He was already telling someone about this...Pointing out the contradictions. Telling how he was tricked into the plot. What is it called, a patsy?" (400–401). Moreover, his coconspirator never takes credit for hitting his mark. We are simply told that he "got off the shot" and fled the scene (402). Of course, whether or not Lee fired the fatal shot is ultimately irrelevant to the "movie" in which Lee envisions himself. Despite his efforts at crafting an alibi, Lee continues to behave like the assassins he has seen on television. He hides his rifle not because he expects to elude capture but because doing so is "the expected thing" (404). "What do I look like?" he asks himself repeatedly as he leaves the scene; "Do I look like someone leaving the scene?" (406).

Shortly thereafter, Lee draws attention to himself by "taking evasive tactics" at the sight of a police cruiser (409). When a police officer asks him to produce identification, Lee jumps to the conclusion that he has been apprehended in connection with the assassination and initiates a Hollywood-style shoot-em-up in which he kills the officer. From there, Lee retreats to a movie theater where another of his coconspirators plans to shoot him during the "noise and cries" of the action onscreen because "that's the way they do it in the movies" (412). Lee, however, is arrested before anyone can shoot him, and in the ensuing media frenzy comes to realize that he is no longer simply Lee Oswald, a zero in the system, but Lee Harvey Oswald, the historic figure he once dreamed of becoming.

In "*Libra* as Postmodern Critique," Frank Lentricchia notes that "on the weekend of 22 November 1963, Lee Oswald...thanks to the fathering power of the media becomes rebaptized, forever now 'Lee Harvey Oswald,' a triple-named echo of another media child, 'John Fitzgerald Kennedy'" (Lentricchia 197). Moreover, as the assassination's "major plotters virtually disappear" from the narrative, the reader must confront the mystery of Lee's identity (203). Because *Libra* is "more about Oswald than about conspiracy," Lentricchia argues, "we learn that the question is not what happened in Dallas on 22 November 1963...The question is not even who is this Oswald? It is, who is *Lee Harvey Oswald?*" (203, Lentricchia's emphasis). One factor that makes this question particularly difficult to answer is that even Lee himself regards Lee Harvey Oswald as a stranger:

> Lee Harvey Oswald. It sounded extremely strange. He didn't recognize himself in the full intonation of the name. The only time he used his middle name was to write it on a form that had a space for that purpose. No one called him by that name. Now it was everywhere. He heard it coming from the walls. Reporters called it out. Lee Harvey Oswald, Lee Harvey Oswald. It sounded odd and dumb and made up. They were talking about somebody else. (416)

For Osteen, Lee's sense of estrangement from his media alter ego signals "that he is again a zero in the system: he is the plot's scapegoat, a cipher who makes the entire system possible" (Osteen 162). In other words, Lee is completely overshadowed by "Lee Harvey Oswald." Like Jack Gladney in *White Noise*, Lee is "the false character that follows the name around" (DeLillo, *White Noise* 17). Ultimately, then, Lee Harvey Oswald does not exist. Or, more accurately, "Lee Harvey Oswald" is a signifier with no referent, or at best a signifier whose referent is a zero in the system. As a result, "Lee Harvey Oswald" can only draw attention to the void behind the name and underscore the impossibility of answering Lentricchia's question. Nonetheless, answering the unanswerable is exactly what retired CIA analyst Nicholas Branch tries to do throughout the novel.

Commissioned to write a secret history of the assassination, Branch finds himself inundated with information. Yet despite his access to seemingly limitless data, including the FBI's 125,000 page file on the assassination and the Warren Report ("with its twenty-six accompanying volumes of testimony and exhibits, its millions of words"), Branch "hasn't written all that much" (DeLillo, *Libra* 181, 59). As he continues to accumulate data, the problem Branch faces is not a lack of information but the absolute profusion of it. "Everything is here," we are told: "Baptismal records, report cards, postcards, divorce petitions, canceled checks, daily timesheets, tax returns, property lists, postoperative x-rays, photos of knotted string, thousands of pages of testimony" (181). Indeed, the Warren Report alone contains so much minutia that Branch comes to think of it as "the megaton novel James Joyce would have written if he'd moved to Iowa City and lived to be a hundred" (181). According to DeLillo, this description is particularly apt insofar as the report serves not only as a "masterwork of trivia" regarding the assassination but also because it includes "the testimony of dozens and dozens of people who talk not only about their connection to the assassination itself but about their jobs, their marriages, their children" (DeCurtis 54). Nonetheless, the Warren Report does little to shed light on what Branch describes as "the seven seconds that broke the back of the American century" or on the question Lentricchia poses: who is Lee Harvey Oswald (DeLillo, *Libra* 181)?

Branch's failure to make sense of the Kennedy assassination is indicative of what Baudrillard refers to as the "fantastic burden" of postmodernity ("Fatal Strategies" 189). In "Fatal Strategies," Baudrillard argues that the "hysteria of causality...which corresponds to the simultaneous effacement of origins" results in an "obsessive search for origins, for responsibility, for reference" (189). Because all origins have been effaced, however, all references refer only to each other, and, as with Branch's quest, what develops is an interpretive system lacking "any relation to its objective" (189). To explain this effacement of origins, Baudrillard proffers a report prepared by the Exxon corporation to explain its activities throughout the world. When the US Government requested this report, Exxon responded with "twelve 1,000 page volumes, whose reading alone, not to mention the analysis, would exceed a few years of work" (190). Far shorter than the FBI's 125,000 page file on the Kennedy assassination or the twenty-six volumes accompanying the Warren Report, the Exxon report contains no information precisely because the sheer mass of documentation eclipses any point of reference beyond that specific text. As with Lee, whose carefully laid and frequently self-contradictory paper trail causes no end of consternation for Branch, the voluminous Exxon report overshadows any event the US Government might wish to investigate. For Baudrillard, this virtual disappearance of otherwise "real" events under seemingly endless reams of documentation renders such events perfectly suited to the postmodern realm of consumer culture. "Perfect is the event or the language that assumes, and is able to stage, its own mode of disappearance," the theorist writes, for in so doing, such events acquire "the maximal energy of appearances" (192). In other words, events that lose all substance the moment they occur are particularly adaptable to the marketplace of images insofar as they become signs without referents, and are therefore unfettered by any connection to the real.

Given Branch's conundrum—an overabundance of documentation yielding an absolute paucity of information—the Kennedy assassination can be read as a template for the kind of "perfect" event

Baudrillard describes; the "magic bullet" theory alone speaks volumes for the incantatory nature of the Warren Commission's findings. Similarly, "Lee Harvey Oswald" emerges from *Libra* as a mere ghost, the aftereffect of Lee's efforts to become a part of history. The irony, of course, is that this ghost—this object, this sign with no discernable referent—derives almost entirely from Lee's desire to confront consumer ideology as a historical subject. Because he cannot gain ascendancy in the order of objects, Lee plots to destroy that order. Steeped in a culture of television and advertising, however, Lee can only conceive of himself as a commodity. As such, he can do no more than mount a massive ad campaign for his own estrangement and discontent, the denouement of which is the assassination of Kennedy. Rather than subverting the system of signs that renders him a zero, Lee strengthens that system by giving birth to the "perfect" postmodern media figure, "Lee Harvey Oswald." "Lee Harvey Oswald," however, has no basis in reality. "Lee Harvey Oswald" is a construct. And ultimately, "Lee Harvey Oswald" is a sign—not only of Lee Oswald's desperation, but of what Baudrillard describes in *The Consumer Society* as "the tangled void of human relations" in the shadow of consumption (196).

In *The Subject as Action*, Alan Singer argues that the novel's historical importance is that it has an affinity for "the conceptual tasks of ideology critique" and that this affinity gives the novel the potential to free "historical subjects from the stasis of self-deluded history" (74). For Baudrillard, on the other hand, consumer ideology has become so pervasive that the only delusion the historical subject might suffer is that she is, in fact, a subject. From this perspective, history has reached a point of stasis, and no amount of critique will alter ideology. Like Baudrillard, DeLillo recognizes the pervasive nature of consumer ideology so much so that *Libra* shares some of Baudrillard's pessimism regarding the position of the subject in consumer society. Seduced by the ethos of consumption, Lee unwittingly embraces what Baudrillard calls fatal strategy when he reinvents himself as "Lee Harvey Oswald," a name with no discernable person behind it, a sign with no referent, an object of history. Despite this apparent pessimism, however, DeLillo also shares Singer's optimism regarding the novel's affinity for breaking the stasis of history.

The novelist, DeLillo explains in his interview with DeCurtis, attempts to redeem the despair of the otherwise overwhelming confusion of postmodernity by bringing order to chaos (DeCurtis 56). In so doing, the novelist also offers a perspective from which the reader might better recognize and critique (rather than acquiesce to) the seductive nature of consumer ideology. In *Libra*, Branch personifies this perspective: while his investigation into the Kennedy assassination renders him increasingly silent throughout the novel, his silence underscores the inherent emptiness of consumer culture. As a historian, Branch can say nothing about Lee because all he has is information on "Lee Harvey Oswald." As a novelist, on the other hand, DeLillo can transcend Branch's silence by recognizing the distinction between Lee and his doppelganger. In so doing, he draws attention to the "tangled void of human relations" Baudrillard sees operating within consumer culture. Whether the ambivalence that results from such a perspective can indeed be revolutionary speaks to the question of whether the novelist in particular or the artist in general can serve as a stronger historical force than the terrorist or the assassin. As the following chapter demonstrates, DeLillo further explores this question in *Mao II.*

CHAPTER 6

ONE BEAT AWAY
FROM ELEVATOR MUSIC:
MAO II AND THE ARTIST
IN OPPOSITION

In a 1993 interview with Adam Begley, DeLillo noted that while the novel is neither dead nor even "seriously injured," literature is "too ready to be neutralized, to be incorporated into the ambient noise" of Western culture (Begley 290). Hence our need for what DeLillo refers to as "the writer in opposition, the novelist who writes against power, who writes against the corporation or the state or the whole apparatus of assimilation" (290). Literature, according to DeLillo, is "one beat away from becoming elevator music," but the writer who works "in the shadows of the novel's greatness and influence" serves as a bulwark against the apparatus of assimilation he sees working in Western culture (290). Although this prognosis for both the novel and the novelist might best be described as guardedly optimistic, it also speaks of the degree to which "the corporation or the state or the whole apparatus of assimilation" has encroached upon the novelist's domain and rendered it suitable for mass consumption (290). For DeLillo, then, the novelist continues to strive against seemingly insurmountable odds to produce what Bill Gray, the beleaguered protagonist of *Mao II*, refers to as a "spray of talent" rife with "[a]mbiguities, contradictions, whispers, hints" that cannot be assimilated by the powers that be (159). In so doing, the novelist helps to preserve humanity from being assimilated into the apparatus DeLillo describes.

In contrast to DeLillo, Baudrillard argues that all art is dead, and that every element of Western culture has already been absorbed by consumer ideology. In *Symbolic Exchange and Death*, Baudrillard traces the death of art to its elision with the "natural" world. Because the space in which we live is "no longer a space of production, but a reading strip, a coding and decoding strip, magnetized by signs," Baudrillard argues, a "kind of unintentional parody hovers over everything, a tactical simulation, a consummate aesthetic enjoyment…is attached to the indefinable play of reading and the rules of the game" (75). Art, then, is not only everywhere, it is everything. As a result, art is also dead, "since not only is its critical transcendence dead, but reality itself, entirely impregnated by an aesthetic that holds onto its own structurality, has become inseparable from its own image" (75). Moreover, Baudrillard argues, the elision of the artificial and the natural that is endemic to Western culture traces its roots to the invention of the *nouveau roman*, in which the novelist "effaces the contradiction of the real and imaginary" by constructing "a void around the real…in order to give it a pure objectivity" (72). That is, the self-contained world the novelist seeks to create via the written word is very much like the landscape of artifice and images Baudrillard sees as endemic to consumer culture in that both exemplify hyperreality, a state in which the parameters of "reality" are always determined by preexisting models. Baudrillard, then, sees the novelist and the artist as architects of the apparatus of assimilation DeLillo seeks to resist.

Clearly, DeLillo and Baudrillard both see humanity as facing the same threat. What DeLillo terms the apparatus of assimilation is marked by the same quasi-mystical faith in the power of brand names and consumer goods to bring about personal fulfillment that is the hallmark of what Baudrillard terms the system of objects. Yet DeLillo's remarks with regard to the relationship between the novelist and consumer culture suggest a degree of optimism that Baudrillard lacks. For DeLillo, the apparatus has yet to fully assimilate humanity into the system, and the artist has the potential to prevent that apparatus from ever doing so. For Baudrillard, on the other hand, the system has already assimilated all of humanity and rendered us objects. From this perspective, everything within the system can only play by the rules of the system, so even the artist can only produce that which repeats the logic of the system. Consequently, revolution from within the system is impossible, and the only hope for bringing about the collapse of the system must come from beyond Western culture in the form of terrorism. As with art, however, DeLillo differs with Baudrillard regarding the effectiveness of terrorism. Where Baudrillard sees terrorism as having the potential to topple the machinery of consumer ideology, DeLillo sees the terrorist as ultimately reproducing the fascism of the very system he or she wishes to destroy. Which is not to say that DeLillo is entirely blind to the lure of terror. Indeed, much of *Mao II* reads as a debate between proponents of art and proponents of what might be considered traditional acts of terror on the revolutionary merits of each medium.

In *Mao II*, DeLillo depicts the emergence of a reclusive author named Bill Gray into a world in which the novel's power to "influence mass consciousness" has largely been usurped by the act of terror (157). An author whose popularity stems in part from his own refusal to appear in public as he perfects his long-awaited third novel, Bill begins to leave his self-imposed exile when he allows a photographer named Brita Nilsson to include him in her "species count" of living novelists (26). As a direct result of his contact with Brita, Bill finds himself roped into an ill-conceived plot to free a Swiss poet who has been taken hostage by terrorists in Beirut, Lebanon. Agreeing to attend a conference in which the famous novelist is to read the works of the unknown poet, Bill travels to London where his attempts to "create a happy sensation" for the sake of freeing his Swiss counterpart are dogged by acts of political violence (99). Not long after a bomb blast forces the cancellation of the peace conference, Bill's burgeoning relationship with a terrorist sympathizer named George Haddad leads him to Lebanon, where he is struck by a car and eventually dies in complete anonymity, leaving his erstwhile handlers, Scott Martineau and Karen Janney, to maintain his estate and his literary legacy in near perpetuity. While Bill's efforts to free the Swiss poet prove ultimately as fruitless as his debates with Haddad over the relative merits of authorship over terrorism, Brita emerges in the novel's epilogue as the character with the greatest potential to reshape the world. No longer satisfied with photographing authors, Brita now documents "barely watched wars" and "children running in dust" (229). Turning a critical lens toward Abu Rashid, the terrorist responsible for kidnapping the Swiss poet, Brita reveals that the "new future" he wishes to bring about through terrorism operates on the same principles of branding and market saturation that drive consumerism, and also that Rashid's desire to "[m]ake all men one man" can only end in the same failure Bill experienced in his abortive attempts to write the perfect novel (235).

Analysis of *Mao II* has, appropriately, focused on the tension between art and terror that is inherent to the novel. In his volume on DeLillo, Douglas Keesey argues that *Mao II* "expresses the author's mid-career doubts about the effectiveness of fiction in a world largely given over to the electronic media" (177). Other critics, however, have been quick to note that Keesey's reading assumes that DeLillo shares Gray's anxiety over the diminishing power of the novelist in relation to the terrorist. As Ryan Simmons observes in "What Is a Terrorist? Contemporary Authorship, the Unabomber, and DeLillo's *Mao II*," DeLillo and Gray are not of the same mind on this issue, for where Gray views terrorism and authorship as separate phenomena, DeLillo muddles the distinction between these terms throughout the novel (677). Other characters in *Mao II* frequently compare Gray to a terrorist, and Gray's own definition of authorship includes principles similar to those he despises in terrorism: though a champion of the individual voice, Gray, in his capacity as an author, wishes to exert control over the mass mind in much the same way such historical and fictional figures as Mao Zedong, Sun Myung Moon, and the terrorist Abu Rashid do or strive to do throughout the novel (687). For Simmons, Gray's inconsistent position on the relationship between authorship and terrorism also applies to the fictional author's concerns about the commercialization of his work. While Gray defines the author as "influential but never commercial," Simmons argues that such a position is "inconsistent" and deconstructs itself: one cannot be influential in a consumer society without first submitting to the conditions of the market (688).

Building on Simmons' argument, Mark Osteen notes in *American Magic and Dread: Don DeLillo's Dialogue with Culture* that Gray "has been usurped by his brand name which, with its neutrally colored surname and common first name, inscribes his position as a commodity or medium of exchange: he is just a 'bill,' a universal equivalent, a blank counter upon which others can write and from whom others profit" (197). Nonetheless, Osteen argues that Gray's fate does not mean that all authors are "inevitably and irredeemably coopted by commerce" (210). Rather, the author has the ability to challenge the order of consumption from within cultural parameters; for Osteen, the issue DeLillo addresses in *Mao II* is not, as Margaret Scanlan suggests in "Writers Among Terrorists: Don DeLillo's *Mao II* and the Rushdie Affair," whether a novel is complicit with the culture it criticizes, "but rather what one does with this condition" (210). Citing DeLillo himself as a paradigm of the author who challenges the dominant culture from within, Osteen suggests that *Mao II* demonstrates "how novels may push out toward the social order, not to become part of the crowd, but to engage the crowd in remaking that order" (213). Along similar lines, Frank Lentricchia and Jody McAuliffe argue in *Crimes of Art and Terror* that while Bill's rhetoric suggests a set of "false and destructive" binary alternatives—"either selfhood cut off in pain or the prison house of replication"—the Swiss hostage, starved for the commonplace and banal experiences of his former life, underscores a desire for "the kind of collective that nourishes and sustains self within an embracing framework of cooperation and mutuality" (35). Thus while the "transgressive desire beneath many romantic and modernist literary visions" may be, as Lentricchia and McAuliffe note, "for a terrifying awakening that would undo the West's economic and cultural order," DeLillo's vision in *Mao II* emerges as one of moderation (39). Rather than striving to undo the West's cultural order (and, conceivably, replace it with his or her own fascist vision), the author must, as Brita does in the novel's epilogue, examine that order from within and seek a balance between the individual and the mass consciousness.

For Baudrillard, however, there can be no half-measures or moderation in responding to consumer ideology. Only "total revolution, theoretical and practical," he argues in *For a Critique of the Political Economy of the Sign*, can "restore the symbolic in the demise of the sign and of value" (163). This argument stems from Baudrillard's belief that everything within the system he envisions has been reduced to a sign of value. Under these conditions, the potential for meaningful communication has been reduced to zero insofar as all of our efforts are focused on accumulating and displaying signs of affluence. In order to restore humanity's potential for meaningful communication, Baudrillard calls for a mode of exchange that operates independently from the arbitrary code of value that regulates consumer culture. This mode of exchange, which Baudrillard calls "symbolic exchange," hinges on the concept of ambivalence. According to Baudrillard,

> Ambivalence is not the dialectical negation of value: it is the incessant potentiality of its annulment, of the *destruction of the illusion of value*. It is not with an opposing code that the ambivalent and symbolic confront the discourse of value. Against value's positive transcendence, the symbolic opposes its radicality. Against the logic of sublimation and generality (of abstraction) are opposed the radicality of the nonfulfillment of desire and symbolic exchange. (209, Baudrillard's emphasis)

From a theoretical perspective, Baudrillard argues, the cultivation of ambivalence will draw attention to the fact that the object of consumerism "is nothing, and that behind it stands the tangled void of human relations, the negative imprint of the immense mobilization of productive and social forces which have become reified in it" (Baudrillard, *Consumer Society* 196). On a practical level, however, Baudrillard is generally at a loss to explain how to cultivate ambivalence from within consumer culture: if everything within that culture is bound up in duplicating the logic of the system, then how can anything generated within the system question that logic?

As A. Keith Goshorn explains in "Jean Baudrillard's Radical Enigma: 'The Object's Fulfillment Without Regard for the Subject,'" the challenge for Baudrillard's thesis, "if it is to have any use beyond fascinating critical description" is "how to envision a change in the affective dimension of what is left of the 'subject'" within the system Baudrillard describes (214). In other words, how can anyone incite social change in a culture where, again quoting Goshorn, "[s]ocial processes have subtly eroded or vacated previous senses of subjective agency" (219)? Independent of Baudrillard, this is also the question DeLillo approaches in the prologue to *Mao II*, in which Karen, the younger of Bill's assistants, participates in a mass-wedding at Yankee Stadium under the guidance of the Reverend Sun Myung Moon. Watching from the stands, Karen's father cannot help but feel "uneasy" at the sight of his daughter becoming part of the "undifferentiated mass" of Moon's followers below (3). Where he once saw Karen as "possessed of a selfness, a teeming soul, nuance and shadow, grids of pinpoint singularities," the father now sees her as being integrated into a single "sculptured object...a toy with thirteen thousand parts," unburdened of "free will and independent thought" (7).

To a large extent, her father's observation is well founded insofar as Karen has spent the preceding weeks and months packed into a van with "fifteen, sixteen sisters...singing you are my sunshine, row row row, chanting their monetary goal" (12–13). At the same time, however, a narrative shift to Karen's perspective reveals that her father has also been absorbed into a separate but equally oppressive undifferentiated mass. Consciously "immunized against the language of self," Karen sees her father as a slave to the illusory "old college logic" that allows the denizens of consumer culture to believe that they are any different from the followers of Moon with regard to their own freedom of thought and action (8). From this perspective, Karen's father is part of a fallen, irrational world in which people "sit at desks and stare at office walls," "smell their shirts and drop them in the hamper" and "bind themselves into numbered seats and fly across time zones...knowing there is something they've forgotten to do" (8, 16). While this characterization of the world is certainly in line with that of Baudrillard, it is a characterization whose accuracy DeLillo interrogates throughout *Mao II.*

The cultural landscape of *Mao II* closely resembles that of DeLillo's sardonic paean to consumerism, *White Noise.* Where the characters in *White Noise* spend much of their time navigating the aisles of supermarkets and are prone to chanting the names of consumer products in their sleep, the main action of *Mao II* begins with Scott, the older of Bill's assistants, walking the aisles of a bookstore and later viewing "signs for Mita, Midori, Kirin, Magno, Suntory," words he interprets as "part of some synthetic mass language, the esperanto of jet lag" (23). Against this backdrop, Scott visits an Andy Warhol exhibit where he admires "repeated news images of car crashes and movie stars" and a "room filled with images of Chairman Mao" for being "unwitting of history" (20, 21). As Baudrillard argues in "Transpolitics, Transsexuality, Transaesthetics," however, such art as Scott enjoys (or "anti-art" as he calls it, citing Warhol as a prime example) amounts to nothing more than "an infinite proliferation of signs, an infinite recycling of forms past and present" in which the notion of value has become "inflamed in the absence of all value judgment" (Baudrillard, "Transpolitics" 10, 15).

Quoting Warhol via Baudrillard, "all artworks are beautiful" (19), or, to borrow a popular phrase, "It's all good!" Under such conditions, however, there can be no criteria for critiquing art, nor can art critique the society from which it emerges. Moreover, as Baudrillard argues in "Revolution and the End of Utopia," because traditional art has "disappeared for the benefit of a pure circulation of images," what remains "does not produce a critical point of view. It only produces a sort of positivity, an imminent operationality which is self-justified and self-fulfilling" (238, 240). Thus as Bill begins to rebel against Scott, who wishes the author's third novel to go unpublished and remain, in its own way, "unwitting of history," he also moves toward challenging Baudrillard's position on art's potential to interrogate the society from which it emerges. Unlike Jack Gladney, whose position as a professor of Hitler Studies renders him a sometimes unwitting, sometimes helpless, and ultimately complicit (albeit inquisitive) pawn of consumer culture in *White Noise*, Bill's role as a highly commodified author brings to a head the issue of whether he has either the potential to break free from the grip of consumerism or the capacity to reshape his culture from within.

As Brita begins to photograph him, her warning that once his picture is published, Bill will be expected to look just like it, closely resembles Baudrillard's description of the third order of simulacra, a state in which "simulation models come to constitute the world" (Kellner 79). Drawing heavily on Walter Benjamin, Baudrillard argues in *Symbolic Exchange and Death* that technology allowing for the serial repetition of objects and images has resulted in a world in which nature has been entirely overwritten by artifice (55–56). Advances in serial reproduction have caused the world in which we live to consist neither of what we might regard as nature (or the "real" world) nor of models based on nature (or some preexisting reality), but of models based on models (57).

Existing in a state of what Baudrillard terms "operational simulation," we are now forced to live at the pace of objects and must, as Brita suggests to Bill, adapt to their rules in order to survive. For Bill, however, this state of affairs is far less than inspiring. Overshadowed by his own photograph, the author laments that he "used to think it was possible for a novelist to alter the inner life of the culture" but now realizes that everything within that culture "tends to channel our lives toward some final reality in print or film" (DeLillo, *Mao II* 41, 43). "There's the life and there's the consumer event," Bill explains; "Nothing happens until it is consumed. Or put it this way. Nature has given way to aura...All the material in every life is channeled into the glow" (43, 44). While Bill's talk of "aura" here is certainly reminiscent of Benjamin's provisionally optimistic vision of a world in which mechanical reproduction brings about a democratization of art by stripping away its aura or uniqueness (i.e., that which makes the work special or holy), it also reveals what Benjamin failed to consider: that, to paraphrase the third law of thermodynamics, aura can neither be created nor destroyed; it can only be displaced. As Bill formulates the problem, then, aura has not only been leeched away from individual works of art but from individuals as well, and has in turn been reabsorbed by the system, rendering it the only object worthy of attention. From this perspective, "the glow" of consumption has become its own greatest spectacle.

Despite his wariness toward the glow of consumer culture, however, Bill remains largely naive with regard to the more subtle rules of the media game. Early in the photo session, Brita notes that he has failed to give any thought to the image he wants to project for her camera, and as the shoot progresses, she must constantly remind Bill to raise his chin in order to present his best possible self. Withdrawn from society and unphotographed for years, Bill finds himself unable to channel his "private language" of "self-exaggeration" into a public image capable of eclipsing the legends that have sprung up in response to his self-imposed exile (37). As Scott recognizes, the ultimate effect of Brita's photos and the publication of Bill's third novel can only damage Bill's reputation. "Bill is at the height of his fame," Scott explains, "[b]ecause he hasn't published in years and years and years...It's the years that made him big. Bill gained celebrity by doing nothing...We could make a king's whatever with the new book. But it would be the end of Bill as a myth, a force. Bill gets bigger as his distance from the scene deepens" (52).

Yet where Scott understands how to use Bill's absence from the literary scene to his commercial advantage, Brita points out that Bill has more at stake than maintaining his status as a legend. The purpose of publication, she argues, is not necessarily to "make a king's whatever," but simply to "show people what you've done" (52). Willing to allow for the possibility that "the life" might resist giving

way to "the media event," Brita believes that publication "is exactly
what [Bill] needs" to shake his suspicion that the "secret force that
drives the industry is the compulsion to make writers harmless" (47).
Under Scott's influence, however, Bill cannot conceive of a world in
which he is anything more than a commodity who, along with his
fellow writers, has long since surrendered his power to shape society
to "bomb makers and gunmen" (41).

What Scott seems to grasp almost intuitively and Bill fails to
appreciate is fatal strategy, a mode of survival Baudrillard describes
whereby what was once considered the subject concedes the supremacy of the object and adopts its strategies in order to thrive within
the system of objects. That is, Scott realizes that Bill's long-standing
disappearance from the public eye ultimately amounts to a glori-
fied publicity stunt that has rendered the author a much sought-after
commodity. As a commodity, however, Bill is powerless to shape his
world, and Scott's world-weary acceptance of this fact speaks to the
cynicism of his position. Similarly, Baudrillard himself admits that
fatal strategy is, at heart, cynical:

> This will to spectacle and illusion, in contrast to every will to
> knowledge and power, is another form of fundamental cyni-
> cism. It is alive in the hearts of people, but haunts just as well
> the processes of events. In the raw event, in objective informa-
> tion, in the most secret thoughts and acts, there is something
> like a drive to revert to the spectacle, or to climax on stage
> instead of producing oneself originally. (Baudrillard, "Fatal
> Strategies" 201)

Hence the power Bill attributes to terrorism: where the novel may be
read as an attempt at producing oneself originally, the act of terror
gives itself much more freely to climax on stage. "What terrorists
gain, novelists lose," Bill explains later in the novel as he debates
the issue with Haddad; "The danger they represent equals our own
failure to be dangerous" (DeLillo, *Mao II* 157). Yet when Haddad
presses the issue by suggesting that Bill sees terrorists as "the only
possible heroes for our time," Bill flatly denies the allegation. The

"terrorist as solitary outlaw" is a myth, he argues, since most terror groups are "backed by repressive governments...perfect little totalitarian states" that "carry the old wild-eyed vision, total destruction and total order" (158). For Bill, then, the ascendancy of terrorism over authorship represents a double lament: not only has terrorism usurped the relevance of the novel, but it has also done so at the expense of the independence, individuality, and subjectivity that his romantic vision of the novel represents.

Like Bill, needless to say, Baudrillard does not romanticize the terrorist as a solitary outlaw struggling to effect what Bill describes as a "democratic shout" of any kind (159). As William Stearns and William Chaloupka explain in *Jean Baudrillard: The Disappearance of Art and Politics*, "Baudrillard will never be understood politically if we insist on confirming him within the modern sepulcher of rational will formation and political action...The place of politics can no longer be occupied by subjects. Political objects now demand their rights" (4). Among such political objects, Baudrillard argues in *The Spirit of Terrorism*, are terrorists, whose response to Western globalization "goes far beyond hatred for the dominant world power among the disinherited and exploited," and reflects the West's own desire for self-destruction (6–7). "They" may have carried out the attack, Baudrillard notes, "but we *wished for* it" insofar as the impulse to "reject any system as it approaches perfection or omnipotence" comes naturally to humanity (5, 7, Baudrillard's emphasis). This is not, however, to say that the impulse Baudrillard describes represents an element of subjectivity or any kind of romantic heroism within humanity. Rather, the will to resist globalization is, ironically, a function of globalization itself, and the West, according to Baudrillard "has become suicidal and declared war on itself" (7). Thus there is nothing unique, self-directed, or heroic about the act of terror from Baudrillard's perspective; indeed, it might better be understood as a symptom, the concrete manifestation of the globe's resistance to globalization regardless of ideology (9, 12). Moreover, the West's suicidal appetite for terror is simultaneously both satisfied and stimulated by the media apparatus that drives consumerism; "the media are part of the event," Baudrillard argues; "they are part of the terror, and they work in both directions" (31). Despite being implicated in the media-driven machinery of the system, however, the act of terror is also distinct from other events in that it embodies ambivalence, the only force Baudrillard deems capable of tearing that system asunder.

Terrorism, Baudrillard argues, "is the act that restores an irreducible singularity to the heart of a system of generalized exchange" (9). In other words, the act of terror introduces an element that cannot be reduced to a sign of value to a system that can only deal in signs of value. For Baudrillard, this element is the terrorist's own death, which amounts to "an absolute weapon against a system that operates on the basis of the exclusion of death" (16). Hence the impact of the terror attacks of September 2001, which Baudrillard describes in *The Spirit of Terrorism* as "the absolute event, the 'mother' of all events, the pure event uniting within itself all the events that had never taken place" (4). Where the system allows only for a kind of pseudodeath, or a death that signifies nothing more than the system's own control over death, the "real" death of the terrorist via suicide (i.e., death on the terrorist's own terms) is an event the system cannot integrate or reduce to a sign of value. Such death, Baudrillard argues, represents "an excess of reality," a "gift" to which the system "cannot respond except by its own death" (18, 17). Such is also the strategy in the case of hostage taking, in which the hostage serves as the alter ego of the terrorist (Baudrillard, *Symbolic Exchange* 37). As with the suicide strike, what is at stake in the hostage situation is "death without any possibility of negotiation" (37). While the system can "easily compute every death, even war atrocities," it is incapable of computing the "death-challenge" issued by terrorists because the kind of death the terrorists offer (again, "real" death, or death beyond the control of the system) "has no calculable equivalent" (37). Because "[n]othing corresponds with death," the system itself is "driven to suicide in return" (37). From this perspective, the terrorist agenda is not to demand political action from within the system, but to strike a lethal blow to the system itself by revealing the concept of value that undergirds it as entirely illusory.

Where Baudrillard imputes an exceptional degree of theoretical wherewithal to the terrorist, *Mao II*'s Haddad rephrases the theorist's argument in more pedestrian terms. Western culture "hasn't yet figured out how to assimilate" the terrorist, he explains; "It's confusing when they kill the innocent. But this is precisely the language of being noticed, the only language the West understands. The way they determine how we see them. The way they dominate the rush of endless streaming images" (157–158). Yet the sadistic torture privately endured by the Swiss poet throughout the novel belies the fact that his captors are not playing by the "rules" Baudrillard and Haddad describe. Beating the hostage with iron rods, depriving him of sleep, and attempting to remove his teeth go far beyond simply killing him to confuse the enemy. Moreover, Bill argues, such disregard for human life can only result in fascism:

> The question you have to ask is, How many dead? How many dead during the Cultural Revolution? How many dead after the Great Leap Forward? And how well did he hide his dead? This is the other question...
>
> The point of every closed state is now you know how to hide your dead. This is the setup. You predict many dead if your vision of the truth isn't realized. Then you kill them. Then you hide the fact of the killing and the bodies themselves. This is why the closed state was invented. And it begins with a single hostage, doesn't it? The hostage is the miniaturized form. The first tentative rehearsal for mass terror. (163)

As Bill's commentary suggests, even if Western culture is totalitarian in nature, replacing it with another totalitarian system will amount to neither a cultural revolution nor a great leap forward. Moreover, terrorism's increasing proficiency in what Haddad calls "the language of being noticed" is a double-edged sword. While spectacular acts of terror certainly have the capacity to "dominate the rush of endless streaming images," entering into that rush of images can also diminish the effectiveness of such acts (158). As J. Kinnear notes in DeLillo's *Players*, media coverage has reduced the act of terror to "another media event" akin to a publicity stunt (180). A similar sentiment appears in *Mao II* as Bill dubiously explains the reasoning behind his publisher's plan to free the Swiss poet from captivity: "Your group gets press, our group gets press, the young man is sprung from his basement room, the journalists get a story, so what's the harm" (98). The harm, of course, is that by providing fodder for the media, the act of terror ultimately reinforces the system it aims to destroy because such publicity stunts as the publisher has in mind can only contribute to the endless stream of media images that have rendered Bill's profession irrelevant.

Despite the apparent despondency Bill displays with regard to his profession, he continues to champion the novel as a viable alternative to the act of terror—if not for effecting the kind of total revolution for which Baudrillard demands, then at least as a means of resisting complete assimilation into the system. For Gray, the novel represents a "democratic shout" (159). In Bill's words, "almost any amateur off the street" can write "one great novel" and, in so doing, produce "[o]ne thing unlike another, one voice unlike the next" (159). Such potential for uniqueness stands in contrast to the totalitarian vision Haddad espouses, in which, according to Bill, the voice of the individual would be destroyed. From Baudrillard's perspective, of course, Bill's position is markedly naive; consumer culture allows for no true freedom of expression or individuality, the theorist argues, and within that culture every form of language can only repeat the logic of the system.

Whereas the kind of "democratic shout" Bill sees as operating in the novel serves primarily as a means of what Osteen calls "finding authentic expression," all language under the conditions Baudrillard describes is invested in reflecting one's ongoing accumulation of prestige and, as such, serves, again to borrow Osteen's phrasing, as "a way to promote power" (208). Yet what might either be termed Bill's naiveté or his optimism suggests that, in his view at least, consumerism has not yet destroyed all potential for meaningful communication and has not yet rendered every utterance a commodity.

While the media landscape he inhabits certainly promotes style over substance (*á là* Andy Warhol), the world in which he lives is not yet the totalitarian and linguistically impoverished state Baudrillard envisions. Which is not to say that language and the author are not in danger. As DeLillo's assertion that literature is one beat away from elevator music suggests, the state Baudrillard envisions is not far off, and the artist serves as one of very few lines of defense against the total elimination of the potential for a "democratic shout."

The totalitarianism that threatens the "democratic shout" throughout *Mao II* takes many forms. Moon's brand of spiritual fulfillment comes at the expense of "free will and independent thought" (7). Maoist China's social order hinges on "a cruelty and unyieldingness that's fully formed" (158). As with the projects of Moon and Mao, Rashid's terrorist organization is attempting to create a new world order in which all men act as one (235). Perhaps more subtle than the totalitarianism of its Eastern counterparts, the West's totalitarianism is no less insidious. Rather than moving toward a world in which all men act as one man, consumerism eliminates free will and independent thought by rendering interchangeable commodities of its adherents—as evidenced, for example, by Bill's appearance in Brita's catalogue of authors. In each of these regimes, value stems from a code that is entirely arbitrary; to be "good" is to march in lockstep with the system because it is assumed that the system itself is inherently good. While proffering codes and maintaining values is certainly a function of any culture, the danger Baudrillard sees in the media-saturated realm of consumerism is that "the system" represents a single, unbending code with no basis in reality. That is, the system amounts to a massive third-order simulacrum, which maps out its own "reality" without regard to anything beyond the scope of its own logic of accumulation.

In the consumer age, Baudrillard argues, we have become "a society of generalized, totalitarian competition, which operates at all levels" (Baudrillard, *Consumer Society* 182). That is, we have entered into a game in which the most important rule is that we must continually strive for social ascension. Because the rules of this game demand constant gains in all fields, they forbid the recognition of loss and preclude meaningful communication insofar as the terms of any exchange are never negotiated between parties but are, instead, always a function of the rules of the game. Always deferring to these rules, moreover, the human subject ceases to exist as such and becomes instead an object devoid of any significant sense of agency. Allowing for loss, however, would disrupt the game and allow parties to negotiate the terms of exchange independent from the dictates of the system. Or, to reverse the equation, disrupting the game by revealing the system of value that undergirds it as illusory would allow for loss and restore the potential for real negotiation.

In *Mao II*, Bill's struggle for authentic self-expression parallels Baudrillard's call for a mode of exchange that might operate without regard (or perhaps with only limited regard) to consumer culture's demand for constant gains in all fields of social ascendancy. From Osteen's perspective, this struggle leads Bill to champion the novelist as "the moderator of an ongoing debate who incites rather than quells the proliferation of meanings" (208). Yet for Baudrillard, inciting the proliferation of meaning is not enough to disrupt the logic of value that undergirds consumer ideology. As Baudrillard argues in *Symbolic Exchange and Death*, inciting such proliferation can only add supplemental meaning to that of value, whereas truly ambivalent language would reveal the entire logic of value as illusory (216–217). Thus, the linguistic polyvalence Osteen sees operating in Bill's vision of the novelist cannot undermine what Baudrillard calls "the functional and terrorist organization of the control of meaning under the sign of the positivity of value" (Baudrillard, *For a Critique* 163).

Nonetheless, Osteen's observation that Bill desires to view words as "material objects" as opposed to Haddad's "weightless electronic signs" suggests that Bill's sympathies do lie with Baudrillard, who argues that recognizing the material reality of words would allow us to experience their loss and, consequently, amount to a means of effecting ambivalence. For example, in *Symbolic Exchange and Death*, Baudrillard describes a theoretical zone in which "words cannot be gratuitously multiplied or uttered" (Baudrillard, *Symbolic*

Exchange 203). Within this zone, words take on the status of objects insofar as their number is limited: each word must be both given and returned in order to stay in circulation (204). In this restricted economy of language, speaking the word results in its loss, and meaning derives from the exchange itself rather than what Baudrillard refers to in *For a Critique* as "a final relation of value" (212). Because words in this type of economy are not bound by the positive transcendence Baudrillard associates with value, they symbolize "real" relationships among those who speak them. That Bill appears to be striving toward such a mode of communication suggests that his discussions with Haddad have not yielded the ultimate definition of authorship he seeks to formulate but have brought him closer to it.

Nearing the end of his journey, Bill dies from an internal injury suffered earlier in the novel, and all identifying documents are stolen from his corpse. While Osteen notes that Bill's anonymous death "may be his only way out of captivity [insofar as] he is finally free from the tyranny of 'Bill Gray' and the rapacities of his interpreters," he is quick to note that Nilsson's photos have "turned Bill into Bill II, an icon subject of the exegeses of the apostles who own his texts, his photos, and even his name" (Osteen 209, 210). In other words, Bill remains a commodity despite his own death. Reading this death and the subsequent thievery of Bill's documentation in light of Baudrillard's comments in *Symbolic Exchange and Death*, however, suggests otherwise: "Death demands to be experienced immediately, in total blindness and in total ambivalence. But is it revolutionary? If political economy is the most rigorous attempt to put an end to death, it is clear that only death can put an end to political economy" (187). Yet for death to yield ambivalence, it must also evoke a sense of loss that is incompatible with consumer culture. Thus, Baudrillard argues, modern funeral homes exist not only to ward off death but also "to ward off [the] sudden loss of signs that befalls the dead, to prevent there remaining, in the *asocial* flesh of the dead, something which signifies nothing" (181). Stripped of identifying documents, Bill's body foregoes the formalities of the modern funeral home and tangibly experiences the sudden loss of signs Baudrillard describes. As a result, his anonymous body signifies nothing. No longer "Bill Gray" the famous writer, the author's corpse stands only for itself, substituting the referent for the term and abolishing their separation. To borrow Baudrillard's terminology, Bill's anonymous death explodes the arbitrary nature of signification in a poetic act *par excellence*: putting the signifier "Bill Gray" to death by its own referent. Thus while photographs of Bill continue to circulate throughout the system of objects along with his "two lean novels," Bill himself escapes that system, however unwittingly.

While Bill's anonymous death allows him to escape the totalitarian system Baudrillard describes, it does little, if anything, to alter that system; even after the author disappears, Scott and Karen continue to go about the "great work" of maintaining the illusion that he is still alive and remains a viable commodity (DeLillo, *Mao II* 223). Likewise, local militias continue to wage what amount to violent advertising campaigns against each other in Beirut. Militants issue press credentials to reporters in order to gain free coverage in the press, and they fire gunshots at portraits of each other's leaders against a backdrop of ads for Coke II and vacations in Tahiti (227–230). Upon arriving on this scene, Bill's one-time photographer, Brita, immediately draws a connection between the ads for Coke and the Maoist terror group she has come to photograph:

> Now there are signs for a new soft drink, Coke II, signs slapped on cement block walls, and she gets the crazy idea that these advertising placards herald the presence of the Maoist group...The placards get bigger as the car moves deeply into cramped spaces...and the signs are clustered now, covering almost all the wall space...and Brita gets another crazy idea that these are like the big character posters of the Cultural Revolution in China—warnings and threats, calls for self-correction. (230)

"Crazy" though her idea may seem, Brita's intuition proves correct when she arrives at the bunker of the terrorist leader Rashid and finds his image, like those of Mao in post-revolution China and the Coke II logo on the streets of Beirut, emblazoned everywhere. As with Coke II in the context of consumer culture, the image of Rashid serves as a sign of value, and Rashid's followers signify their loyalty to the terror chief (i.e., their value not only to him but to his organization as well) by pinning reproductions of his photograph to their shirts (231). According to Rashid's translator, this practice is evidence that under Rashid, all men will be "one man," and that for his followers, the "image of Rashid is their destiny" (233). Following the logic of consumer culture, then, Rashid is aiming for total market saturation, and he wants his own image to become the ultimate sign against which all others are judged. Yet where Rashid's followers are all engulfed in the cult of personality surrounding the terrorist, Brita uses her camera to cast a critical eye upon the value with which they have endowed him.

When a young boy enters Rashid's bunker wearing a hood, Rashid's interpreter explains that the hood signifies that Rashid's followers "don't need their own features or voices" (234). Ironically, however, Rashid's interpreter also notes that the terrorist organization exists because the Western presence in Beirut threatens his followers' sense of self-respect and identity (235). This argument falls in line with Baudrillard's argument that the terrorists who perpetrated the attacks of September 2001 did so in response to humiliations inflicted upon the East by the West (Baudrillard, *Spirit of Terrorism* 26). Yet where Baudrillard argues that the act of terror engenders ambivalence insofar as it embodies a "dual, personal relationship" that allows the terrorist to confront the opposing power in a "genuinely adversarial," face-to-face relationship, the hoods worn by Rashid's followers suggest otherwise (25, 26). Always deferring to the will of their leader, Rashid's followers are, like the denizens of consumer culture Baudrillard describes, locked in a system that precludes negotiation.

Recognizing the totalitarian nature of Rashid's mode of governance, Brita impulsively unveils one of his followers and snaps his photograph. In the tense moment that follows, neither party has recourse to ideology: Brita is completely out of her element, and

Rashid's follower reels at the notion of a foreign woman daring to transgress against his leader's dictates. In this moment, Brita looks the terrorist in the face and sees, for the first time, not simply a terrorist or the blank face of an ideological movement, but an individual. Which is not to say that DeLillo romanticizes the confrontation; the terrorist immediately strikes Brita and is about to strike her again when he is dismissed by Rashid. Nonetheless, Brita attempts to reveal herself as more than an anonymous agent of a particular ideological regime when she "walks over to Rashid, shakes his hand, actually introduces herself, pronouncing her name slowly" (237). While this incident does not bring about the collapse of consumer ideology, it does subordinate ideological dictates to interpersonal relations and, as such, reveals the inherent value Rashid and his followers impute to their ideological system as illusory.

As the novel concludes, Brita is awakened by the rumble of a passing tank. The tank, however, does not portend a looming battle but the passage of a wedding party through the streets of Beirut. The image of this wedding party is unlike that of the mass wedding depicted in the novel's prologue. Where the participants in the earlier wedding are absorbed into an undifferentiated mass, the members of the Beirut wedding party remain distinct:

> The bride and groom carry champagne glasses and some of the girls hold sparklers that send off showers of excited light. A guest in a pastel tuxedo smokes a long cigar and does a dance around a shell hole, delighting the kids. The bride's gown is beautiful, with lacy appliqué at the bodice, and she looks surpassingly alive, they all look transcendent, free of limits and unsurprised to be here. They make it seem only natural that a wedding might advance its resplendence with a free-lance tank as escort. (240)

As the party parades past her balcony, Brita raises a glass of melon liqueur to the bridegroom, and he returns the gesture. That this act echoes Brita's earlier face-to-face confrontations with Rashid and his follower underscores the notion that ideology need not preclude what Baudrillard terms dual, personal relationships. While the wedding can certainly be read as an event steeped in tradition, the members of this particular wedding party are neither hiding behind that tradition nor walking in mindless lockstep with its dictates. Rather, they are confronting each other and the outside world (as embodied by Brita) with limited, but not total, recourse to ideology. Yet as the wedding party passes out of sight, Brita sees bright flashes in the distance and is reminded of the ongoing ideological conflicts spiraling out of control all around her—faceless soldiers firing at each other in order to promote one brand of cultural hegemony over all others. On close scrutiny, however, Brita realizes that the flashes she sees in the night are not gunshots but camera flashes, and that someone in the distance, like Brita herself, has the potential to reveal the face of "the other" and, in so doing, pave the way for a negotiation of differences that does not hinge entirely on blind recourse to ideology.

As Brita does, needless to say, so too does DeLillo. By turning a critical eye not only toward consumer culture *per se* but also toward the blind push for total market saturation that the logic behind that culture demands, DeLillo effects his own version of a democratic shout and places a further beat between the artist and the apparatus of assimilation that would otherwise reduce all forms of art to elevator music. Where terrorism ultimately reproduces the objectifying logic of the very system it aims to destroy by substituting one totalitarian system of value for another, DeLillo examines the individuals behind those movements. Indeed, this focus on individuals, fictional though they may be, sets DeLillo apart from Baudrillard, the broad theoretical sweep of whose own writing largely precludes attention to the particular. Yet attention to the particular is what allows DeLillo to enact the ambivalence for which Baudrillard calls. By putting a face on the individual behind or within the movement, he demonstrates that the artist has the power to do what the terrorist cannot: place dual, personal, and genuinely adversarial relationships ahead of ideology. While this strategy does not completely eradicate consumerism as Baudrillard demands, the fact that it can be implemented demonstrates that subjectivity remains intact and that consumer ideology, while certainly a threat, has yet to reach critical mass and render objects of all within its purview. Thus while the future may, as one character in *Mao II* laments, belong to crowds, DeLillo demonstrates that the present remains, if only provisionally, in the hands of individuals who must continue to view each other as such in order to prevent the lifeless world Baudrillard envisions from becoming a reality. Significantly, as DeLillo demonstrates, it is not the terrorist who prevents this totalitarian vision from becoming a reality, but the artist.

CHAPTER 7

TO VANDALIZE THEIR EYEBALLS: *UNDERWORLD*'S GRAFFITI INSTINCT

Grieving over the death of fellow graffiti artist Skaty 8, *Underworld*'s Moonman 157 (a.k.a. Ismael Muñoz) meditates on the nature of his art. There is "no art in bombing platforms and walls," Moonman notes (435). "You have to tag the trains. The trains come roaring down the rat alleys all alike and then you hit a train and it is yours, seen everywhere in the system, and you get inside people's heads and vandalize their eyeballs" (435). That the artist refers to his craft as "bombing" draws attention to its violent nature. Yet his mode of violence is markedly different from the kind perpetrated by terrorists in *Players*, *Libra*, *Mao II*, and other works by DeLillo in which kidnapping, bombing, and assassination fail to dismantle the infrastructure of capitalist ideology and consumer culture. Rather than aiming to destroy, Moonman's intention is to create. Riding the Washington Heights local, he observes that every car is as follows:

> tagged with his own neon zoom, with highlights and
> overlapping letters and 3-D effect, the whole wildstyle thing
> of making your name and street number a kind of alphabet
> city where the colors lock and bleed and the letters connect
> and it's all live jive, it jumps and shouts—even the drips are
> intentional, painted supersharp to express how the letters
> sweat, how they live and breathe and eat and sleep, they dance
> and play the sax. (433)

The effect of this living, breathing art is twofold. First, commuters react to the train with a mixture of shock and admiration; in Moonman's words, "their heads [go] wow" (434). Second, as Timothy L. Parrish observes, by "'spray-paint scrawling' the fact of their urban ethnic existence all over the city," Moonman and other graffiti artists assert identity as an act of defiance against a "system" that includes city politicians who wish to preserve the city's cleanliness and "the CIA and Dow Chemical, whose alliance creates a chemical solvent more effective than orange juice in erasing art from the trains" (Parrish 716).

The real triumph of Moonman's art, according to Parrish, "is the unlikely connections it establishes among different classes and races of people who ordinarily refuse to acknowledge each other's existence" (716). In establishing these connections, Moonman effects a shift in the way commuters view the objects that surround them and enacts a constructive and forceful version of what Jean Baudrillard describes in *The Consumer Society* as the "violent irruptions and sudden disintegrations" that will inevitably destroy consumerism when the masses come to realize that "the Object is nothing and that behind it stands the tangled void of human relations" (196). Through Moonman, DeLillo implies that art presents a form of violence that is capable of wreaking more than superficial damage on consumer culture. At the same time, however, DeLillo depicts artists throughout *Underworld* as fragile purveyors of violence who are in constant danger of being co-opted by that culture. At issue, then, is how the artist as depicted by DeLillo subverts consumer culture and avoids becoming a part of what Baudrillard calls the system of objects.

One way to understand the system of objects as Baudrillard envisions it is to consider the opening sentences of Nick Shay's narrative in *Underworld*:

> I was driving a Lexus through a rustling wind. This is a car assembled in a work area that's completely free of human presence. Not a spot of mortal sweat except, okay, for the guys who drive the product out of the plant—allow a little moisture where they grip the steering wheel. The system flows forever onward, automated to a priestly nuance, every gliding movement back-referenced for prime performance. Hollow bodies coming in endless sequence. There's nobody on the line with caffeine nerves or a history of clinical depression. Just the eerie weave of chromium alloys carried in interlocking arcs, block iron and asphalt sheeting, soaring ornaments of coachwork fitted and merged. Robots tightening bolts, programmed drudges that do not dream of family dead. (63)

Here, the lack of human presence and seeming speed with which the system produces vehicles underscores a concern Baudrillard voices in *The Consumer Society* regarding the relationship between humanity and the objects that constitute our cultural landscape:

> There is all around us today a kind of fantastic conspicuousness of consumption and abundance, constituted by the multiplication of objects, services and material goods, and this represents something of a fundamental mutation in the ecology of the human species. Strictly speaking, the humans of the age of affluence are surrounded not so much by other human beings...but by *objects*. Their daily dealings are not so much with their fellow men, but rather—on a rising statistical curve—with the reception and manipulation of goods and messages. (25)

By rendering the world a "sweeping vista of perpetual shopping," Baudrillard argues, mass production has allowed the "eternal substitution of homogenous elements" to "reign unchallenged" (30). Moreover, because communication is predicated on what Baudrillard calls "the living interconnection of distinct elements," the proliferation of homogeneous commodities has emptied the world of meaning and short-circuited the symbolic function of communication (30). As a result, human interaction has suffered, and the species has become increasingly, as Nick puts it, "factually absent from the scene" (DeLillo, *Underworld* 63). Indeed, that another character eventually identifies Nick as "the Lexus" validates Baudrillard's concern; the conflation of man and car is symptomatic of the degree to which consumption has become less a matter of satisfying actual needs than of signaling one's prowess at consuming (79). That is, everything within consumer culture serves primarily as a sign of value—a dictum that applies not only to luxury cars, but to art as well.

In his introduction to *The Consumer Society*, George Ritzer notes that "Baudrillard holds to the dream of an art that instead of being in the thrall of consumer society, would be able to decipher it" (16). Consumer ideology, however, reduces the likelihood that art of this nature will emerge. "Art, jeans and burgers all acquire their meaning and their value relative to one another as well as to the entire system of consumer objects," Ritzer explains (16). Because consumer culture attaches value to the work of art as systematically as it attaches value to the article of clothing, the food item, or the home appliance, the work of art serves primarily as a sign of value that positively reflects the social status of its possessor and can be substituted for any commodity of equal value.

According to Baudrillard, the marketing of art, particularly that which is mass produced, "delivers up to the logic of consumption (*i.e.,* to the manipulation of signs) certain contents or symbolic activities which were not previously subject to that logic" (106). As a result of mass production, works of art "no longer stand opposed, as *works* and as semantic substance—as *open* significations—to other finite objects" (107). Rather, they have become "finite objects themselves and are part of the package, the constellation of accessories by which the 'socio-cultural' standing of the average citizen is determined" (107). Demonstration of one's acculturation, then, is bound up in the exchange of signs, and individuals adept at this mode of exchange, "like designed objects, are better integrated socially and professionally" (109). "Culture" in this context, Baudrillard notes, is no more than a functional rationalization of texts and images that promises but fails to deliver a means of deciphering our age "without being abolished in it" (109). Rather than deciphering the consumer age, the commodified work of art serves only to exemplify its basic premise: to be acculturated is to consume well. What suffers when art serves only to indicate the sociocultural standing of the individual who either possesses or appreciates it is a sense of confrontation. Rather than interrogating consumer ideology, the work of art serves only to reinforce that ideology. To appreciate the work of art is to accept and reaffirm its value and, in turn, to legitimate the practice of using commodities to signal social standing.

While Nick seems more or less comfortable with his (and humanity's) diminishing role in the world of objects, his former lover, Klara Sax, has a vested interest in reversing the trends Baudrillard describes. An artist once dubbed "the bag lady" for her use of discarded aerosol cans, sardine tins, shampoo caps, and mattresses, Klara now works with abandoned B-52 long-range bombers, employing a small army of volunteers to strip the planes of their original coats of paint and to repaint those planes one at a time, in some cases by hand. The purpose of this project, Klara explains, is to "unrepeat" the Cold War weapons systems that, like Nick's Lexus, "came out of the factories and assembly halls as near alike as possible, millions of components stamped out, repeated endlessly" (DeLillo, *Underworld* 77). Through these acts of unrepeating, Klara hopes to recover what she refers to as both "a sort of survival instinct" and "a graffiti instinct—to declare ourselves, show who we are" (77).

That survival and graffiti go hand in hand is a truth Klara elucidates in a lengthy monologue on the "nose art" that once decorated many of the bombers she has acquired. Historically, such art included unit insignia, snarling animal mascots, and "sexy" women painted on the noses of war planes as charms against death. These charms were meaningful, Klara explains, because the men who flew the planes "lived in a closed world with its particular omens and symbols" (77). In other words, the sweeping vista of perpetual shopping Baudrillard describes did not hold sway over their lives. Rather, their isolation from consumer culture and heightened awareness of death's likely imminence afforded the men Klara describes a greater appreciation for the power of the symbolic to convey meaning beyond that of sign value. This power is essential to Klara's project, and she notes that her goal is to keep the scope of her work "small and human" despite its apparent enormity (78). Ironically, Klara makes these comments to a reporter from a French television station, so despite her interest in the "small and human," she has no qualms about explaining the significance of her work via mass media. This tension appears in many of DeLillo's works, and *Underworld* is no exception. Following their own graffiti instincts, artistic figures throughout the novel struggle to reclaim the "small and human" even as they engage the massive systems that dehumanize the species.

Unlike the self-assured "unrepeater" of massive weapons systems depicted in the first chapter of *Underworld*, the younger Klara of the novel's "Cocksucker Blues" section has doubts about her identity as an artist. Envious of the buzz her protégé, Acey Greene, is generating in the art world, Klara begins to recognize the limits of her own artistic sensibilities. Although she respects and even envies art "in which the moment is heroic, American art, the do-it-now, the fuck-the-past," Klara cannot "place hand to object and make some furious now, some brilliant jack-off gesture that asserts an independence" (377). Yet throughout "Cocksucker Blues," such gestures serve only to reinforce conservative, consumer-driven ideologies. On television, Richard Nixon gestures with a "hand-jerk over the head" as if to say, "here I am, you bastards, still alive and kicking," and in a documentary also titled *Cocksucker Blues*, the "whole jerk-off monotonic airborne erotikon" of a Rolling Stones tour proves less than subversive when Mick Jagger et al. are described as a "band of emaciated millionaire pricks" (475, 384, 385).

Jack-off, jerk-off, hand-jerk: all three terms indicate masturbation and suggest that figures like Nixon, Jagger, and the kinds of artists Klara envies are engaged in solitary acts of self-gratification and are uninterested in effecting social change. Which is not to say that all instances of masturbation in *Underworld* are solitary, nor that solitary acts are incapable of effecting social change, particularly with regard to consumer ideology. In a passage describing the graffiti artist at work, DeLillo juxtaposes images of Moonman's first homosexual experience with those of his *modus operandi* to suggest that the graffiti instinct itself is a kind of jerk-off gesture. "The man who reached around and said excuse me," reads one brief paragraph that is shortly followed by another: "The crew shook the cans and the ball went click" (439). As with Jagger and Nixon, Moonman's jerk-off gesture is one of defiance. This defiance, however, is not marked by the self-indulgence of the solitary masturbatory act or the sense of isolation Baudrillard sees as stemming from consumer ideology. Rather, Moonman's sexual initiation introduces him to an underground world that allows for a sense of intimacy the world above prohibits. Similarly, the work of tagging trains is not a solitary endeavor for Moonman; his crew consists of young "hopefuls" who, among their other duties, shake spray cans, stand guard while Moonman paints, and brace their arms to support his weight when he needs to reach the upper parts of cars (438). Additionally, the purpose of Moonman's work is not to promote or aggrandize himself as an artist, but to tell a story of tenement life, "good and bad but mostly good" (440). Imagining himself "an unknown hero of the line," Moonman comes closest to autographing his work when a tourist photographs his tag, and "Ismael sidle[s] to the open door so he [can] be in the picture, too, unknown to the man" (434). In that moment, Parrish notes, "the pathos of Moonman's at once deeply public and terribly private work is almost unbearable" (Parrish 717). Nonetheless, this delicate balance between public and private is exactly what artists throughout *Underworld* continually struggle to achieve.

Using language similar to DeLillo's, Baudrillard offers a fairly lengthy "reading" of graffiti as a phenomenon of the early 1970s and explains the ways in which it subverts the logic of signification that supports consumer culture. Discussing a "spate of graffiti" that "broke out" in New York in 1972, Baudrillard notes that the content of the work was neither political nor pornographic (*Symbolic Exchange* 76).

As in *Underworld*, the graffiti consisted solely of "surnames drawn from underground comics such as DUKE SPIRIT SUPERKOOL KOOLKILLER ACE VIPERE SPIDER EDDIE KOLA and so on, followed by their street number" (76). These names, Baudrillard argues, altered the terrain of the city, which had, by the latter half of the twentieth century, been transformed from a politico-industrial zone to a "zone of signs, the media and the code" (77).

As factories disappeared from urban landscapes, cities ceased to be zones of production and became zones of consumption, importing the codes of consumer culture via television and advertising. Under these circumstances, Baudrillard argues, "radical revolt effectively consists in saying 'I exist, I am so and so, I live on such and such street, I am alive here and now' " (78). Moreover, that the graffitists opposed anonymity with pseudonyms rather than their own names suggests that retaliation against the system consisted not in regaining identity but in turning indeterminacy against the code: "SUPERBEE SPIX COLA 139 KOOL GUY CRAZY CROSS 136 mean nothing, it is not even a proper name, but a symbolic matriculation number whose function is to derail the common system of designations" (78). "Invincible due to their own poverty, they resist every interpretation and every connotation," Baudrillard argues; "In this way, with neither connotation nor denotation, they escape the principle of signification and, as empty signifiers, erupt into the sphere of the *full signs* of the city, dissolving it on contact" (79).

In addition to dissolving the signs that constitute the city, graffiti also dissolves boundaries imposed by architecture and urban planning:

> Graffiti runs from one house to the next, from one wall of a building to the next, from the wall onto the window or the door, or windows on subway trains, or the pavements. Graffiti overlaps, is thrown up, superimposes… Its graphics resemble the child's polymorphous perversity, ignoring the boundaries between the sexes and the delimitation of erogenous zones. Curiously, moreover, graffiti turns the city's walls and corners, the subway's cars and the buses, into a *body*, a body without beginning or end, made erotogenic in its entirety by writing

just as the body may be in the primitive inscription (tattooing). Tattooing takes place on the body. In primitive societies, along with other ritual signs, it makes the body what it is—material for symbolic exchange: without tattooing, as without masks, the body is only what it is, naked and expressionless. By tattooing walls, SUPERSEX and SUPERKOOL free them from architecture and turn them once again into living, social matter, into the moving body of the city before it has been branded with functions and institutions. (82)

Thus art dealer Esther Winship's promise to give Moonman a wall if she ever finds him poses a threat to the subversive force of his work even if, as Klara speculates, the promise of the wall is "the first stage of saying I'll give him a building, I'll give him a city block" (DeLillo, *Underworld* 377). Described as "stupidly out of touch" and "sealed in a safer frame of reference," Esther wears a safari jacket as she seeks out Moonman, and Klara admits that she is ill at ease with the idea of tagging trains, an activity she likens to a "romance of the ego, poor kids playing out a fantasy of meretricious fame" (392). As far as Moonman is concerned, however, egotism is a moot point; far from wishing to see his name or face in newspapers, his goal is to stay "totally low and out of sight" because he can "easily envision a case where the whole gallery scene is a scam by the police to get writers out of the tunnels and train yards and into the open, identified by name and face" (436). While this suspicion stems from Moonman's fear of arrest, it also speaks to his suspicion of "the establishment" in general. Anonymity is power for Moonman because it allows him to avoid being co-opted or interpreted by those in the "gallery scene." Because graffiti, in Baudrillard's words, is "made to be given, exchanged, transmitted and relayed in a collective anonymity," it lacks a signature and attacks the ego-centered mode of artistic production with which Esther and Klara are familiar (Baudrillard, *Symbolic Exchange* 79). Consequently, in order for Klara to get in touch with her own graffiti instinct, she must strive to conquer her own egocentrism by confronting her professional envy of Acey Greene's rising profile in the art world.

Predicting that Acey will be assassinated within six months, Klara's lover Miles Lightman describes the up-and-coming artist as "too famous to live" (DeLillo, *Underworld* 397). Later, however, Miles qualifies his opinion by noting that Acey's work is "a cut above total shit" and that her fame is the direct result of "pandering to white ideas about scary blacks" (479). Realizing that in her praise of Acey's work she has been "waiting all along for someone to disagree," Klara experiences a mixture of joy and guilt at her lover's assertion; she wants Miles to keep talking, regardless of whether his assessment of Acey's work is correct (480). Subsequently, while vacationing in Los Angeles, Klara receives word that Acey's work has been panned by critics as well. Eager to read the stinging reviews of Acey's show, Klara's friends speak "with controlled excitement" and wait for her "to rejoice in kind," an expectation that makes her feel "sleazy as hell" (491). The following day, however, she experiences a kind of rebirth when she visits the Watts Towers, about which all she knows is that the man who created them "worked alone, an immigrant, for many years, a sort of unimaginable number of years, and used whatever objects he could forage and scrounge" (492). Deeming the environment a "place riddled with epiphanies," Klara rubs her palms over bright surfaces and feels "a kind of static in her body" that feels to her like "laughing helplessly as a girl" (492). Inspiring in her a sense of artistic rebirth, Klara's experience at the Watts Towers brings to fruition a pair of smaller epiphanies she experienced earlier in the novel.

Watching a woman caresses herself on a hotel bed in *Cocksucker Blues*, Klara realizes that the men in the film "stay men," while "the women become girls except maybe the woman who rubs her pussy and licks it and says something inaudible because the whole point of sound in a film like this is to lose it in the corners of the room" (385). Like Moonman's tag, the woman's words refuse to yield meaning, and like Moonman himself, the woman engages in a masturbatory act that is distinct from the "jerk-off monotonic airborne erotikon" of "millionaire pricks" at play. In contrast to the band and its assortment of groupies who "all do the same things, dope, sex, picture taking," the woman who touches herself is not engaged in an act of consumption but one of defiance; by pleasuring herself, she withholds her body from the system of objects and turns away from the ethos of consumption that renders other women interchangeable commodities within that system. All at once, the simultaneously public and private nature of her act—onscreen self-gratification—confronts consumer ideology and denies its hegemony. Because her words fail to signify and her sexuality refuses to yield to consumer demands, both carry symbolic weight insofar as neither depends upon a final relation of value for meaning.

The above reading, however, is at odds with the distrust toward all forms of mass media that Baudrillard voices in *For a Critique of the Political Economy of the Sign*. The media support consumer ideology "not as vehicles of content, but in their very form and operation," Baudrillard argues in a chapter titled "Requiem for the Media" (*For a Critique* 169). Because the mass media do not allow for reciprocal exchange of speech and response, they induce a state of noncommunication that is inimical to symbolic exchange. Lulled into idleness by the media's exclusion of responsibility, the consumer's only options are to accept or reject what the media present, and engaging the media becomes nothing more than a referendum marked by the control of rupture (171). Everything that passes through the mass media becomes a sign of the mass media's power to produce and reproduce what we consider reality. As a result, subversive acts cannot be mass mediated. Rather, under the media's collective gaze, the subversive act becomes nothing more than a model for reproduction and exists only "as a function of its reproducibility" (174).

The message of the media is structured by a code that allows for communication to flow in one direction only, from the transmitter to the receiver (178). This mode of communication excludes "the reciprocity and antagonism of interlocutors, and the ambivalence of their exchange" because there is no code for ambivalence (179). That is, because ambivalence is predicated not on the circulation of information and semantic content (i.e., value) but on the negation of these concepts, it can neither be encoded nor decoded and therefore cannot be mass mediated. Hence graffiti is transgressive insofar as it allows for ambivalence—"not because it substitutes another content, another discourse, but simply because it responds, there, on the spot, and breaches the fundamental role of non-response enunciated by all the media" (183). In contrast, such phenomena as independent films either reinforce this role of non-response or result in "a kind of personalized amateurism, the equivalent of Sunday tinkering on the periphery of the system" (182). In short, no revolution will ever be televised because real revolution is predicated on the restoration of response that television, film, and other forms of mass media prohibit. Nonetheless, Klara's reaction to *Cocksucker Blues* suggests that the film does allow for viewer response, as does her reaction to a screening of Sergei Eisenstein's *Unterwelt* at Radio City Music Hall.

Described as "the movie people had to see" despite never having heard of it "until the Times did a Sunday piece," *Unterwelt* exemplifies the work of art that has become part of what Baudrillard describes in *The Consumer Society* as "the constellation of accessories by which the 'socio-cultural' standing of the average citizen is determined" (DeLillo, *Underworld* 42; Baudrillard, *Consumer Society* 107). "I don't need to see the movie. I already love it," Esther declares, waving a handbag when she arrives at the screening, clearly revealing that her motivation for attending the event has less to do with viewing the film than demonstrating her prowess as a consumer (DeLillo, *Underworld* 425). Even so, DeLillo describes "an ambivalence" that energizes those in attendance:

> There was an ambivalence that vitalized the crowd. Whatever your sexual persuasion, you were here to enjoy the contradictions. Think of the relationship between the film and the theater in which it was showing—the work of a renowned master of world cinema screened in the camp environment of the Rockettes and the mighty Wurlitzer. But a theater of a certain impressive shapeliness, a breathtaking place, brass on the outer walls and handsome display cases in the ticket lobby and nickel bronze stair rails here in the foyer, a space that

resembled the hushed and sunken saloon of an ocean liner. And possibly a film, you're not likely to forget this, that will be rid-dled with mannerisms whatever the level of seriousness. (425)

While DeLillo's use of the term may not be as precise or theoreti-cally loaded as Baudrillard's, both senses of ambivalence are predi-cated upon contradiction and the nonfulfillment of desire. Implied in the "camp environment" of Radio City Music Hall is the promise of entertainment, but the somber tone of *Unterwelt* refuses to deliver on that promise. "I want to be rewarded for this ordeal," Esther says halfway through the movie (431), but no reward is forthcoming. Indeed, Klara realizes that although the film largely fails to enter-tain, its "remote and fragmentary" nature promotes "a giddy kind of total confusion" that makes her squirm and foreshadows the "near helplessness" she will experience in the presence of the Watts Towers later in the novel (430, 491). Moreover, the film's silence is suggestive of the inaudible woman in *Cocksucker Blues*; what is "this murky film, this strange dark draggy set of images," Klara wonders, "if not a statement of outrage and independence?" (431).

When a subway running beneath the theater is revealed to be one of Moonman's, the parallel becomes clear: *Unterwelt* is Eisenstein's attempt to vandalize the eyeballs of his audience (433). That he succeeds in doing so through film suggests that ambivalence can indeed be effected via mass media. Like Moonman's graffiti, *Unterwelt* is (to borrow Parrish's phrase) "at once deeply public and terribly private" insofar as it communicates without signify-ing or pandering to audience expectations of what art should do *á là* Acey Greene. Thus Klara's epiphany at the Watts Towers and her subsequent realization that she is, in fact, an artist despite her qualms about tagging trains suggests that what characterizes the graffiti instinct is not the "do it now, fuck the past" attitude of the art she both fears and admires, but the "freshet of life" that instinct engenders in an otherwise lifeless world (494). One can vandalize eyeballs, Klara realizes, without jerking off.

A "statement of outrage and independence," Eisenstein's film helps to demonstrate the relationship Klara begins to see between art and ideology. "This is a film about Us and Them," the narrator observes as *Unterwelt* nears its abrupt conclusion, "They can say who they are, you have to lie. They control the language, you have to improvise and dissemble. They establish the limits of your existence. And the camp elements of the program, the choreography and some of the music, now tended to resemble sneak attacks on the dominant culture" (444). In the context of consumerism, the dominant culture does not stop at placing limits on one's existence but eradicates humanity altogether: we are all, Baudrillard argues, homogeneous elements in a vast network of interchangeable commodities. Everything within this network serves as a sign, and each sign designates value, the common denominator that renders all things interchangeable. Within these parameters, the language of consumer culture is nothing more than a means of signaling social status, and its "message" always reinforces what Baudrillard calls the positive transcendence of value: the proliferation of signs in consumer culture precludes the possibility of loss insofar as even a commodity that is "lost" or destroyed can be replaced with a dollar amount equal to the commodity's value.

Through *Unterwelt*, however, Eisenstein engenders a vision that is distinct from that of consumer culture: "All Eisenstein wants you to see, in the end, are the contradictions of being. You look at the faces on the screen and you see the mutilated yearning, the inner divisions of people and systems, and how forces will clash and fasten, compelling the swerve from evenness that marks a thing lastingly" (444). As a result of this vision, Klara experiences a "curious loss" when the film ends, "that thing you used to feel as a child when you walked out of the movie house in the middle of the day and the streets were all agitation and nasty glare, every surface intense and jarring, people in loud clothing that did not fit" (445). Moreover, as her friends concern themselves with where to get "the best cheesecake" and "onion soup that makes you think you're in Les Halles," Klara feels as if their conversation is occurring "in a room three rooms away" or "over there somewhere" (445). In effect, conversation in the register of consumerism has ceased to be meaningful to Klara. Or, in Baudrillard's terms, ambivalence has brought about the collapse of sign exchange: thinking in terms that are completely alien to her friends, Klara cannot converse on their level.

Which is not to say that Baudrillard's suspicion of the mass media's potential for allowing ambivalence is entirely misplaced. Although Klara experiences a curious sense of loss after viewing *Unterwelt*, her companions remain unaffected because they regard the film in terms of what Baudrillard refers to as "ideological categories that express a certain type of social relation, namely, in which one speaks and the other doesn't" (Baudrillard, *For a Critique* 179). Within this relationship, Baudrillard notes,

> two terms are artificially isolated and artificially reunited by an objectified content called a message. There is neither reciprocal relation nor simultaneous mutual presence of the two terms, since each determines itself in relation to the message or code, the "intermedium" that maintains both in a respective situation (it is the code that holds both in "respect"), at a distance from one another, a distance that seals the full and autonomized "value" of the message (in fact, its exchange value). (179)

Because messages allow information to flow in only one direction, no immediate reciprocity exists between the transmitter of the message and its receiver. Film, for example, transmits a message to the receptive audience. While this message unites or allows for a connection between the film and the audience, it only does so by placing itself between both parties. Moreover, the unidirectional nature of "messaging" precludes responsibility (i.e., the potential for response) between the film and the audience. Accustomed to this mode of communication, Klara's companions are faced with two options with regard to *Unterwelt*: they can accept the film's "message" or they can reject it. They cannot, however, respond to the film. That is, they cannot give anything back or even lose anything to *Unterwelt*. Yet the "curious loss" Klara experiences as a result of watching *Unterwelt* suggests that its lack of a coherent message has allowed a kind of unmediated communion between the artist and the film. Like the woman Klara admires in *Cocksucker Blues*, *Unterwelt* "speaks" without signifying, but its failure to reach Klara's companions underlines the difficulty of effecting symbolic exchange via the mass media: if no apparent message is forthcoming, which is to say that the medium has no inherent value, then the masses are more likely to reject that medium than to attempt to engage it in any fashion.

The viability of ambivalence as an alternative to the vacuous positivity of consumer culture remains problematic throughout *Underworld*. That Klara is the only member of her party capable of recognizing *Unterwelt*'s symbolic weight suggests that ambivalence is reserved for an elect caste of artistically minded individuals, and the woman touching herself in *Cocksucker Blues* comes off as somewhat regressive insofar as masturbation is generally perceived not as a means of exchange but as a form of self-gratification. Moreover, Baudrillard's reading of graffiti tends to romanticize vandalism. While graffiti may indeed blur the boundaries between public and private property, and may also exemplify a mode of communication that short-circuits "the non-response enunciated by all the media," the graffiti artist remains, at heart, a consumer: even Moonman prefers Perrier to tap water (439). Such complications underline the conundrum at the heart of effecting the kind of revolution Baudrillard describes. The masses must learn to appreciate ambivalence in order to restore symbolic exchange, but in order for the masses to appreciate it, ambivalence must be packaged in a way that makes it palatable to them. That is, for ambivalence to gain ascendancy, it must first be commodified, and thus rendered impotent.

In "Symbolic Exchange and Hyperreality," Deborah Cook observes that Baudrillard's conundrum leaves us with few, if any, options. Indeed, Cook argues, the only mode of symbolic exchange Baudrillard allows the masses is silence; through silence, the masses mirror the media's irreversibility and in so doing effectively return to the media their own logic of nonresponse (152). In Baudrillard's words, "This absence of power may be understood, no longer in the least as the strategy of power, but as a counterstrategy of the masses themselves in confrontation with power" (qtd. in Cook 152). The problem with Baudrillard's position, according to Cook, is that silence represents the symbolic death of the masses: "the masses no longer will themselves to be subjects but rather lifeless objects; they abandon all responsibility and make a mockery of whatever autonomy they may have preserved" (154). This problem is augmented by the fact that Baudrillard speaks too broadly of "the masses" and their relationship to consumer culture; Cook argues that "Baudrillard's often hyperbolic statements do not allow one to make the fine distinctions necessary for analysis of everyday speech and behavior, and the effects which the media have had on them" (155). While Baudrillard seeks an immediate mode of communication that allows for genuine response, his overwhelming interest in the mass media precludes any chance of mapping out ways in which such a mode of communication might operate.

To be sure, sketching a means of effecting symbolic exchange, even on a personal level, is no easy task. Indeed, to reduce ambivalence to a simple formula is to return to the conundrum at the heart of Baudrillard's call to arms; doing so would more likely serve than cripple consumerism insofar as the formulaic generally lends itself to commodification. Moreover, following what Klara refers to as the graffiti instinct is an endeavor fraught with tension and ambiguity. As in Parrish's reading of Moonman's work, the distinction between public and private acts begins to dissolve as the artist's desire for recognition competes with an urge to communicate. Yet by exploring such tensions, the novel breaks new ground where Baudrillard falls short in that it explores the relationship between the media and everyday speech and behavior. In so doing, *Underworld* allows for the fine distinctions Cook sees as lacking in Baudrillard's work and charts some of the territory through which the artist must travel in order to effect symbolic exchange and, in turn, subvert consumer culture.

Particularly revealing in this regard is DeLillo's depiction of Lenny Bruce in Part Five of *Underworld*, "Better Things for Better Living Through Chemistry: Selected Fragments Public and Private in the 1950s and 1960s." On tour during the Cuban Missile Crisis, "the infamous sick comic" agonizes nightly over his act and its relationship to the looming potential for nuclear Armageddon:

> Because the Russians had put missiles into Cuba. And President Kennedy's grim speech still formed a kind of grim auditory wall running through the room. Nuclear strike capability. Full retaliatory response. Such resonant and carefully crafted terms. This was an audience accustomed to a different level of dread…And they all needed Lenny to help them make the transition to the global thing that's going on out there with SAC bombers rumbling over the tarmac and Polaris subs putting to sea, like *dive dive dive*, it's dialogue from every submarine movie ever made and it's all factually happening but at the same time they find it remarkably unreal—Titans and Atlases being readied for firing. (504)

In order to make the unfolding events and the imminence of nuclear war seem more real to his audience, Bruce employs parody to work away at the wall of "resonant and carefully crafted terms" Kennedy makes use of to reassure his fellow citizens that their world order will remain intact.

"Good evening, my fellow citizens," Bruce begins, echoing the President's opening line (504). Yet mimicking the President himself is too obvious, Bruce decides, and he "kills the bit before it begins" despite having won a few laughs with his impersonation (505). Turning against his audience, Bruce plays on their desire to be seen as seedy hipsters in order to explain the difference between real and perceived life on the edge: "Yeah, I know you smoke some grass on Saturday night. Making the scene. Plus you accidentally drove through Watts one night, and you can't stop talking about it. Made the shorthairs stand on end. Negroes in porkpie hats. No, yes, this thing here, let me tell you what the edge is. The true edge is not where you choose to live but where they situate you against your will" (505). True life on the edge, Bruce further explains, "is having twenty-six guys from Harvard deciding our fate" (505). His monologue then shifts to an overt attack on conspicuous consumption and the Kennedy administration. In addition to belonging to eating clubs and secret societies, all the President's men, Bruce informs his audience, "wear boxer shorts with geometric designs that contain the escape routes they've been assigned when the missiles start flying" (505). He then goes on to describe the bunker that will house the President, the Secretary of State, and the Joint Chiefs of Staff in the event of a nuclear strike:

> Picture it...Twenty-six guys in Clark Kent suits getting ready to enter a luxury bunker that's located about half a mile under the White House and the faggot decorator's doing a last-minute checklist. Let's see, peach walls, stunning. Found the chandelier in a little abbey outside Paris. None of that Statler Hilton dreck in *my* bomb shelter...
>
> Rugs, fabulous, the purest Persian slave labor. Arched windows, okay we're twelve stories underground but the curtain fabric was irresistible so just shut up. Dining table, plantation mahogany, eleven bottles of Lemon Pledge. Centerpiece, designed it himself, the highlight of his career. A huge mound of crabmeat carved in the shape—they're gonna love this, it's so forceful and moving—yes, Kennedy and Krushchev wrestling in the nude. Lifesize. (506)

Returning to his opening line, Bruce mimics Kennedy a second time and launches into what will become his catchphrase for the remainder of the tour: *"We're all gonna die!"* (506).

Rather than mystifying his audience with such opaque technical jargon as "[n]uclear strike capability" and "[f]ull retaliatory response," Bruce cuts to the heart of the matter with a version of Kennedy's address that is to the point and distinctly more heartfelt than the original. Although DeLillo separates Bruce's setup from his punch line in order to describe the sense of anticipation building among his audience, the revised address reads in its entirety, "Good evening, my fellow citizens...*We're all gonna die!*" As his monologue continues, Bruce likens Kennedy to a pitchman "for insect repellant or throat spray" whose references to "[s]wift and extraordinary buildup" evoke more concern for the greasy buildup soiling America's ovens than for nuclear proliferation. Each time he returns to his punch line, however, Bruce offers a vision of the President that is decidedly at odds with Kennedy's public persona. The historical Kennedy ceases to function as a positive sign of rational government because Bruce negates that sign with his own Kennedy. Which is not to say that Bruce's Kennedy replaces the historical Kennedy in the collective imagination of his audience, but that the signifying nature of "Kennedy" is altered. Signifying both national security and its opposite, "Kennedy" gains symbolic stature in that "Kennedy," as revealed by Bruce, is not only a pitchman for preparedness but also an embodiment of national panic. Both extremes cancel each other out, and the President ceases to be a positive sign of American strength and resolve. Initially, this transformation causes the members of Bruce's audience to "bust their guts laughing" (509). After the performance, however, they drive through the night "at first morose and then angry and then fatalistic and then plain shaking scared, chests tight with the knowledge of how little it would take to make the thing happen" (508). Imparting both fear and laughter, Bruce inspires a sense of ambivalence in his audience that eliminates the veneer of calm proffered by Kennedy's "resonant and carefully crafted terms" (504).

Yet throughout this portion of the novel, Bruce remains painfully aware of his own potential for commodification. While his act certainly represents an attack on what might be considered the mainstream American lifestyle, this attack also serves to render Bruce a commodity within beatnik culture. "The whole beat landscape was bomb-shadowed," DeLillo's narrator informs us. "It always had been. The beats didn't need a missile crisis to make them think about the bomb. The bomb was their handiest reference to the moral squalor of America, the guilty place of smokestacks and robot corporations" (545). In other words, the bomb is a sign, and although beatnik counterculture appears to stand opposed to mainstream, corporate America, both factions are beholden to the logic of signification because both are heavily invested in the manipulation of signs for the purpose of indicating social status. By playing up his own fear of nuclear annihilation, Bruce uses the bomb to gain an audience among beatnik circles. "Lenny was showbiz," we are told, "he was suited and groomed and cool and corrupt, the mortician-comic, and the bomb was part of a scary ad campaign that had gotten out of hand" (546). By placing the bomb at the center of his act, Bruce indicates to his beatnik audience that he is hip to their scene. In so doing, Bruce places himself in danger of reversing the transubstantiation he performed upon Kennedy. That is, where Bruce's impression of the President transforms "Kennedy" from a positive sign into an ambivalent symbol, the comedian's interest in gaining the approval of his audience has the potential to transform "Lenny Bruce" from an ambivalent symbol of discord and uncertainty within American culture into a positive sign of the beatniks' perceived resistance to the mainstream.

Ultimately, however, Bruce is not beholden to the expectations of his hipster audience. What motivates the comic is his interest in "the loaded words" of his culture (585). Reciting such nonsensical strings of forbidden verbiage as "Mick spic hunky junkie boogie" and "Fuck suck fag hag gimme a nickel bag," Bruce thrills to the fact that many people in his audience have never heard these words spoken aloud and takes further delight in using these words to reveal "an odd turn of truth, a sense of unleashing perhaps, or disembarrassment" (585). "When the radiation makes you too sick to vomit, they hand our rubber vomit, for morale," Bruce explains before moving onto an exegesis of the slang term "smack" for the benefit of the Yiddish-speaking obscenity investigators in his audience (593):

> And you cops on special duty. The linguists in the crowd. There's something you ought to know. The word smack, or heroin? Comes from the Yiddish word *shmek*. You know this, experts? A sniff, a smell, like a pinch of snuff. Dig it, he's got a two hundred dollar *shmek* habit. Next time you bust a junkie who's a coreligionist…and you stick your rubber glove up his ass to check what kind of stash he's got in there, that smell

you smell is *shmek*, my friend. Which is just another name for ordinary life. (594)

Drawing an olfactory link between heroin and feces, Bruce underscores the basic absurdity of life: it may stink, but we keep living it. This, of course, stands in contrast to the positive logic of consumer culture, which does not allow for such contradictions. Where consumer culture distributes rubber vomit in order to maintain the illusion of meeting human needs, Bruce gives his audience dry heaves and ambivalence. His exploration of "loaded words" reveals that they are not simply overrun with connotation but rife with contradiction. Perhaps ironically, revealing the ways in which consumer culture is blind to such contradictions is Bruce's stock in trade. By drawing attention to these contradictions, Bruce sanctions ambivalence and in so doing neutralizes the value-laden logic of signification that provides the only means of communication within consumer ideology.

Locating himself in what he calls "the invisible middle" (592), Bruce is able to employ his own version of the counterstrategy Baudrillard describes in *Simulacra and Simulations*. "*We're all gonna die!*" the comedian cries time and again, underscoring not only his own lack of power but also that of those who are allegedly in power. Far from signaling what Cook considers the symbolic death of the masses, Bruce's response proves liberating. By describing the "true edge" of their existence (i.e., their genuine nearness to death), he reveals to his audience the spurious nature of consumer ideology; where consumer ideology proffers the illusion that individuals might demonstrate their own unique positions within society through the commodities with which they surround themselves, Bruce's audience can hear "the obliteration of uniqueness and free choice" as well as "the replacement of human isolation by massive and unvaried ruin" in his giddy shriek (507). Striking a balance between fear and amusement, Bruce explores the contradictions of life in the nuclear age and in so doing gives voice to the largely unspoken ambivalence of his day.

Throughout *Underworld*, DeLillo's project is much like that of Bruce. Confronted with what Baudrillard sees as the unrelenting and vacuous positivity of consumer culture, DeLillo explores the contradictions inherent in that culture in order to reclaim what Klara Sax refers to as the "small and human" from the massive systems that threaten to co-opt humanity. Where Baudrillard sees consumer culture as reducing everything and everyone within its purview to a commodity or sign of value, DeLillo struggles against this trend by following his own graffiti instinct and engaging in his own mode of "unrepetition." To this end, he refrains from presenting a simple solution to the problematic relationship between art and commodification. Instead, he explores this relationship from a number of perspectives. In so doing, DeLillo demonstrates that there can be no single or systematic approach to defending against consumerism and that such an approach would only, as Baudrillard intimates, reproduce the homogenizing logic of the very system it aims to dismantle. Moreover, where Baudrillard's focus on the relationship between the system and the masses does not allow for what Cook refers to as the fine distinctions necessary for analyzing the relationship between individuals and the mass media, DeLillo's attention to specific cases underscores the need for individuals—artists, in particular—to develop their own strategies for declaring human existence in the face of an otherwise-dehumanizing system. If the capacity to develop and deploy such strategies is the mark of the artist, then *Underworld* demands that we all live as artists in order to cultivate, each in our own way, the fragile "freshet of life" that separates us from the commodities that constitute our world.

CHAPTER 8

"SLOW, SPARE AND PAINFUL": BODY TIME AND OBJECT TIME IN *THE BODY ARTIST*

Shortly before *The Body Artist* draws to a close, DeLillo presents a review of *Body Time*, the performance piece for which protagonist Lauren Hartke has been preparing through much of the novel. The aim of the piece, the review explains, is to allow the audience "to feel time go by, viscerally, even painfully" (104). To this end, Lauren silently glides through a series of transformations that "begins with an ancient Japanese woman on a bare stage, gesturing in the stylized manner of Noh drama" and "ends seventy-five minutes later with a naked man, emaciated and aphasic, trying desperately to tell us something" (105). Exactly what this wordless "something" might be is the question at the heart of *The Body Artist* and a matter upon which Lauren comments within the review of *Body Time*: "Maybe the idea is to think of time differently...Stop time, or stretch it out, or open it up. Make a still life that's living, not painted. When time stops, so do we. We don't stop, we become stripped down, less self assured. I don't know" (107).

Like *The Body Artist* itself, *Body Time* is heavily invested in rethinking the notion of time in a way that "flies" its audience, like the naked figure of Lauren's performance piece, "out of one reality and into another" (108). As the title of Lauren's piece might suggest, this second reality is that of body time, an organic conception of time that stands in contrast to what Baudrillard describes as object time. Where body time passes in a "slow, spare and painful" manner that allows Lauren's audience to experience a visceral passage from one moment to the next, object time, according to Baudrillard, is not "a succession of natural moments in a cycle" but a "functional mechanism" that forces us to "live at the pace of objects, live to the rhythm of their ceaseless succession" (DeLillo, *Body Artist* 103–104; Baudrillard, *Consumer Society* 154, 25). Thus while experiencing time in as visceral a fashion as Lauren intends imposes a certain degree of discomfort upon the members of her audience, "flying" from a state of object time to a state of body time serves as an exercise with the potential to release one's perceptions of both time and the body from the objectifying strictures of consumer ideology.

By asserting an intimate link between time and the body, *Body Time* underscores the ways in which common perceptions of time— its division into measurable units, for example, or its division into a past present and future—are largely artificial. In so doing, Lauren's performance also calls into question that aspect of time which Baudrillard identifies in *Symbolic Exchange and Death* as a form of value that is "accumulated in the phantasm of death deferred" (146). Even those who do not believe in a personal eternity, Baudrillard notes, do, in fact, "believe in the infinity of time as they do in a species of capital of double-compound interest" (146). In other words, the passage of time as measured in artificial and largely arbitrary units allows interest to accumulate long after the capitalist's death, resulting in "the eternity of a productive system no longer familiar with the reversibility of gift-exchange, but instead with the irreversibility of quantitative growth" (146). By carrying Lauren's audience beyond the artificial demarcations consumer culture uses to its advantage with regard to time, however, *Body Time* halts the endless accumulation Baudrillard describes and effectuates what the theorist refers to throughout his body of work as ambivalence, or the incessant potential for the destruction of the illusion of value. As such, *Body Time* has the potential to inflict more damage to consumer ideology than such acts generally associated with terrorism as hostage taking, suicide bombing and murder.

In contrast to DeLillo's previous novel, *Underworld*, the narrative structure of *The Body Artist* is fairly straightforward: after the suicide of her husband, Lauren retreats to a rented vacation home where she discovers the mentally impaired man who inspires *Body Time*, the performance piece described shortly before the novel's conclusion. Discussing DeLillo's *Mao II* in *American Magic and Dread: Don DeLillo's Dialogue with Culture*, Mark Osteen notes that photographer Brita Nilsson's relationship with deceased author Bill Gray "seems to confirm the death of the old authorship and her resigned acceptance of a future given over to crowds of people and images. And yet it may also represent a glimmer of hope—if a compromised and ambiguous one—that authentic authorship and opposition are not dead" (210). Likewise, Lauren's relationship with her deceased husband—filmmaker Rey Robles—offers a similar hope; putting away the pages of the "bullshit autobiography" she had been helping Rey compile, Lauren begins a slow return to the medium for which she is best known, her own body. In so doing, Lauren continues the work of authorship and opposition begun by Nilsson at the conclusion of *Mao II*.

Where the photographer enacts what Osteen calls "oppositional authorship" through the interrogation and dilution of authoritarian power structures, the body artist does so by confronting the structure of time itself, particularly as it relates to her body. Indeed, that the review of *Body Time* included in the novel refers to Lauren's ability to "fly" her audience out of one reality into another echoes Hélène Cixous' call in "The Laugh of the Medusa" for all women to recognize their powers of flight in order to take pleasure in "dislocating things and values, breaking them all up, emptying structures, and turning propriety upside down" (344). Associating woman's power of flight with signification, Cixous locates both phenomena within the whole of the feminine body as opposed to the singularity of the phallus, in which man concentrates all of his anxieties as well as the power to signify.

Emphasizing the political dimension of Cixous' observation, Ann Rosalind Jones explains in "Writing the Body: Toward an Under-standing of *L'écriture Féminine*" that the immediacy with which the body is supposedly experienced by women, as described in the writings of such Feminist critics as Cixous, Julia Kristeva, and Luce Irigaray, "promises a clarity of perception and a vitality that can bring down mountains of phallocentric delusion. Finally, to the extent that the female body is seen as a direct source of female writing, a powerful alternative discourse seems possible: to write from the body is to recreate the world" (361). Jones, however, is quick to warn against the potential for mystifying that which makes women's writing a revolutionary alternative to writing that might be described as phallocentric. Women's writing, Jones explains, "will be more accessible to writers and readers alike if we recognize it as a conscious response to socioliterary realities, rather than accept it as an overflow of one woman's unmediated communication with her body" (367). In order to engage in such a conscious response, the woman writer must adopt two interdependent strategies: a critique of phallocentrism "in all the material and ideological forms it has taken," and a quest for "new representations of women's consciousness" (367–368). Calling on women to examine "the words, the syntax, the genres, the archaic and elitist attitudes toward language and representation that have limited women's self knowledge and expression during long centuries of patriarchy," Jones argues that a concerted attack on phallocentric modes of expression will erode the "sociosexual arrangements that keep us from our own potentials and from each other" (368).

Examining the ways in which consumerism keeps us from the potentials Jones describes, Baudrillard decries contemporary society in particular for rendering the body a network of signs organized around the fetishization of the phallus:

> The entire contemporary history of the body is the history of its demarcation, the network of marks and signs that have since covered it, divided it up, annihilated its difference and its radical ambivalence in order to organize it into a structural material for sign exchange, equal to the sphere of objects, to resolve its playful virtuality and its symbolic exchange (not to be confused with sexuality) into sexuality taken as a determining agency, a *phallic* agency entirely organized around the fetishization of the phallus as the general equivalent. (*Symbolic Exchange* 101)

Through a program of what Baudrillard terms "planned narcissism," consumer ideology reduces sexuality to a matter in which the fulfillment of desire "becomes negotiable in terms of signs and exchanged phallic values" (103). Just as capital represents for Baudrillard "the total system of exchange-value under the general equivalent of money," so too does the body represent a system of signs organized around the general equivalent of the phallus (111).

Given the analogy he draws between money and the phallus, it is not surprising that Baudrillard views contemporary attitudes toward sexuality as yet another set of symptoms related to consumer ideology's capacity for rendering objects of its adherents. Under the conditions Baudrillard describes, a woman must cover herself with phallic substitutes (rouged lips, for example, or the tight fitting bracelet around the arm or ankle) in order to answer society's summons "to produce a phallus from her own body, on pain of perhaps not being desirable" (110). In other words, society calls on the subject to become an object of desire as defined in relation to what Baudrillard terms the phallus exchange standard (116). Yet this standard is entirely arbitrary, an organizational model instituted by the "repressive politics of desublimation" as well as the tendency of contemporary psychoanalysis to "officialize" sex and the body (117). "Liberating" the body from the ambivalence of sexuality, psychoanalysis proffers the pleasure principle as a legitimate and positive rationale behind sexual subjectivity. The body organized around the pleasure principle, however, is highly prone to commodification insofar as it is bound up in what Baudrillard frequently describes as the vertiginous nature of consumerism: the liberated libido is always hungry, always consuming, always dissatisfied despite consumer ideology's insistence that satisfaction is not only plausible but the norm. Hence Baudrillard's call for a return to ambivalence, particularly in the realm of sexuality; if we recognize that the lack symbolized by the phallus will never be filled, we will abandon the phallus exchange standard espoused by consumerism in relation to sex, and, in so doing, begin to escape the vertiginous cycle of accumulation that is endemic to consumer ideology.

Where contemporary society organizes the body around the phallus exchange standard, archaic society views the entire body as a whole. For Baudrillard, this archaic understanding of the body is best exemplified by "the Indian's" attitude toward nudity:

> When the Indian...says 'everything is a face to me,' in response to the white man's questions as to why he is naked, he is saying that his entire body...is given over to symbolic exchange, while for us, nudity has a tendency to be reduced to a single face and a single look. For the Indian, bodies gaze at each other and exchange all their signs. These signs are consumed in an incessant relaying and refer neither to a transcendental law of value, nor to a private appropriation of the subject. (107)

Though not explicitly tied to the issue of gender, this "archaic" view of the body parallels that of Cixous, Jones, and other Feminist critics who seek nonphallocentric modes of expression insofar as divorcing the body form the phallus exchange standard allows for a mode of interpersonal exchange that is not bound up in anxiety over maintaining subjectivity through constant appropriation and reappropriation of the phallus. Rather than exchanging signs of greater or lesser phallic value in an effort to accumulate an irrational and ultimately meaningless excess of such signs, those bodies not bound by the phallus exchange standard become, in Baudrillard's words, "just like gods and women, material for symbolic exchange" (107).

In the absence of the phallus exchange standard, the entire body, rather than a fetishized network of signs representing the body, becomes the material for exchange. Such is the case with the mysterious Mr. Tuttle, who visits Lauren after the death of her husband in *The Body Artist*. Apparently mentally handicapped, Tuttle has no concept of the arbitrary demarcations that might otherwise divide his body; he "unbashfully" allows Lauren to bathe him, and as she does so, Lauren begins to "wordlessly" name and number "his parts for him" (68). Yet in this naming and numbering, Lauren does not divide Tuttle's body into arbitrary zones or organize his understanding of the body around his own phallus. Indeed, Lauren handles Tuttle's penis and testicles as easily as she handles the rest of his body, and as she traces "his nose and brows and the rim of his ear," Lauren marvels at the ways in which everything, to borrow a phrase from DeLillo's *Underworld*, is connected (68).

Not a child but "[no]t quite a man either," Tuttle falls "outside the easy sway of either/or" and inspires Lauren to reorganize (or perhaps de-organize) her body in anticipation of her next performance as a body artist (69). To this end, she embarks upon a regimen of exfoliation, depigmentation, haircutting, and bleaching that renders her "a blankness, a body slate erased of every past resemblance" (84). Consequently, Lauren begins to resemble "someone who is classically unseen, the person you are trained to look through, bled of familiar effect, a spook in the night static of every public toilet" (84). In other words, she begins to resemble Tuttle, whom Lauren later describes as "someone you could easily miss...someone you technically see but don't quite register in the usual interpretive way" (95).

One result of her transformation is that Lauren transcends the dichotomy of gender: as noted, *Body Time*, in which Lauren is the sole performer, begins with a Japanese woman on a bare stage and ends with a naked man standing alone on the same stage, "trying desperately to tell us something" (105). Moreover, Lauren's interviewer, Mariella Chapman, confesses that she can almost believe that Lauren is "equipped with male genitals" or "that she has trained her upper body to deflate and her lower body to sprout" (109). "At times she makes femaleness so mysterious and strong that it encompasses both sexes and a number of nameless states," Chapman further explains (109). Stated another way, Lauren's attempt to render her body "a blankness" allows her to transcend the fetishization of the phallus and divorce herself from what Baudrillard calls the phallus exchange standard; rather than making herself up to increase her phallic exchange value, she makes herself down, so to speak, thus rendering herself nonphallic. Immeasurable in terms of the phallus exchange standard, Lauren's sexuality ceases to function as a sign of phallic value. As a result, Lauren becomes, like Tuttle, "unseen," or at least invisible to the culture that would just as soon interpret all phenomena in terms of value. Or, in Baudrillard's terms, Lauren's body regains its radical ambivalence: it is not valued; it simply is.

In addition to inspiring Lauren to reconceptualize her body, Tuttle inspires her to rethink her understanding of time. Early in *The Body Artist*, Lauren views time as linear, as demonstrated by the novel's opening sentence: "Time seems to pass" (7). Echoing Bucky Wunderlick's observation in DeLillo's *Great Jones Street* that time can not only "seem to pass" but also "build, slowly gathering weight," the opening sentence of *The Body Artist* underscores Baudrillard's understanding of time as a form of value "accumulated in the phantasm of death deferred" (DeLillo, *Great Jones Street* 126; Baudrillard, *Symbolic Exchange* 146). Indeed, Lauren's impulse in the days following her husband's funeral to "organize time until she [can] live again" suggests that an orderly sense of time can hold death at bay (or, at the very least, distract one's attention from it) (DeLillo, *Body Artist* 37). At the same time, her awareness of her rental agreement's pending expiration points up the relationship Lauren intuitively draws between time and money (32). Additionally, Lauren's interest in a live-streaming video feed from the edge of a two-lane road in Kotka, Finland, demonstrates the degree of comfort she finds in linear time. Most interested in "the dead times," or those stretches during which no motion disrupts the scene, Lauren is constantly reminded of the passage of time by a digital display in the corner of the screen, which provides for her "a sense of organization" and allows her to believe that she sees Kotka "in its realness, in its hours, minutes and seconds" (38).

Lauren's estimation of the phenomenon notwithstanding, what she perceives as the natural passage of time is, on the contrary, an artificial construct. The screen thrives on the circumstance of nothing going on precisely because the "nothingness" heightens the screen's significance; what matters is not what is happening on the screen, but how the screen frames each moment. Juxtaposed with the "sense of organization" imposed by the "unyielding frame" of time, what Lauren perceives as "the fact of Kotka" ceases to be simple. Rather than depicting Kotka "in its realness," the clock in the corner of the computer screen reduces the town to an accumulation of the "hours minutes and seconds" Lauren so admires (38). Moreover, by imposing such arbitrary divisions on the two lane road in Kotka, the clock renders time the same measurable commodity upon which Lauren's rental agreement is based; that Lauren takes comfort in the fact that her husband is survived by "debts cascading on other debts" lends credence to Baudrillard's assertion that regardless of one's position on the existence of a personal eternity, one cannot deny the infinity of time as it applies to double-compound interest (94).

Unlike Lauren, however, Tuttle cannot conceive of time in linear terms. During their first conversation, he proves incapable of even distinguishing between past and future. "It rained very much," he says, speaking of an impending storm (44). Subsequently, Lauren emphasizes the distinction she sees between past and present when she explains to Tuttle that "[i]t did not rain. It *will* rain" (45). This distinction, however, is lost on Tuttle. As she continues to interrogate him, Lauren realizes that she hears "something at the edge" in his voice, something "unconnected to income levels or verb tenses or what his parents watch on TV" (50). Later, Lauren speculates that

> [m]aybe this man experiences another kind of reality where he
> is here and there, before and after, and he moves from one to
> the other shatteringly, in a state of collapse, minus an identity,
> a language, a way to enjoy the savor of the honey-coated toast
> she watches him eat.
>   She thought maybe he lived in a kind of time that had no
> narrative quality. (64–65)

While Lauren acknowledges that Tuttle's understanding of time
and language might render him incapable of savoring the taste of
honey, she also speculates that his mode of perceiving the world
around him allows Tuttle to exist in what she terms "the not as if
of things" (90). In other words, Tuttle's inability to recognize what
Lauren later comes to see as "arbitrary divisions" in time and space
grants him communion with something akin to a Lacanian Real—
existence beyond the arbitrary mediation of language. As Cornel
Bonca notes in "Being, Time and Death in DeLillo's *The Body Artist*," this perspective allows Tuttle to experience being and time neither "as awareness of individual, angst-provoking finitude" nor as
"a teleological leaning toward death...but transpersonally, as if he
were Being itself, mysteriously conscious of Its own pathos, pointing [Lauren's] way back to Being" (65). Nonetheless, the mysterious
consciousness Bonca describes presents a major obstacle in terms of
representation: the logical impasse of expressing through language
that which is beyond language—hence Lauren's attempt to convey
what she has learned from Tuttle not via the written or spoken word,
but through her own body.

Exploring the link between time and the body in "Women's Time,"
Kristeva argues that a woman's experience of "cycles, gestation" and
"the eternal recurrence of a biological rhythm" allows her to appreciate "the massive presence of a monumental temporality, without
cleavage or escape, which has so little to do with linear time (which
passes) that the very word 'temporality' hardly fits" (445). This observation corresponds with Lauren's intuition that Tuttle is a "walking
continuum" and that he senses time as a "continuous whole" (DeLillo,
Body Artist 91). Likewise, Lauren realizes that, as with his body,

Tuttle is incapable of "making arbitrary divisions" in time (91). That she comes to this realization while performing exercises in preparation for her as-yet-unnamed performance piece forces Lauren to consider the relationship between time and her own body. On one hand, Lauren insists to herself that she is "made out of time," that time "is the only narrative that matters," and that it "stretches events and makes it possible for us to suffer and come out of it and to see death happen and come out of it" (92). Yet on the other hand, Lauren recognizes that Tuttle exists "in another structure, another culture, where time is something like itself, sheer and bare, empty of shelter" (92). While this sense of time may indeed be empty of shelter, that Lauren conceives of it as a function of Tuttle's alien culture suggests that her own sense of time may itself be a cultural myth, thus underscoring Kristeva's point. If linear time, "which passes," is only one form of time, then the opening sentence of *The Body Artist* holds especially true in that while time "seems to pass," it can also stand still or operate in cycles, as Lauren demonstrates in *Body Time*.

Against a video backdrop displaying the two-lane highway in Kotka, Finland, Lauren adopts several identities over the course of her performance, including that of a "woman in executive attire, carrying a briefcase, who checks her wristwatch and tries to hail a cab" (106). Repeating this action "countless times" while the mechanical voice of a telephone answering machine plays relentlessly over the sound system, Lauren juxtaposes cyclic time with linear time (106). As Chapman notes in her review of the piece, this juxtaposition can have one of two effects on members of the audience: either a sense of feeling "mentally suspended" or one of frustration in which the individual might cast a glance at her own watch and "go slouching down the aisle and into the night" (106). Yet those who resist the urge to glance at their own watches—that is, the urge to retreat from the monumental slowness and repetition of *Body Time* in favor of the sheltering comfort of linear time—come to a "stripped down, less self-assured" sense of time that is akin to that experienced in "dreams or high fevers" or when "doped up or depressed" (107). While such states may be less than ideal for engaging in such practical activities as hailing taxi cabs, they do, as Chapman points out, allow for a blurring of past and future (107). Moreover, Chapman observes that this sense of time is intimately linked to language, as demonstrated when Lauren transforms herself into a naked man who is "stripped of recognizable language and culture" (107). As with time throughout the piece, language fails to provide a comfortable context for the naked man's existence as his verbs and pronouns "scatter in the air" and he begins to convulse (107). Yet this unsettling sense of time and language is also what allows the naked man—and, by extension, Lauren's audience—to fly "out of one reality and into another" in which distinctions between past, present, and future hold no sway (107).

Like *Body Time*, Kristeva's "Women's Time" not only draws a connection between time and the body, but also extends this connection to language. According to Kristeva, female subjectivity poses a problem "with respect to a certain conception of time: time as project, teleology, linear and prospective unfolding; time as departure, progression and arrival—in other words, the time of history" (446). Such a linear conception of time, Kristeva adds, "renders explicit a rupture, an expectation, or an anguish which other temporalities work to conceal" (446). This expectation or anguish centers on the imminence of death and is reflected in the structure of linear time in the enunciation of the sentence: "noun + verb; topic—comment; beginning—ending" (446). Yet for Baudrillard, what makes this enunciation so remarkable is that it separates life and death even as it underscores the imminence of the latter; in *Symbolic Exchange and Death* he argues that much of Western culture exists to "dissociate life and death, to ward off the ambivalence of death in the interest of life as value, and time as the general equivalent" (147). Early cultures, according to Baudrillard, allowed life and death to exist concurrently in a "collective theatre of death" in which death was "not yet buried in individual consciousness" but an integral part of lived experience (146). In modern times, however, death is not an immediate presence; rather, death is deferred.

No other culture, Baudrillard notes, has held a "distinctive opposition of life and death in the interests of life as positivity: life as accumulation, death as due payment" (147). Moreover,

[n]o other culture has had this impasse: as soon as the *ambivalence* of life and death and the symbolic reversibility of death comes to an end, we enter into a process of accumulation of life as value; but by the same token, we also enter the field of the *equivalent* production of death. So life-become-value is constantly *perverted* by the equivalent of death. Death, at the same instant, becomes the object of perverse desire. Desire invests the very separation of life and death. (147)

In other words, life and death are no longer concurrent social phenomena but separate phenomena experienced individually; whereas society as a whole can experience life and death simultaneously insofar as both states permeate the aggregate, the individual can only experience life, and then death. Thus when Baudrillard speaks of the "ambivalence" of life and death, he is referring to the way in which both states strike a concurrent balance—an impossibility within the structure of linear time as reflected in the enunciation of the sentence as described by Kristeva.

According to Baudrillard, when ambivalence ceases to function, death becomes deferred, and the "balance" must be paid upon dying. As a result, the individual "accumulates" life while alive and "cashes in" at death, to borrow a popular phrase. Death, then, becomes the general equivalent *against* which life is measured, and time the general equivalent *by* which life is measured. Thus, Lauren's desire to "organize time until she [can] live again" in the days following Rey's suicide can be seen as an attempt at distancing herself from death in that by dividing time into increasingly smaller units, she can tender the illusion of deferring death infinitely and, in so doing, seemingly add to the value of her own life. Yet as Baudrillard might predict, Lauren's attempts at deferring death result in a desire for it.

Throughout the first days following Rey's funeral, Lauren is haunted by the memory of her deceased husband:

When she was downstairs she felt him in the rooms on the second floor. He used to prowl these rooms talking into a tiny tape recorder, smoke in his face, reciting ideas about some weary script to a writer somewhere whose name he could never recall. Now he was the smoke, Rey was, the thing in the air, vaporous, drifting into every space sooner or later, unshaped, but with a face that was somehow part of the presence, specific to the prowling man...

She stepped slowly through the rooms. She felt him behind her when she was getting undressed, standing barefoot on the cold floor, throwing off a grubby sweater, and she half turned toward the bed. (32, 33)

Here, Lauren's relationship to Rey's death lacks what Baudrillard refers to as "symbolic reversibility" (*Symbolic Exchange* 147). That is, because life and death exist as separate rather than concurrent phenomena within contemporary Western culture, no interplay can occur between them. As a result, Lauren can only conceive of her husband as having ceased to exist in one state and having entered another, which is inaccessible except through her own death—hence Lauren's desire to "disappear in Rey's smoke, be dead, be him" (DeLillo, *Body Artist* 34). Unlike Lauren, however, Tuttle is apparently unable to recognize the division between life and death and can, as a result, commune with the dead. Shortly before his exit from the novel, Tuttle executes a word-for-word recitation of Lauren's last conversation with Rey (86). Which is not to say that Tuttle is remembering the conversation but bearing witness to it. Watching him "struggle in his utterance," Lauren realizes that Tuttle is "only reporting, helplessly," what he hears "in his refracted time" (87). While Rey is not, as Lauren initially wants to believe, "alive now in this man's mind, in his mouth and body and cock," he is no less present for Tuttle because Tuttle cannot make what Lauren sees as such "arbitrary divisions" as "this from that, now from then," or even life from death (87, 91).

For Baudrillard, Western culture's propensity for recognizing the so-called arbitrary divisions that demarcate time and the body as they separate life from death stems from our mode of language—that is, signification. In *For a Critique of the Political Economy of the Sign*, Baudrillard argues that the logic of signification provides the structure for an all-encompassing system of communication that reduces everything (and everyone) to a commodity by grounding all forms of exchange in the seemingly rational circulation of value (147). Because the structure of the sign as defined by Ferdinand de Saussure is "at the heart" of the structure of the commodity form as defined by Karl Marx, the commodity itself has become the *"system of communication* administering all social exchange" (146, Baudrillard's emphasis). Likewise, because value is the concept at the heart of the commodity, value becomes the myth that governs the exchange of signs within Western culture. Thus, Baudrillard argues, the logic of signification names everything in terms of the code of value that regulates political economy (147).

The code of value Baudrillard describes, moreover, may be what Lauren has in mind when she realizes that what is missing when Tuttle speaks is "a code in the simplest conversation that tells the speakers what's going on outside the bare acoustics" (DeLillo, *Body Artist* 65). This, however, is not to say that Tuttle is incapable of meaningful exchange. Although he cannot signify, Tuttle is capable of engaging in what Baudrillard terms symbolic exchange, which is exchange predicated on loss. The "meaning" of what Tuttle says does not depend upon a final relation of value between a sign and its referent (as in the case of signification) but upon the continued giving and countergiving of the terms in play among those engaged in the act of exchange. For example, when Lauren speculates that Tuttle might speak a language different from her own, she instructs him to "say some words" (55). In response, Tuttle parrots the phrase back to her: "Say some words" (55). In so doing, Tuttle demonstrates that while he does not speak another language, he does use language in a unique way. For him, the purpose of speaking is not to convey information but to present each word as a kind of gift. Accordingly, after one seemingly nonsensical exchange, Tuttle is described as "not pleased exactly, but otherwise satisfied" with what he has said, whereas Lauren pores laboriously over his words, frustrated that she cannot glean meaning from them (48). That is, Lauren wants Tuttle's words to operate as a kind of currency in an economy of signification in which words are "invested" with meaning and yield a "wealth" of information.

In Baudrillard's terms, Lauren wants Tuttle's words to operate according to a final relation of value among signs and referents; she wants them to signify. Practical and universally accepted within Western culture as signification may be, however, it does not always yield meaning. Throughout the first chapter of *The Body Artist*, Lauren and Rey's final conversation is particularly vapid, a fact underlined by Lauren's eventual regret that her last words to Rey consisted of an exegesis of the Ajax toilet cleaner brand name (87). Such exchanges, she later realizes, amount less to genuine communication than to a kind of jockeying for social position: "You don't know how to love the ones you love until after they disappear. Then you understand how thinly distanced your were from their suffering, how sparing of self you often were, how rarely unguarded of heart, working your networks of give and take" (116).

In contrast to the mode of communication shared by Lauren and Rey, Tuttle's mode of communication—symbolic exchange—does not allow its participants to be sparing of self. As a result, Lauren cannot distance herself from Tuttle's suffering; she must confront it head-on. One night, for example, she stands outside Tuttle's room and listens to him whimper. Though Lauren initially denies knowing how to interpret these whimpers, she immediately reverses her position: "Of course she knew. He had no protective surface. He was alone and unable to improvise, make himself up. She went to the bed and sat there, offering touches and calming sounds, softenings of the night" (90). Living in what Lauren thinks of as "the not-as-if of things," Tuttle is incapable of metaphor, and thus incapable of signification. Although his inability to signify means that Lauren will never know for sure whether what she "knows" about the workings of Tuttle's mind is true, his whimpering, like much of his seemingly nonsensical babble, engenders a greater sense of intimacy between himself and Lauren than exists between Rey and Lauren throughout the conversations depicted earlier in the novel.

Lacking a final relation to value, Tuttle's mode of language remains completely alien to Lauren through much of the novel, a fact that is, again, intimately linked with his sense of time and death. One reason Lauren cannot understand Tuttle is that their discussions have no "time sense" and lack "all reference at the unspoken level, the things a man speaking Dutch might share with a man speaking Chinese" (66). More to the point, Lauren realizes,

> [t]here is nothing he can do to imagine time existing in reassuring sequence, passing, flowing, happening—the world happens, it has to, we feel it—with names and dates and distinctions.
>
> His future is unnamed. It is simultaneous, somehow, with the present. Neither happens before or after the other, and they are equally accessible, if only in his mind. (77)

In fact, Baudrillard might argue, it is precisely *because* Tuttle's future is unnamed that it is simultaneous with his present; as with life and death, he can appreciate the bar that separates past from present no more than he can take advantage of the one that stands between signifier and signified within the structure of the sign.

Ultimately, then, Lauren's preparations for *Body Time* amount to an extended self-tutorial in Tuttle's mode of expression. As she becomes better versed in this new mode of expression, her attitude toward language changes. Early in the novel, Lauren can lose herself in the "strange contained reality" of the printed page and deems the newspaper a particularly satisfying means of communication; looking at the page and distinguishing "one line from another," she imagines herself capable of having conversations with people "halfway around the world, who speak another language" (19). These conversations, however, take place at the expense of Lauren's involvement with her immediate environment. Wile reading the paper, she forgets to taste her food and, more poignantly, only occasionally looks up to see the half glass of juice in her husband's hand (19). In contrast to her earlier view of language, however, her experience with Tuttle causes Lauren to lose all interest in newspapers and the people she might "meet" on the printed page. Upon looking at the front page of a newspaper in town, she realizes that what it offers is not true intimacy with anyone but "another framework altogether, a slick hysteria of picture and ink, the world so fleetingly easy to love and hate, so reliable and forgettable in its recipes and wars and typographical errors" (115). Turning away from the signifying force of the printed page, Lauren begins to think less in terms of signs than "motive forms" and "faces," and, in effect, enters the "not-as-if" world inhabited by Tuttle (117).

Within this "not-as-if" world, Lauren becomes increasingly less engaged in separating life from death. Whereas her initial strategy for dealing with the suicide of her husband is to organize time and thus, according to Baudrillard's model, render life and death mutually exclusive phenomena, Lauren's post-*Body Time* strategy is to invite death into her life. In one instance, she holds the nozzle of a spray gun to her head and imitates her husband's suicide (114). In another, she wonders, pointedly, "Why not sink into it? Let death bring you down. Give death its sway" (116). Although this line of reasoning is suggestive of suicide, Lauren is less interested in ending her own life in this passage than allowing Rey's death to bring her "into some scandal of garment rending grief" (116). "Why should you accommodate his death?" she asks; "Or surrender to it in thin-lipped tasteful bereavement? Why give up if you can walk along the hall and find a way to place him within reach?" (116). Or, in Baudrillard's terms, why not seek the symbolic reversal of death? As if in response to these questions, Lauren moves through the halls of her vacation home feeling "exposed, open, something you could call unlayered" as she refuses to "yield to the limits of belief" (121, 122). Pausing before the bedroom she once shared with Rey, Lauren imagines that once she steps inside, "she will already have been there, at night, getting undressed" (122). Her husband is sitting on the bed, we are told, and Lauren feels "two real bodies" in the room (122). Dismissing this perception as one of false anticipation, however, Lauren nearly decides not to enter the room at all because doing so would be "pathetic" (123). Her change of heart, however, suggests that Lauren's perception of two real bodies may not have been entirely imagined, and the room's emptiness affords her the opportunity to confront

Rey's death in an ambivalent fashion: because he is both a real body to Lauren in the collapsed time of Tuttle's world and absent in "real" time, Lauren experiences his life and death simultaneously.

Yet Tuttle's mode of exchange is no substitute for sign exchange, particularly for the purposes of conveying information. Although Lauren's exchanges with Tuttle might be described as meaningful insofar as they encourage a social relation beyond value and engender in Lauren a greater appreciation for the "not-as-if of things," they also prove frustrating in that Lauren can never find a single, sensible message among Tuttle's words. Moreover, as Lauren slips more deeply into the "not-as-if of things" following Tuttle's disappearance, she begins to dissolve: "I am Lauren," she realizes late in the novel, "[b]ut less and less" (117). Beyond the realm of signification, she lacks both the capacity and the desire to make the kinds of demarcations that would otherwise allow her personality to remain intact. What prevents Lauren from dissolving entirely, however, is finding herself in a situation in which she is forced to signify.

Confronted by her landlord, Lauren must accurately "read the situation, fix its limits," and in so doing begins the work of redrawing the boundaries that have begun to fade from her perception of reality (117). As the landlord explains that the house still belongs to him, Lauren begins to feel as if she is "fitting into something, becoming comfortable out here, in the driveway, with the owner of the house" (118). Although Lauren eventually withdraws from the conversation, the fact that it takes place at all is significant in that it demonstrates that she is capable of what might be considered "code-switching" between symbolic and sign exchange. Equally adept at both modes of language, Lauren has the power to withhold the "gift" of signification, which places the landlord in the frustrating position of interpreting her silence. At the same time, however, the power to signify allows Lauren to reassert her identity and fix the limits of her being. Rather than depicting her slow dissolution into the "not-as-if of things," the novel concludes with Lauren standing by an open window, wanting to feel "the sea tang on her face and the flow of time in her body, to tell her who she was" (124).

Time no longer "seems to pass" in the novel's final passage; it does, in fact, pass. And in so passing, time allows Lauren to recognize her own identity in terms of mortality rather than a final relation to value. In other words, Lauren is no longer beholden to the mechanistic order of what Baudrillard terms object time, but is instead open to a more visceral experience of time's passage—that of what she herself calls body time and Kristeva considers women's time. Thus while DeLillo may not, strictly speaking, be considered a Feminist author, many issues he raises in *The Body Artist* resonate strongly with those of such clearly Feminist theorists as Cixous, Irigaray, Jones, and Kristeva. Indeed, *The Body Artist* in many ways answers Kristeva's call in "Women's Time" for an attempt "to break the code, to shatter the language, to find a specific discourse closer to the body and emotions" (451–452). Such efforts, Kristeva argues, are akin to acts of terror in that they can lead us to deadly violence, cultural innovation, or "both at once" (452). The violence to which Kristeva refers, moreover, is largely violence against the ideological underpinnings of Western culture, and its ultimate end is not simply to destroy that culture but "to nourish our societies with a more flexible and free discourse, one able to name what has thus far never been an object of circulation in the community: the enigmas of the body, the dreams, secret joys, shames, hatreds of the second sex" (457). Engendering such a free and flexible discourse is as much DeLillo's project in *The Body Artist* as it is Lauren's project in *Body Time*. By rethinking the relationships among time, the body, death, and language, DeLillo, like Lauren, engages in the slow, spare, and painful work that many (as in the case of Lauren's fickle audience) may lack the patience to endure, but whose stakes, to borrow a phrase from Kristeva, "are of epochal significance" (452).

CONCLUSION

AN ELEMENT OF DOUBT:
COSMOPOLIS AND THE
SPECTER OF AMBIVALENCE

In an unfavorable review of *Cosmopolis*, Michiko Kakutani writes that the novel amounts to the story of a "comic-strip capitalist pig" whose cross-town trip to the barber "turns out to be a long day's journey into tedium" that is marred by flat, tired dialogue and "the sort of rote recitation of status items found in 'Lifestyles of the Rich and Famous' " (Kakutani E-10). What this review fails to recognize, however, is that Eric Packer, the novel's protagonist, is keenly aware of the flat and tired nature of his own lifestyle and is in many ways desperate to escape the tedious comfort of the status items that constitute his universe. In his anxious effort to experience even a hint of life amidst the deadening landscape of "smart spaces built on beams of light," Eric voluntarily submits to a blast from his bodyguard's stun gun, shoots himself in the hand with a revolver and revels in the knowledge that a clandestine aggressor poses a credible threat to his life (102).

A chronic insomniac, Eric seeks out pain and death in order to remind himself that he is alive. At the same time, however, Eric's role as a billionaire asset manager and currency trader gives him every reason to support the very system that is the source of his ennui. Moreover, the tension inherent in Eric's desire to both maintain and escape his lifeless lifestyle drives *Cosmopolis* forward as it gives rise to an ambivalence that struggles to find expression throughout the novel. As a steward of consumerism, Eric can only speak a language of upward mobility and financial gain, a language from which the notion of ambivalence is precluded insofar as the concept is inimical to the exclusively vertiginous nature of Eric's socioeconomic outlook. Yet as the lifeless system of mathematically generated economic models Eric so passionately admires tightens its apparent stranglehold on society, Eric's ambivalence begins to express itself violently, as does that of his assassin Richard Sheets (a.k.a. Benno Levin). In many ways, then, *Cosmopolis* demonstrates the point with which Baudrillard concludes *The Consumer Society*: the ambivalence that consumer ideology has long and systematically repressed will erupt violently and inevitably to tear asunder the "white Mass" of consumerism (196).

As with the majority of the author's works, the world DeLillo depicts in *Cosmopolis* bears many similarities to the world Baudrillard envisions throughout his *oeuvre*. The sole resident of a forty-eight-room penthouse triplex that overlooks Manhattan's East River, Eric's investment in such frivolously expensive commodities as a lap pool, a card parlor, a shark tank, and a borzoi pen solidly roots the young billionaire in the system of objects Baudrillard describes in his first major work. Moreover, the "self-haunted and synthetic" nature of his existence reinforces the notion that in an effort to accumulate and arrange commodities in a way that reflects his continuing advances in social status, Eric has himself become a commodity within a self-contained constellation of objects that insulates him from meaningful interaction with the outside world (6). Further insulating Eric within a self-contained reality is the limousine he appreciates for being "not only oversized but aggressively so, metastasizingly so, a tremendous mutant thing that [stands] astride every argument against it" (10). Within this limousine, Eric monitors world events by watching an array of visual display units that offer him "medleys of data," "flowing symbols," "alpine charts," and "polychrome numbers pulsing" (13). While all of this data appears on one level to be contingent upon world events, Eric also knows that world events are contingent upon the decisions he makes using the "ratios, indexes, whole maps of information" at his disposal (14). A self-proclaimed visionary, Eric can only agree with an advisor who notes that his role in society is to "acquire information and turn it into something stupendous and awful" (19). In other words, Eric examines economic models in order to influence world economies in a way that will improve his financial prospects as reflected in the economic models he examines. Eric's reliance on models places him in what Baudrillard describes as a state of hyperreality, or a closed system of signs that protects itself "from the referential and the anxiety of the referential, as well as from all metalanguage" by "operating its own metalanguage, that is, by duplicating itself as its own critique" (*Symbolic Exchange* 74).

As if to demonstrate the degree to which Eric has been absorbed into the model world of charts, graphs, and information to which he continually looks for guidance, the video monitors in his limousine appear to predict his every move, as when he realizes that he has placed his thumb on his chin full seconds after seeing himself perform the same action onscreen (DeLillo, *Cosmopolis* 22). More ominously, Eric also watches his own death and interment in the video display built into his wristwatch shortly before he is murdered (206). As with the models Eric uses to predict the ebb and flow of world currencies, the computer-generated images that haunt the billionaire throughout the novel suggest that the "reality" in which he lives amounts to what Baudrillard refers to as a third-order simulacrum, or a model based upon other models rather than upon reality.

Confirming Baudrillard's theory that the rapid growth of capitalism (and, in turn, consumerism) has ushered Western culture into a hyperreal state of third-order simulation, Eric's "chief of theory," Vija Kinski, warns Eric that he is "dealing with a system that's out of control. Hysteria at high speeds, day to day, minute to minute" (85). People who live in seemingly "free" societies, Vija continues, do not have to fear "the pathology of the state" because they create their own frenzies and mass convulsions as they allow themselves to be "driven by thinking machines that [they] have no final authority over" (85). For Vija, even the protestors who rock Eric's limousine while she tries to sip vodka are part of the system she envisions. The protestors are themselves an element of the free market economy, she explains: "These people are a fantasy generated by the market. They don't exist outside the market. There is nowhere they can go to be on the outside. There is no outside" (90). Yet as Eric begins to accept that a "shadow of transaction" does, as Vija intimates, exist "between the protestors and the state" and that "the market culture's innovative brilliance" is the power to "shape itself to its own flexible needs, absorbing everything around it," one of the protestors immolates himself and, in so doing, shakes Eric's faith in the system (99). The market cannot absorb or assimilate the starkness and horror of self-immolation, Eric tells Vija, who brushes off his protest with the observation that the act they have both witnessed is "not original" but an "appropriation" of an act that has already been repeated "endlessly" by "Vietnamese monks, one after another, in all their lotus positions" (100).

On one hand, Eric's horror at the sight of the burning man is in line with Baudrillard's position in *Symbolic Exchange and Death* that a suicidal act of protest can amount to defying the system "*with a gift to which it cannot respond save by its own collapsed and death,*" and that the system must "*commit suicide in response to the multiplied challenge of death and suicide*" in order to save face (37, Baudrillard's emphasis). Vija's cold response to the self-immolation, on the other hand, resonates with Baudrillard's assertion in *The Spirit of Terrorism* that if terrorists merely use their own deaths to combat the system, they will "disappear...in a useless sacrifice" (21). Indeed, the uselessness of the burning man's sacrifice becomes especially apparent when an ambulance crew removes his charred body and Eric, having regained his composure, persists in his quest for a haircut

(DeLillo, *Cosmopolis* 103). The hustle and bustle of the world at large continues despite the protestor's apparent death, Vija explains, because the "creed of the new culture" is that people "will not die;" rather, they will "be absorbed in streams of information" (104).

Rather than comforting Eric, Vija's assurance that the "new culture" has conquered death leaves Eric feeling cold and isolated; try as he might, Eric cannot fathom connecting to his chief of theory on a human level. Vija's eyes are described as "unrevealing," "remote," and "unalive" to Eric, and he pointedly wonders where the theorist's life is as she holds forth on the topic of microchips so small and powerful as to allow humans and computers to merge (104–105). Evoking the Cheshire cat of Lewis Carroll's *Alice's Adventures in Wonderland*, DeLillo describes Vija as a "voice with a body as afterthought, a wry smile that sail[s] through heavy traffic" (105). As Mark Osteen notes in his discussion of "Moholean relativity" in DeLillo's *Ratner's Star*, Carroll's Cheshire cat speaks of a self-contained reality in which everybody is mad, or, in the context of DeLillo's novel, "a realm of dreams that constantly change according to the dreamer's needs or desires" (Osteen 78). These are also the conditions of the reality Vija describes, a reality in which Eric's needs are always anticipated and met by the economic system in which he places his faith and through which the young billionaire can only spiral ever more deeply into self-absorption and alienation from the world at large.

Ensconced in his self-contained world, Eric is unable to make meaningful connections with the people around him. Although he tries to imagine spending an intimate evening alone with Vija, Eric knows that she is no more than an employee (DeLillo, *Cosmopolis* 104). Likewise, "his wife of twenty-two days, Elise Shifrin, a poet who [has] right of blood to the fabulous Shifrin banking fortune of Europe and the world" remains a stranger to Eric throughout the novel; Eric barely recognizes Elise whenever he sees her, and Elise spends the greater part of their time together blocking Eric's sexual advances (15). Beyond the sexual realm, Eric's most constant companion is his chief of security, Torval, who refuses to speak Eric's name throughout the novel, and whom Eric shoots on a whim (146). In fact, Eric arguably comes closest to engaging in intimate conversation when he discusses the shape of his prostate with his assassin, a conversation which produces in Eric "a sense of warmth, of human involvement" that goes unmatched throughout the novel (199). Too guarded in every sense of the word, Eric distances himself from the people who populate his world; his mode of conversation is generally cold and calculating, and it amounts to nothing more than the kind of clever, competitive banter that characterizes many of the conversations depicted throughout DeLillo's novels. Yet where Lyle Wynant might turn to terrorism to escape the deadening effect of such talk in *Players* or Klara Sax might turn to art for the same purpose in *Underworld*, neither alternative proves viable for Eric. Just as the protestors who rock Eric's limousine are an element of the market they ostensibly seek to overthrow, so too is art, in Eric's eyes, a mere, if particularly valuable, commodity.

Confirming Baudrillard's observation in *The Consumer Society* that our "generalized neo culture" sees no difference "between a delicatessen and an art gallery," Eric counters his art dealer's suggestion that he buy "an important Rothko" with the demand that she acquire for him the entire Rothko Chapel, a place of worship and meditation inspired by the works of American abstract expressionist Mark Rothko (Baudrillard, *Consumer Society* 28; DeLillo, *Cosmopolis* 27). While Eric insists that the acquisition of the chapel will serve, like the twin elevators in his apartment building, as an undeniable sign of his ability to spend "major money" at will, his art dealer, Didi Fancher, insists that the power of art lies not so much in its price as in the sense of mystery art can evoke (29). "Don't you see yourself in every picture you love?" Didi asks; "You feel a radiance wash through you. It's something you can't analyze or speak about clearly. What are you doing at that moment? You're looking at a picture on a wall. That's all. But it makes you feel alive in the world. It tells you, yes, you're here. And yes, you have a range of being that's deeper and sweeter than you knew" (30).

In a word, the deeper, sweeter range of being that Didi mentions can be described as doubt: where Eric was once, according to the art dealer, a "commanding presence" whose "talent and drive" were constantly "put to good use," Didi now observes that "an element of doubt" has crept into his life (31). In other words, rather than adhering to consumer ideology's dictum to strive continually for more and greater signs of wealth, Eric has begun—in Didi's estimation, at least—to question both the value of unceasing upward mobility and the accuracy of the computer models that define his life. Yet despite Didi's admiration for Eric's burgeoning capacity to doubt and her insistence that doubting requires more courage than does faith, the young billionaire persists in what Didi refers to as his "crude" assessment of art—that it serves as nothing more than a sign of his ever-growing wealth within a purely rational and predictable economic system (33, 28).

Ostensibly beholden to "the zero-oneness of the world, the digital imperative that define[s] every breath of the planet's living billions," Eric initially denies that his faith in the system can ever be shaken on the grounds that "[t]here is no doubt" and that "[n]obody doubts anymore" (24, 31). Reaffirming this sentiment when Eric admits to her that an element of doubt has, indeed, crept into his worldview, his chief of theory reprimands him for capitulating to the concept: "Doubt? What is doubt? You don't believe in doubt. You've told me this. Computer power eliminates doubt" (86). Yet while the purpose of Eric's computers is to eliminate doubt by charting an ideal world of ever-increasing economic returns, the computer's predictions can only come to fruition if Eric places all of his faith in the models it generates—that is, if he refuses to doubt. For Baudrillard, this solipsism is at the heart of hyperreality, which exercises social control by means of "prediction, simulation, programmed anticipation and indeterminate mutation," and in which every image, media message, and functional object serves as a test of one's compliance with the code of value that regulates consumer ideology (Baudrillard, *Symbolic Exchange* 60, 63). To doubt under such conditions is to undermine the authority of the models upon which hyperreality is based, and thus to undermine hyperreality itself. Hence Eric's hesitation to acquiesce to his doubts: if he fails to comply with the dictates of his computer-generated models, he will call the entire system upon which his fortune is built into question, and, in turn, both the system and his fortune will, he fears, collapse. Even as Eric attempts to repress whatever traces of doubt he may be experiencing, however, the disgruntled employee plotting his death cannot help but to allow his own sense of doubt to come roiling violently to the surface.

Writing under the *nom de guerre* Benno Levin, Eric's assassin, Richard, reveals in the "Confessions of Benno Levin" sections of the novel that he left a job as a professor of computer applications in a community college to "make [his] million" in the corporate world (DeLillo, *Cosmopolis* 56). Yet in the corporate world, Richard notes, his million was not immediately forthcoming, and his supervisors rendered him a disposable "minor technical element" in Eric's corporation (60). "I was generic labor to them," Richard explains; "And I accepted this. Then they let me go without notice or severance package. And I accepted this" (60). In these instances, Richard's unquestioning acceptance of his disposable nature suggests that, at least initially, he recognized the apparent sensibility of the decision to let him go: described by his employers as having "problems of normalcy," he was an ill-fitting cog in an otherwise smoothly running machine and as such did not contribute to the efficient execution of the corporation's directives.

What Richard's position assumes is that the corporation's directives and, more importantly, the economic system in which those directives function are perfectly reasonable. In other words, Richard's initial acceptance of his dismissal stems from the same faith in the system that once inspired him to make his million in corporate America, a faith in the twin possibilities of ever-increasing economic gains and infinite upward social mobility. Richard's faith in the system, however, is not as strong as Eric's. Where Richard describes Eric as being "always ahead, thinking past what is new," he sees himself as being susceptible to what he calls "*susto*, or soul loss," which fills him with doubt not only with regard to the system in which he once toiled so faithfully, but also with regard to himself (152). Indeed, Richard is so filled with doubt that even his plan to assassinate Eric—arguably his sole interest in post-corporate life—is riddled with uncertainty. "I'm ambivalent about killing him," Richard explains shortly before putting his plan into action; "Does this make me less interesting to you, or more?" (154).

That Richard characterizes himself as "ambivalent" about his plan to kill Eric is significant in that ambivalence is the term Baudrillard uses to denote the incessant potential for the destruction of the illusion of value that is at the heart of consumer ideology. Richard's ambivalence, however, is not a matter of choice. Rather, it stems from his inability to play by the rules of consumer culture. Describing this inability to Eric as the novel draws to a conclusion, Richard notes somewhat disjointedly, "I thought all these other people. I thought how did they get to be who they are. It's banks and car parks. It's airline tickets in their computers...I'm helpless in their system that makes no sense to me. You wanted me to be a helpless robot soldier but all I could be was helpless" (195).

Unable to participate in what Baudrillard terms "the White mass" of consumer culture, Richard is markedly different from the protesters who appear earlier in the novel in that where the protestors counter the signs of global capitalism with signs touting the superiority of their own positions, Richard is incapable of proffering signs of any kind and thus occupies the space "outside the market" whose existence Vija denies (90). Hence the world Richard occupies is not the weightless landscape of "smart spaces built on beams of light" Eric envisions but one that embodies a "practical life of starting over" in a condemned building with only an iron writing desk and a defective exercise bike to call his own (102, 58). From this position, Richard can do what the protestors cannot: deny the legitimacy of value and thus undermine the entire system within which the protesters and the forces of advanced global capitalism do battle to no apparent end. If, as Baudrillard argues in *Symbolic Exchange and Death*, the system will never fall to a "direct, dialectical revolution of the economic or political infrastructure" because everything produced within the system "will only feed back into the mechanism and give it impetus, following a circular distortion similar to a Moebius strip," only someone like Richard, who has been barred from the system, can bring about its demise (36). Or, more accurately, only someone like Richard can give voice to the ambivalence that will undermine the system's authority.

As noted, Richard does not come about his sense of ambivalence by choice but by chance. On one hand, this fact suggests an answer to the issue of Baudrillard's apparent failure to present either a theory of the subject as an agent of social change or a theory of class or group revolt, which Douglas Kellner raises in *Jean Baudrillard: From Marxism to Postmodernism and Beyond* (18). In Richard's case, ambivalence is not an attitude to be cultivated by the individual but one that occurs naturally, an attitude to which a minority are prone while the vast majority are not. From this perspective, those who lack the ability to manipulate the signs that constitute the consumer landscape will be the first to acknowledge, in Baudrillard's words, "that the Object is nothing and that behind it stands the tangled void of human relations," and therefore will also be the first to instigate the "violent irruptions and sudden disintegrations" the theorist predicts (Baudrillard, *Consumer Society* 196). On the other hand, this perspective ignores the potential for those who are capable of manipulating signs to decline from doing so. After all, Eric's decision to repress his doubts is exactly that—a decision. Moreover, that his art dealer encourages Eric to succumb to his sense of doubt suggests that doing so may already be a decision that she has made for herself, and that in so doing, she has allowed herself to be "receptive to the mysteries" of life beyond consumerism despite having "learned how to make money and spend it" (30, 29). Ultimately, then, it is Eric's decision to place all of his faith in the market, to believe in "the game," that locks him in the vertiginous grip of consumerism and also seals his doom. This decision, however, is not one Eric makes alone and (given the vast numbers who make the same decision and, in so doing, legitimize consumer ideology) is, in many ways, the most rational decision to make.

As Barry Schwartz explains in *The Paradox of Choice: Why More is Less*, the decision to run in the "rat race" and pursue consumer goods is akin to being in a crowded football stadium and trying to watch an important play: "A spectator several rows in front stands up to get a better view, and a chain reaction follows. Soon everyone is standing just to see as well as before. Everyone is on their feet rather than sitting, but no one's position has improved. And if someone, unilaterally and resolutely, refuses to stand, he might just as well not be at the game at all" (194). Likewise, for Eric to doubt the legitimacy of his virtual world would put him out of the game and relegate him to the same position of social irrelevance that Richard occupies. Yet his failure to doubt is also what leads Eric to his doom. As DeLillo points out in an April 2003 interview with Paul Gediman, *Cosmopolis* is set in a time when capital markets were surging, multinational corporations seemed more influential than governments, the Dow kept climbing, the Internet kept getting swifter and more inclusive, and ordinary people entertained dreams of individual wealth (Gediman 9). At the same time, however, DeLillo notes that all of the phenomena he describes "began to end (as it does in the novel) in the spring of the year 2000" (9). In other words, although *Cosmopolis* depicts a culture that perfectly mirrors the vertiginous and hyperreal world that Baudrillard has described throughout his career, it also depicts the collapse of that world—not the total collapse, to be sure, but at least a significant deflation of its sovereignty.

Riding through the streets of Manhattan in a stretch limousine mere hours before his death, Eric sees an electronic billboard announce that "A SPECTER IS HAUNTING THE WORLD—THE SPECTER OF CAPITALISM" and immediately recognizes the statement as a "variation on the famous first sentence of *The Communist Manifesto* in which Europe is haunted by the specter of communism" (96). Although he dismisses both statements out of hand, what Eric fails to consider is something DeLillo has insisted upon throughout his career: that a haunting is indeed occurring. For Eric, this haunting takes the form of a growing doubt in the computer-generated models that define his world—a doubt, moreover, that is brought violently to life in the person of his assassin. More than just a disgruntled employee, Richard is disgruntled with an entire system that he cannot, for the life of him, manipulate. Although the vast majority of individuals who populate Richard's world—and, if Baudrillard is to be believed, our world as well—have the blind faith and wherewithal to proffer and arrange empty signs in a way that signals their respective social positions in relation to each other, Richard cannot do so. Likewise, he cannot participate in the shared and voluntary illusion of infinite upward social mobility at the heart of that world and, as a result, cannot fathom an existence in which someone like Eric can go so far as to drive himself to "fail more, lose more, die more than others" in order to convert what might otherwise be perceived as losses into positive signs of his unceasing upward mobility.

In short, Richard's inherent lack of faith in the system results in an inability to participate in the increasingly vertiginous quest for more and greater signs of wealth that is endemic to consumer culture. Unable to accept the artificial delirium of constant social and financial gain that drives people like Eric ever forward, Richard experiences ambivalence, which is forbidden by the system insofar as it calls into doubt and thus undermines the ethic of infinite growth upon which the system is based. Forbidden and largely repressed though it is, however, ambivalence, as Baudrillard predicts and Richard demonstrates, will indeed erupt violently and inevitably into our virtual lives to tear asunder the fabric of consumerism. In this context, *Cosmopolis*—like many of DeLillo's novels—can be read as a warning: unlike Eric, we must allow ourselves to be "receptive to the mysteries" of life beyond the artificial confines of consumer culture, or, like Eric, we will realize too late that we are not only dead in the virtual world, but that our lives in "original space" are in jeopardy as well. What haunts the world, then, is neither the specter of Communism nor the specter of Capitalism but the growing specter of ambivalence. As DeLillo has insisted throughout his career, however, whether this ambivalence surfaces with the blunt violence of Richard's rage or, as in *The Names*, with an awestruck appreciation for "the nightmare of real things, the fallen wonder of the world" is entirely up to us (339).

CREATING A STRUCTURE OUT OF WILLFUL TRIVIA: *FALLING MAN* AND THE UNBEARABLE AMBIVALENCE OF BEING

In the opening pages of DeLillo's *Falling Man*, Keith Neudecker emerges from the destruction wrought by the terror attacks of September 11, 2001, as if waking from a dream. Dazed by the violence unfolding around him, he walks almost without purpose, unsure, at least on a conscious level, of where he is going. In this respect, he is very much like the Alzheimer's patient who, later in the novel, loses her bearings and wanders the streets of New York, "desperate, separated from everything" (93). As with the Alzheimer's patient whose disease strips her of all points of reference to the world with which she was once accustomed, the collapse of the World Trade

Center and the chaos that ensues ushers Keith into "a time and space of falling ash and near night" (3). And, again, as with the Alzheimer's patient, the change Keith experiences in relation to his world is not temporary but permanent: in the wake of the destruction he has witnessed, he can never return to the perceived position of safety and relative insulation from world events that his old life afforded him. To borrow a phrase from Slavoj Zizek, who himself borrows the phrase from the Wachowski brothers' film *The Matrix*, the destruction of the World Trade Center welcomes Keith and his fellow New Yorkers to "the desert of the real" (Zizek, *Welcome* 15). Yet even though Keith's emigration into the desert of the real provides him with the opportunity to interact with his world in a way that Baudrillard might term ambivalent—that is to say meaningful insofar as interaction within this context allows for the possibility of loss, of true give and take—the vulnerability and uncertainty inherent in his new worldview proves unbearable. As a result, Keith cannot help but reconstruct and retreat into his own version of the ideological framework from which he was so violently torn at the beginning of the novel—suggesting, in essence, that for all of the public rhetoric insisting that September 11 "changed everything," the world remains, at least from an ideological perspective, largely the same.

Ghosts of DeLillo's previous novels haunt *Falling Man*. Evoking shades of *The Names*, Keith's wife Lianne is editing a scholarly volume on ancient alphabets, and his son Justin speaks in a monosyllabic jargon that is reminiscent of Tap Axton's adoption of Ob in the earlier novel. In a nod to Jack Gladney of *White Noise*, Keith's mother-in-law Nina Bartos is a "So-and-So Professor of Such-and-Such" who attempts to "accommodate the true encroachments of age by making drama of them, giving herself a certain degree of ironic distance" (9–10). Then there is Falling Man, the performance artist for whom the novel is named and who, like Lauren Hartke of *The Body Artist*, uses his own body as a medium for drawing people out of the tedium of their daily lives. Most notable, however, are the Twin Towers of the World Trade Center—a looming presence through much of *Underworld*, now tragically reduced to rubble. Far from signaling a lack of imagination on DeLillo's part, the return of these tropes and figures signals the transfiguration of the novelist's psychic landscape. In *Falling Man*, we are no longer in the playful realm of speculation as we were in *White Noise* or, for that matter, the meticulously constructed but no less fantastic *Libra*; rather, we have crossed over into a desolate, shattered world where the worst nightmares of DeLillo's previous works have come to fruition. The "gestures of sodden collapse" that mark the innocent students in the opening paragraphs of *White Noise* have given way to the genuine article as "two women sobbing in their reverse march…both in running shorts, faces in collapse" move slowly through the wreckage in the corresponding passage of *Falling Man* (*White Noise* 3; *Falling Man* 4). In short, where *White Noise* et al. may well represent dress rehearsals for disaster, *Falling Man* serves as a cogent meditation on coping with the real thing.

The world lost to Keith in the collapse of the Twin Towers might best be described as hyperreal since it, like many of the worlds DeLillo describes throughout his *oeuvre*, is one in which signs and mathematical models precede reality—a world, we are told, of "routine stimulus" and "streaming forms of office discourse" (*Falling Man* 65). From Baudrillard's perspective, the hyperreality of this world stemmed from the binary structure of the towers (or "perfect parallelepipeds," as he describes them) in which Keith worked (Baudrillard, *Spirit* 43). Signifying "the end of any real reference," the perfect similitude of each tower to the other indicated that "architecture, like the system, was now merely a product of cloning, and of a changeless genetic code" (43–44). In other words, because the towers were shaped "in the pure computer image of banking and finance, (ac)countable and digital," they existed first and foremost as copies of each other and therefore underscored the fact that there was no "original" (45). Working within this environment, moreover, Keith lived according the logic of the system embodied by the towers. Less of a man than, in his mother-in-law's words, "an archetype," he served as "a model of dependability for his male friends, all the things a friend should be" (DeLillo, *Falling Man* 59). Like the towers themselves, in other words, Keith was the embodiment of a code, the prime example of what might be termed, in some circles, the ideal man. Given his strict adherence to this code, Keith lacked a capacity for intimacy and was thus, again in his mother-in-law's words, "sheer hell on women," a notion borne out by the "extended grimness" of his marriage to Lianne (59, 7). With the collapse of the towers, however, comes the collapse of the code they embodied, and Keith is consequently forced to adapt to the new world in which he finds himself.

As the hyperreal world embodied by the towers starts to unravel at the start of the novel, the real world begins to intrude. This fact emerges when Keith and one of his fellow survivors recall seeing a man "carrying a long iron implement, like something to pry open an elevator door" on their way out of the building (57). That neither can initially remember the name of this implement, which is later revealed to be a crowbar, suggests that it is completely alien to both Keith and Florence Givens, his fellow survivor. And naturally so, Baudrillard might argue, for in the realm of the hyperreal, utensils do not exist. That is, tools with true utility, tools that demonstrate a working relationship between humanity and the physical world, are superfluous in hyperreality because all that matters in hyperreality is the manipulation of signs (Baudrillard, *System of Objects* 86). In this context, the materialization of the initially unnamed crowbar can only portend imminent disaster for the system insofar as the very existence of the real-world need that the crowbar meets reveals the illusory and frivolous nature of everything the system has heretofore deemed significant. Along similar lines, the fact that neither Keith nor Florence can initially name the so-called "implement" demonstrates that, in a clear reversal of the logic that regulates hyperreality, its function comes first, and its name—which is to say its handle, or the linguistic sign by which it might easily be identified—is an afterthought. Hence the double-trauma of the moment: the survivors of the tragedy are in a state of utter shock, sitting among the rubble "like dreamers bleeding," not only because they have witnessed the physical destruction of the towers but also because the safe, self-contained, and artificial universe generated by the system in which they had placed all of their faith has ceased to matter (DeLillo, *Falling Man* 58).

As the shock of surviving the collapse of the towers begins to dissipate, Keith enjoys a temporary reprieve from the emptiness that marked his life prior to the terror attacks. In addition to the opportunity to reconcile with his wife and son, he also gains a greater appreciation for the minutia of the physical world around him and a more organic sense of the passage of time. Beginning to think "into the day, into the minute," Keith notices that such minor details as "how he licked his thumb and used it to lift a bread crumb off the plate and put it idly in his mouth" seem "clearer to the eye" than they did amidst the ceaseless rush of his former life (65). Regaining the "small lost strokes" of each passing day and minute, moreover, he experiences something highly akin to the sense of so-called "body time" that Lauren Hartke strives to generate throughout *The Body Artist*—that is, a stretched or opened-up sense of time that causes the subject to feel "stripped down, less self assured" (*Falling Man* 65; *Body Artist* 107). Likewise, Keith's new apprehension of time's passage is, much like Lauren's experience of body time, slow, spare, and, in many ways, painful insofar as it causes him to view his own life in an unfamiliar light that makes him feel "strange to himself" (*Falling Man* 65). Yet while Lauren's artistic predisposition all but forces her to seek out and embrace a similar sense of self-estrangement in *The Body Artist*, a yearning for the comfort Keith associates with the relative ignorance of his former life causes him to recoil from the discomfort of living so viscerally within his own skin. Without recourse to the code embodied by the towers, the code that had allowed him to live as an archetype rather than as a man, he is rendered vulnerable in his dealings with the world at large.

One way of reading Keith's newfound vulnerability is in terms laid out by Emmanuel Levinas in *Totality and Infinity*. In this work, Levinas argues that the only way to know whether we are "duped by morality" is by testing morality against the moral summons of the face-to-face relation (21). In this relation lies a state of being "more naked than nudity," in which both parties experience what Levinas describes as the morality of mutual obligation, as opposed to a morality based on an arbitrary and potentially illusory external code (199). In Levinas' words, "The face opens the primordial discourse whose first word is obligation" (199). For Keith, however, the absence of the arbitrary code that once regulated his life appears to be permanent, so whether or not that code ever "duped" him is, in his current state, a moot point. Perpetually "more naked than nudity," he has no choice but to conduct all business, both personal and otherwise, according to the primordial discourse of mutual obligation that Levinas describes. While this mode of discourse does, on one hand, allow Keith to establish an intimate relationship based upon open and guileless communication with Florence, it also presents him with the difficult proposition of explaining that relationship to Lianne—a proposition that, in Keith's estimation, represents both "the right thing to do" and a potentially bad idea insofar as it can lead either to "an understanding of clean and even proportions, long lasting, with a feeling of reciprocal love and trust" or to prompting Lianne to "get a steak knife and kill him" (161, 162). In any event, what is not an option for Keith regardless of whether he tells his wife about his affair with Florence is seeking an alibi in a specific code of behavior. He must, in other words, admit, if only to himself, that he acted of his own volition and not according to the dictates of an external and arbitrary code.

While the collapse of the system may indeed rob Keith of any recourse to an external code of conduct, his recollection of the poker games he enjoyed before the fall of the towers suggests that he has already experienced the kind of face-to-face primordial discourse that Levinas describes and that he has also participated in a small-scale collapse similar to that which has rattled his world. Recalling the "glazed frenzy" with which they played each hand, Keith remembers that he and his fellow card players were known to watch each other's eyes across the table and, in so doing, regress "to preliterate folkways" whenever they met for their regular game (97). As time passed, however, the players constructed arbitrary rules around the game, "creating a structure out of willful trivia" by voluntarily limiting their own options with regard to which varieties of poker they could play and forbidding any eating or drinking throughout the proceedings (98). When this structure proved too limiting, the players revolted against the very rules they had created, and, as Keith recalls, the system they had designed to maximize the purity of their dedication to the game "fell apart" (100). "Somebody got hungry and demanded food," we are told; "Somebody else pounded the table and said *Food food*. This became a chant that filled the room" (100). As a result of this chanting, moreover, "[t]hey rescinded the ban on food...Other prohibitions fell, banned words were reinstated. They bet and raised, ate and drank, and from that point on resumed playing such games as high-low, acey-deucy, Chicago, Omaha, Texas hold'em, anaconda and a couple of other deviant strains in poker's line of ancestry" (100).

That Keith recalls the sudden disintegration of the rules that he and his cohorts had developed as a return to the "wallow of wild-man poker" signifies that the game has come full-circle—evolving from a primordial face-to-face affair to one regulated by a set of strict rules before returning to a more-or-less unregulated version of the game. In this sense, the brief history that Keith recalls serves, on a microcosmic level, as a metaphor for the rise and fall of civilizations throughout history, not the least of which is his own. Significantly, then, what this brief history implies is that the demise of Keith's civilization and all of its attendant codes, prohibitions, and rituals arose not from without, but from within. Along these lines, Nina's lover, Martin, argues that the towers that symbolized the order of global capitalism were "built as fantasies of wealth and power that would one day become fantasies of destruction" (116). Hence, from Martin's perspective, the very construction of the towers amounted to a challenge on the part of the culture that built them—to wit: "Here it is, bring it down" (116). Adopting a similar position, Zizek describes video footage of the collapsing towers as being "reminiscent of the most breathtaking scenes in big catastrophe productions" and, in turn, argues that because the so-called "unthinkable which happened was the object of fantasy," America "got what it fantasized about" when the towers collapsed (*Welcome* 16). Likewise, Baudrillard notes that the "fact that we have dreamt of this event—that everyone without exception has dreamt of it" can be measured "by the emotive violence of all that has been said and written in the effort to dispel it" (*Spirit* 5). Distasteful as these assertions might, at first glance, appear, they nonetheless support the notion that just as Keith and his fellow poker players strained to the point of revolt against the limitations they imposed upon themselves, the terror attacks that shook the ideological underpinnings of Keith's world were suicidal in more ways than one.

On the most superficial level, the terror attacks of September 2001 were suicidal insofar as they involved the voluntary deaths of the perpetrators, but as Baudrillard opines, witnessing the destruction of the "global superpower" embodied by the World Trade Center was akin to "seeing it, in a sense, destroying itself, committing suicide in a blaze of glory" (4–5). "It has been said that 'Even God cannot declare war on himself,'" the theorist continues; "Well, He can. The West, in the position of God (divine omnipotence and absolute moral legitimacy), has become suicidal and declared war on itself" (7). While this assertion may seem questionable, particularly in light of the fact that the terrorists were not, strictly speaking, agents of Western ideology, Zizek helps to explain Baudrillard's reasoning when he points out that the totality of global capitalism "means that it is the dialectical unity of itself and of its other, of the forces which resist it on 'fundamentalist' grounds" (Zizek, *Welcome* 51). This notion, moreover, is borne out in *Falling Man* when Justin conflates Eastern and Western nomenclature by confusing "bin Laden" with the distinctly Anglophonic "Bill Lawton." Hoping to find "some important meaning" in their son's error, Keith and Lianne construct an image of a Bill Lawton who "has a long beard…wears a long robe…flies jet planes and speaks thirteen languages but not English except to his wives" (73–74). That this image is conjured in the context of a conversation in which Keith suggests that Lianne would do well to remember not just the "blood and pain" of bearing her own child but that a rival of hers has also experienced the same pain points to the significance of Justin's error: despite their apparent antipathy, the East and West are, as Zizek intimates, caught up in the same struggle and, as such, suffer as one.

While Lianne's initial impulse is to objectify non-Westerners as "the ones who think alike, talk alike, eat the same food at the same time of day," she knows that this is not the case and eventually comes to the realization that on the morning of the attacks, God's name was "on the lips of the killers and victims both" (68, 134). Valid not only with regard to the name of God but in relation to the ideological framework of both parties, this sentiment gains traction as DeLillo imagines Mohamed Atta's rationale in the days leading up to the attacks. While Atta praises his movement for engaging in "face to face" encounters with its enemies, his eventual *modus operandi* is more akin to the virtual mode of confrontation endemic to the very power he intends to overthrow than to anything imagined by Levinas (81). Indeed, as one of Atta's coconspirators immerses himself in American culture in order to carry out his plan, his sense of identity becomes as bound up in his Visa card and frequent flyer number as it is in his blood oath "to kill Americans" (171). Likewise, Atta himself is described as a "nobody from nowhere," the same phrase used to describe Jay Gatsby, who exists in F. Scott Fitzgerald's *The Great Gatsby* not so much as a subject but as a phantom constituted by the sum total of his possessions (DeLillo 172; Fitzgerald 137). Taking on the characteristics of phantoms themselves, Atta and his fellow terrorists become "invisible" to their victims just as their victims become invisible to them (171). As such, the terrorists and their victims become faceless to each other, thus removing Atta from the field of face-to-face confrontation and placing him more firmly in the abstract realm of clashing ideologies.

In the final analysis, Atta's goal as revealed in *Falling Man* is not to replace the ideology of the West with one more firmly rooted in the moral summons of the face-to-face relation but to substitute one arbitrary and dehumanizing code for another. In this sense, Atta's contention that the "world changes first in the mind of the man who wants to change it" reads less as a call to destroy the hyperreal realm of what he considers "the all-enfolding will of capital markets and foreign policies" than as an affirmation of the validity of the hyperreal insofar as the world he imagines is the model upon which he believes the new world should be based (80). What Atta wants, in other words, is not to overthrow the system but simply to change its governing metaphor so that it no longer runs according to the all-enfolding will of capital markets but rather according to the all-enfolding will of God—as imagined both in the pages of the Koran and by Atta himself. To swap metaphors yet again, the exhortation at the beginning of the Koran can thus be read in reference to the ideology of the West as well; just as the Koran is "not to be doubted," nor is the hegemony of capital markets, for only faith prevents either system from collapsing (231). Faith in both systems, however, is exactly what is lost (or, at the very least, shaken) in the destruction of the towers since the event arguably represents a perversion of the tenets of Islam and replaces America with, in Martin's words, "an empty space where America used to be" (193). Consequently, both systems falter as their adherents begin to suspect that the vertiginous accumulation of signs of piety (on one hand) and wealth (on the other) is ultimately meaningless. Bereft of a means of measuring self-worth against the dictates of a code, those who survive the attacks are forced, somewhat ironically, to interact with the world in a way that is identical to that which Atta falsely lays claim: "directly...through eyes, through word and look" (81). Or, in the words of Levinas, "more naked than nudity" (199).

Of course, being more naked than nudity would place anyone in uncomfortable territory, so it seems only natural that Keith should attempt to clothe himself, as it were, in a code with which he has some degree of familiarity: that of the poker games he enjoyed before the fall of the towers. Significantly, the brand of poker Keith plays as he retreats to Las Vegas for long stretches at a time is not the "preliterate" version of the game he enjoyed in his previous life but one in which a strict code structures everything from the rules of the game to the environment in which it is played. Fitting like a cog "into something that was made to his shape," Keith comes to see himself as a "self-operating mechanism" specifically suited to the artificial milieu of the city in the desert (225, 226). Additionally, that he does not know whether the waterfalls he sees in the

casinos of this city are "real or simulated" suggests that the oasis
he has discovered may well be a mirage or, as Baudrillard describes
Las Vegas in *America*, "the absolute simulacrum" (DeLillo 203;
Baudrillard 126). Not that the distinction matters to Keith. As one
of his acquaintances notes, the difference between the real and the
unreal is "not something we're supposed to think about" (204).
Rather, the point of Las Vegas is to serve as its own closed reality, the perfect refuge from the desert of the real. In this respect,
Keith's realization that the city is "all one thing, whatever the venue,
the city, the prize money" indicates a rebirth or, at the very least,
a reawakening of the self-contained hyperreality generated by the
unceasing movement of global capital (204). Finding solace in the
"crucial anonymity" of the constant "check-and-raise" inherent in
poker, Keith loses himself in what is arguably the purest distilla-
tion of the code he thought destroyed in the collapse of the Twin
Towers: a ceaseless exchange of otherwise-meaningless signs in an
endlessly vertiginous quest for "more."

Despite the comfort he finds in "catching planes to go play cards,"
Keith cannot deny "the absurdity, the total psychotic folly" of the
lifestyle he adopts in order to retreat from the desert of the real (216).
Yet while this retreat—like America's vengeful return to conspicuous
consumption in the wake of September 11—amounts, in his wife's
words, to "something very sad," Lianne's fascination with David
Janiak, "the performance artist known as Falling Man," allows her to
avoid following a similar path (216, 219). Adopting a position likely
"intended to reflect the body posture of a particular man who was
photographed falling from the north tower of the World Trade Center," Janiak serves as a constant reminder not only of the collapse
of the towers but of the "lesson," for lack of a better word, that the
collapse conveyed: all of the assumptions inherent in the ideology
of global capitalism were (and continue to be) illusory (221). Thus if
Keith's escape into the highly structured world of gambling is symptomatic of his culture's larger efforts to construct what many pun-
dits described as a "new normal" in the aftermath of September 11,
Janiak's appearances as Falling Man represent a protest against such

efforts and serve as a forceful reminder of the fact that the trappings of global capitalism can be rendered meaningless in the blink of an eye. Reflected in Lianne's relationships with the Alzheimer's patients with whom she works, as well as in her relationship with her mother, this fact is contingent upon the fragility of life (which is to say, the constant nearness of death). Since they afford Lianne very little emotional protection; moreover, these relationships are, like her husband's life in "the days after," painful but also much more fulfilling than anything Keith might find in the "routine run of cards" that constitutes his new life (230, 225). For Lianne, then, Falling Man is an affirmation: her life is meaningful not because she has the potential to accumulate vast sums of money or other signs of wealth but, on the contrary, because it is so fleeting, because she always has the potential to lose everything.

Following the fall of the towers, the composer Karlheinz Stockhausen was reported to have likened the tragedy to a work of art. While Stockhausen later denied such reports, the metaphor bears consideration since, in Zizek's words, "we can perceive the collapse of the WTC towers as the climactic conclusion of twentieth-century art's 'passion for the Real'" (11). Thus while the terrorists who brought down the towers were not artists, their action did have the effect of art: however unwittingly, they shattered our false sense of reality and forced us—for a time, anyway—to live in the so-called desert of the real. This effect, however, was fairly short-lived, as evidenced in Falling Man by Keith's escape to the "zone of purged sensation" he finds in Las Vegas (225). Yet even if the West has responded to the tragedy of September 11 by constructing bigger and better zones of purged sensation so that we all might avoid the seemingly unbearable ambivalence of living in the desert Zizek describes, art continues to remind us that the event occurred and that the desert remains. This is true not only of Falling Man, the performance artist, but of Falling Man, the novel, as well, for like the majority of DeLillo's works, his latest explores the potential for life beyond the soul-numbing artifice of the systems we create even as it acknowledges the value of those systems. If DeLillo's oeuvre is any indication, the potential to live ambivalently—that is, the potential to allow for loss, the potential to engage in meaningful face-to-face relations, the potential to step beyond the limits of the false reality of the ideological systems that surround us and to enter the desert of the real—is always with us (45). The challenge, of course, lies in realizing that potential.

WORKS CITED

Abel, Marco. "Don DeLillo's 'In the Ruins of the Future': Literature, Images, and the Rhetoric of Seeing 9/11." *PMLA* 118, no. 5 (Oct 2003) 1236–1250.

Adorno, Theodore W., and Max Horkheimer. *Dialectic of Enlightenment.* New York: Herder and Herder, 1972.

Barthes, Roland. *The Semiotic Challenge.* 1985. Translated by Richard Howard. Berkeley: University of California Press, 1994.

Baudrillard, Jean. *America.* 1986. Translated by Chris Turner. New York: Verso, 1988.

———. *The Consumer Society: Myths and Structures.* 1970. London: Sage, 1998.

———. *The Ecstasy of Communication.* 1987. Translated by Bernard and Caroline Schutze. New York: Semiotext(e), 1988.

———. "Fatal Strategies." In *Jean Baudrillard: Selected Writings*, edited and translated by Mark Poster 188–209. Stanford: Stanford University Press: 1988.

———. *Fatal Strategies.* 1983. Translated Philip Beitchman and WGJ Niesluchowski. New York: Semiotext(e), 1990.

———. *For a Critique of the Political Economy of the Sign.* 1972. Translated by Charles Levin. St. Louis: Telos, 1981.

———. *The Gulf War Did Not Take Place.* 1991. Translated by Paul Patton. Sydney: Power, 1995.

———. *The Mirror of Production.* 1973. Translated by Mark Poster. St. Louis: Telos, 1975.

———. "Revolution and the End of Utopia." In *Jean Baudrillard: The Disappearance of Art and Politics*, edited by William Stearns and William Chaloupka 233–242. London: Macmillan, 1992.

———. *Simulacra and Simulation.* 1981. Translated by Sheila Faria Glaser. Ann Arbor: University of Michigan Press, 1994.

———. *Simulations.* 1981. Translated by Paul Foss, Paul Patton, and Phili Beitchman. New York: Semiotext(e) 1983.

———. *The Spirit of Terrorism*. Translated Chris Turner. New York: Verso, 2002.

———. *Symbolic Exchange and Death*. 1976. Translated by Iain Hamilton Grant. London: Sage, 1998.

———. *The System of Objects*. 1968. Translated by James Benedict. New York: Verso, 1997.

———. "Transpolitics, Transsexuality, Transaesthetics." In *Jean Baudrillard: The Disappearance of Art and Politics*, edited by William Stearns and William Chaloupka 9–26. London: Macmillan, 1992.

Begley, Adam. "Don DeLillo: The Art of Fiction CXXXV." *Paris Review* 35 (Fall 1993) 274–306.

Benjamin, Walter. *Selected Writings.* Cambridge, London: Belknap Press of Harvard University Press, 1996.

———. *Illuminations.* London: Cape, 1970.

Bonca, Cornel. "Being, Time, and Death in DeLillo's *The Body Artist.*" *Pacific Coast Philology* 37, no. 1 (2002) 58–68.

Butterfield, Bradley. "The Baudrillardian Symbolic, 9/11, and the War on Good and Evil." *Postmodern Culture*. 13, no. 1 (2002): 27 pars. Sep 2002. <http://muse.jhu.edu/journals/postmodern_culture/v013/13.2butterfield.html>.

Carmichael, Thomas. "Lee Harvey Oswald and the Postmodern Subject: History and Intertextuality in Don DeLillo's *Libra*, *The Names*, and *Mao II*." *Contemporary Literature* 34, no. 2 (1993): 204–217.

Certeau, Michel de. *The Practice of Everyday Life.* Berkeley: University of California Press, 1984.

Cixous, Hélène. "The Laugh of the Medusa." In *Feminisms: An Anthology of Literary Theory and Criticism*, edited by Robyn R. Warhol and Diane Price Herndl 334–349. Rutgers: Rutgers University Press, 1991.

DeCurtis, Anthony. "'An Outsider in Society': An Interview with Don DeLillo." In *Introducing Don DeLillo*, edited by Frank Lentrichhia 43–66. Durham: Duke University Press, 1991.

DeLillo, Don. "American Blood: A Journey through the Labyrinth of Dallas and JFK." *Rolling Stone*, Dec 8, 1983, 21–28, 74.

———. *Americana*. Boston: Houghton Mifflin, 1971.

———. *The Body Artist*. New York: Scribner, 2001.

————. *Cosmopolis.* New York: Scribner, 2003.

————. *End Zone.* Boston: Houghton Mifflin, 1972.

————. *Falling Man.* New York: Scribner, 2007.

————. *Great Jones Street.* New York: Vintage, 1973.

————. "In the Ruins of the Future: Reflections on terror and loss in the shadow of September." *Harper's,* Dec 2001, 33–40.

————. *Libra.* New York: Viking, 1988.

————. *Mao II.* New York: Viking, 1991.

————. *The Names.* New York: Knopf, 1982.

————. *Players.* New York: Knopf, 1977.

————. "The Power of History." *New York Times Magazine,* Sep 7, 1997, 60–63.

————. *Ratner's Star.* New York: Knopf, 1976.

————. *Running Dog.* New York: Knopf, 1978.

————. *Underworld.* New York: Scribner, 1997.

————. *White Noise.* New York: Viking, 1985.

Derrida, Jacques. *Of Grammatology.* Corrected Edition. Translated by Gayatri Chakravorty Spivak. Baltimore: Johns Hopkins University Press, 1997.

doCarmo, Stephen N. "Subjects, Objects and the Postmodern Differend in Don DeLillo's *White Noise.*" *Lit* 11 (2000) 1–33.

Duvall, John. "From Valparaiso to Jerusalem: DeLillo and the Moment of Canonization." *Modern Fiction Studies* 45, no. 3 (Fall 1999) 559–568.

Fitzgerald, F. Scott. *The Great Gatsby.* 1925. New York: Simon and Schuster, 1995.

Freud, Sigmund. *Inhibitions, Symptoms and Anxiety.* Translated by Alix Strachey. London: Hogarth Press, 1971.

Frow, John. "The Last Things Before the Last: Notes on *White Noise.*" In *Introducing Don DeLillo,* edited by Frank Lentrichhia. Durham: Duke University Press, 1991.

Gane, Mike. *Baudrillard: Critical and Fatal Theory.* London: Routledge, 1991.

————, ed. *Baudrillard Live: Selected Interviews.* New York: Routledge, 1993.

Gediman, Paul. "A Day in the Life of the Present: Don DeLillo on *Cosmopolis.*" *Inside Borders,* Apr 2003, 8–9.

Goshorn, A. Keith. "Jean Baudrillard's Radical Enigma: 'The Object's Fulfill-ment Without Regard for the Subject.'" In *Jean Baudrillard: The Disappear-ance of Art and Politics*, edited by William Stearns and William Chaloupka. New York: St. Martin's Press, 1992.

Gottdiener, M. *Postmodern Semiotics: Material Culture and the Forms of Mod-ern Life.* Oxford: Blackwell, 1995.

Goux, Jean Joseph. *Symbolic Economies: After Marx and Freud.* Translated by Jennifer Curtiss Gage. Ithaca: Cornell University Press, 1990.

Irigaray, Luce. *This Sex Which Is Not One.* Translated by Catherine Porter. Ithaca: Cornell University Press, 1985.

Jones, Ann Rosalind. "Writing the Body: Toward an Understanding of *L'écriture Féminine.*" In *Feminisms: An Anthology of Literary Theory and Criticism*, edited by Robyn R. Warhol and Diane Price Herndl. Rutgers: Rutgers University Press, 1991.

Kakutani, Michiko. "Headed Toward a Crash, Of Sorts, in a Stretch Limo." *New York Times*, Mar 24, 2003, late ed: E 10.

Keats, John. *Selected Letters of John Keats.* Edited by Grant F. Scott. Cambridge: Harvard University Press, 2005.

Keesey, Douglas. *Don DeLillo.* Twayne's United States Authors Series. New York: Twayne, 1993.

Kellner, Douglas. *Jean Baudrillard: From Marxism to Postmodernism and Beyond.* Cambridge: Polity, 1989.

Kristeva, Julia. *Powers of Horror: An Essay in Abjection.* Translated by Leon. S. Roduiez. New York: Columbia University Press, 1982.

———. "Psychoanalysis and the Polis." *The Critical Tradition.* Edited by David H. Richter. Boston: Bedford, 1998.

———. "Women's Time." In *Feminisms: An Anthology of Literary Theory and Criticism*, edited by Robyn R. Warhol and Diane Price Herndl. Rutgers: Rutgers University Press, 1991.

Knight, Peter. "Everything is Connected: *Underworld*'s Secret History of Paranoia." *Modern Fiction Studies* 45, no. 3 (Fall 1999) 811–836.

Lacan, Jacques. *Ecrits: A Selection.* Translated by Alan Sheridan. New York: Norton, 1977.

Lane, Richard J. *Jean Baudrillard.* Routledge Critical Thinkers Series. London and New York: Routledge, 2000.

LeClair, Tom. *In the Loop: Don DeLillo and the Systems Novel.* Urbana and Chicago: University of Illinois Press, 1987.

Lentricchia, Frank, ed. *Introducing Don DeLillo.* Durham: Duke University Press, 1991.

———. "Libra as Postmodern Critique." In *Introducing Don DeLillo,* edited by Frank Lentrichhia. Durham: Duke University Press, 1991.

Lentricchia, Frank, and Jody McAuliffe. *Crimes of Art and Terror.* Chicago: University of Chicago Press, 2003.

Levinas, Emmanuel. *Totality and Infinity.* Translated by Alphonso Lingis. Pittsburgh: Duquesne University Press, 1969.

Osteen, Mark. *American Magic and Dread: Don DeLillo's Dialogue with Culture.* Philadelphia: University of Pennsylvania Press, 2000.

Parrish, Timothy L. "From Hoover's FBI to Eisenstein's *Unterwelt:* DeLillo Directs the Postmodern Novel." *Modern Fiction Studies* 45, no. 3 (Fall 1999) 696–723.

Poster, Mark, ed. *Jean Baudrillard: Selected Writings.* Stanford: Stanford University Press, 1988.

Saussure, Ferdinand de. "Nature of the Linguistic Sign." *Course in General Linguistics.* 1916. New York: McGraw Hill, 1965.

Scanlan, Margaret M. "Writers Among Terrorists: Don DeLillo's Mao II and the Rushdie Affair." *Modern Fiction Studies* 40, no. 2 (Winter 1994) 229–252.

Schwartz, Barry. *The Paradox of Choice: Why More is Less.* New York: Ecco, 2004.

Shields, Rob, ed. *Lifestyle Shopping: The Subject of Consumption.* New York: Routledge, 1992.

Simmons, Ryan. "What is a Terrorist? Contemporary Authorship, the Unabomber and *Mao II.*" *Modern Fiction Studies* 45, no. 3 (Fall 1999) 675–695.

Singer, Alan. *The Subject as Action: Transformation and Totality in Narrative Aesthetics.* Ann Arbor: The University of Michigan Press, 1993.

Stearns, William, and William Chaloupka, eds. *Jean Baudrillard: The Disappearance of Art and Politics.* London: Macmillan, 1992.

Suzuki, Daisetz T. *Zen and Japanese Culture.* 1959. Princeton: Princeton University Press, 1993.

Tucker, Robert C, ed. *The Marx-Engels Reader.* Second Edition. New York: Norton, 1978.

Wilcox, Leonard. "Baudrillard, DeLillo's *White Noise* and the End of the Heroic Narrative." *Contemporary Literature* 32 (1991) 346–365.

———. "Baudrillard, September 11, and the Haunting Abyss of Reversal." *Postmodern Culture* 14, no. 1 (2003): 32 pars. Sep 2003. <http://muse.jhu. edu/jour nals/pmc/current.issue/14.1wilcox.html>.

Zizek, Slavoj. *The Sublime Object of Ideology*. New York: Verso, 1989.

———. *Welcome to the Desert of the Real*. New York: Verso, 2002.

INDEX

Printed in the United States
202953BV00003B/67/P

9 781604 975048